THE
ABC-CLIO
COMPANION TO

The American Labor Movement

Industrial Workers of the World poster

THE
ABC-CLIO
COMPANION TO

The American Labor Movement

Paul F. Taylor

ABC-CLIO

Library of Congress Cataloging-in-Publication Data

Taylor, Paul F.
    The ABC-CLIO companion to the American labor movement / Paul F. Taylor.
        p.   cm. — (ABC-CLIO companions to key issues in American history and life)
    Includes bibliographical references and index.
    1. Trade-unions—United States—Encyclopedias.   2. Labor movement—United States—Encyclopedias.   3. Labor movement—United States—History—Chronology.   I. Title.   II. Series.
    HD6508.T39   1993   331.88'0973—dc20   93-36557

ISBN 0-87436-687-9 (alk. paper)

00 99 98 97 96 95 94 93   10 9 8 7 6 5 4 3 2 1 (hc)

ABC-CLIO, Inc.
130 Cremona Drive, P.O. Box 1911
Santa Barbara, California 93116-1911

This book is printed on acid-free paper ∞.
Manufactured in the United States of America

To Sue Ann Taylor

ABC-CLIO Companions to Key Issues in American History and Life

The ABC-CLIO Companion to the American Labor Movement
Paul F. Taylor

The ABC-CLIO Companion to the Civil Rights Movement
Mark Grossman

The ABC-CLIO Companion to Women in the Workplace
Dorothy Schneider and Carl J. Schneider

Forthcoming

The ABC-CLIO Companion to the American Peace Movement
Christine Anne Lunardini

The ABC-CLIO Companion to the Environmental Movement
Mark Grossman

The ABC-CLIO Companion to Women's Progress in America
Elizabeth Frost-Knappman

Contents

Preface

After having seen my book *Bloody Harlan*, published in 1990, the editors at ABC-CLIO asked me to write a concise encyclopedia of the American labor movement. I selected the list of topics from materials I have used in teaching American labor history for more than a decade, as well as from my personal research covering nearly 40 years. I have written this book to appeal to both the general reader and the scholar. I hope I have attained that goal.

The *ABC-CLIO Companion to the American Labor Movement* is a guide to the evolution of organized labor from the antebellum years to the present day. It assembles in one volume information on labor leaders, major unions, landmark court decisions and legislation, key events, and the opposition of American business.

The ABC-CLIO Companions series is designed to provide the nonspecialist with concise, encyclopedic guides to key movements, major issues, and revolutions in American history. The encyclopedia entries are arranged in alphabetical order.

Cross-references connect related terms and entries. A chronology of key events provides a handy overview, and a bibliography is provided to facilitate further research.

Many individuals have supported and assisted my work on this book. Dr. Edward J. Cashin, my department chairman at Augusta College, provided released time from teaching so that I could devote more time to writing. The Augusta College Faculty Research and Development Committee allocated funds to expedite necessary travel in order that I might work on the project. Mrs. Carolyn Kershner, secretary to the dean of the School of Arts and Sciences, typed the manuscript from rough, handwritten drafts. My wife and faithful companion of 32 years traveled with me and, in research libraries, assisted in note taking. It is to her, Sue Ann Taylor, that I dedicate this work.

The final product is of my own doing. Any errors that may be discovered are my own.

Introduction

The modern American labor movement is rooted in the decades before the Civil War, with the establishment of early trade unions, local unions, workingmen's associations, and workingmen's parties. During the Jacksonian era, with its multifaceted reform movements, trade unionism developed significantly as political leaders on the state level and in Congress began to address the problems of the working class. As the Industrial Revolution began its sweep across the United States, and as factories, mills, plants, and mines mushroomed, the American labor force, spurred by the influx of immigrants in the post–Civil War era, experienced explosive growth. As the Civil War ended in 1865, national labor organizations and unions began to take shape.

During the Gilded Age labor unions and labor leaders of national status and stature emerged. Both matured as the business tycoons and robber barons of the late nineteenth century consolidated, centralized, and monopolized the American economy and industrial system. As the industrial statesmen developed the oil, iron, railroad, and coal resources of a burgeoning nation, American workers became victims of exploitation. Long hours, low wages, unsafe and unsanitary work places, and brutish foremen were everyday problems facing the toiling masses of the late nineteenth century. Unions, often

led by such charismatic leaders as William Sylvis, organized and evolved as labor struggled to improve its status and to upgrade both the conditions of the working class and its quality of life.

From the National Labor Union of the 1860s to the modern AFL-CIO, the American labor movement has experienced rise and fall, victory and defeat. While organized labor today is not as powerful an interest group as it once was, millions of American workers still look to unions to represent them in the workplace. Virtually all American workers, whether members of unions or not, owe much of the improved conditions of their work—matters often taken for granted, such as safe working environments, the eight-hour day, the forty-hour week, and retirement benefits—to the struggle and sacrifice of union men and women.

Labor unions of today have declined in number and importance, but the theme song of labor, "Solidarity Forever," rings clearly for many workers; both Solidarity Day and Labor Day remain special days for the American working class.

Solidarity forever
Solidarity forever
Solidarity forever
For the union makes us strong

Adair v. United States (U.S., 1908)

In 1898 Congress passed the Erdman Act, which stated that interstate railroads could not require employees to sign nonunion (yellow-dog) contracts. A decade later in the *Adair* case the U.S. Supreme Court ruled the law unconstitutional because it violated both freedom of contract and property rights protected by the Fifth Amendment. Because of the decision, until the 1930s employers could require employees to sign contracts declaring they would not join a labor union.

See also Coppage v. Kansas; Erdman Act; Yellow-Dog Contracts.

Adamson Act (1916)

Enacted by Congress in 1916 as part of President Woodrow Wilson's New Freedom package, the Adamson Act established an eight-hour day for railroad workers engaged in interstate commerce. The eight-hour day was one of labor's chief demands in the late nineteenth century.

See also Eight-Hour Day.

Adkins v. Children's Hospital (U.S., 1918)

In *Adkins* the Supreme Court overturned a District of Columbia minimum wage law for women hospital workers. According to the Court, the law violated the Fifth Amendment. During the next two decades the Court's decisions favored property rights rather than human rights.

AFL-CIO

See American Federation of Labor; Congress of Industrial Organizations.

Akron Sit-Down Strike (1936)

A key weapon in the hands of organized labor during the 1930s was the sit-down strike. The first of these strikes took place in late January 1936 at an Akron, Ohio, Firestone plant. Rubber workers listened to a stirring, impassioned speech by United Mine Workers President John L. Lewis, who urged them to organize, and at 2:00 A.M. on a cold, snowy, blustery night they shut down the plant's conveyor belt. Production at the plant ground to a halt. The excited workers sang loudly about John Brown's body lying a'moldering in the grave, "but his soul goes marching on." On the third day of the sit-down strike and 53 hours after workers had idled plant machinery, Firestone management agreed to negotiate with them. The company met most of the workers' demands, including three hours of pay per day to every worker involved in the sit-down strike. The Akron rubber workers sit-down strike was a victory for employees and a harbinger of future sit-down strikes in the auto, textile, and electrical industries.

See also Sit-Down Strikes.

Alliance for Labor Action

During the Vietnam conflict, AFL-CIO President George Meany was a solid supporter of President Lyndon Johnson's foreign policy of containment. The war created tension between labor's old guard and the young lions of the labor movement. When AFL-CIO leadership remained firm in its support of the Vietnam war, United Automobile Workers (UAW) chief Walter Reuther led the auto workers out of the union. Calling upon labor to organize aggressively and to pursue democratic goals, the UAW joined forces with the Teamsters in the Alliance for

Labor Action, which brought together the nation's two largest unions. In the end the alliance did not work because the UAW was "clean" and democratic while the Teamsters were corrupt and autocratic.

See also International Brotherhood of Teamsters, Chauffeurs, Warehousemen and Helpers of America; United Automobile Workers.

Altgeld, John Peter (1847–1902)

Born of German immigrant parentage, John Peter Altgeld was elected Democratic governor of Illinois in 1892. The Altgeld administration was involved in two labor disputes. At Haymarket Square, Chicago, in 1886 a clash between workers and police left eight policemen and eight workers dead. Although the bomb thrower who hurled a missile into the ranks of policemen was never identified, seven workers were convicted and sentenced to die and another received a 15-

John Peter Altgeld

year prison term. In June 1893 Altgeld pardoned three of the Haymarket rioters, an action that branded him labor's friend. Later, in 1894, Altgeld protested the use of federal troops by President Grover Cleveland in the Pullman Strike. When the army broke the strike, Altgeld supported William Jennings Bryan in the Democratic convention of 1896. For his action in both labor conflicts, Altgeld earned the sobriquet American Radical. He was considered a revolutionary along with Eugene Victor Debs.

As long as Altgeld lived, he was a crusader for the people, the workers, and the farmers. His first venture into politics came in Missouri where, as a People's Party candidate, he was elected prosecuting attorney. Later, in Illinois, he opposed corporate wealth amassed by the monopolies of the Gilded Age. Altgeld supported free silver, favored an income tax, and opposed the injunction law. Near the end of his life, as a law partner of famous defense attorney Clarence Darrow, Altgeld participated in the defense of a labor union against an injunction. A reformer, politician, and man of integrity during the Gilded Age, Altgeld stood out as one who sacrificed his own personal political ambitions in order to promote the general welfare and common good.

Amalgamated Association of Iron, Steel and Tin Workers (AAISTW)

A craft union formed in the late nineteenth century, the Amalgamated Association of Iron, Steel and Tin Workers (AAISTW) rejected membership in the national Knights of Labor because it did not desire to lose its identity as an organization for skilled workers. When the American Federation of Labor was formed in 1886, the AAISTW became a member. At the Homestead, Pennsylvania, plant of Carnegie Steel Corporation in 1892, AAISTW refused to accept wage cuts. In the ensuing strike, Henry Clay Frick, general plant manager, imposed a lockout against the workers. Company guards, Pinkerton detectives, and finally state militia were used to protect company property and break the strike. When the strike ended in November 1892, scabs (strikebreakers) took the jobs of most AAISTW members.

The Homestead lockout was a major defeat for the AAISTW. Carnegie Steel, and later United States Steel, continued to oppose the unionization of its workers. It was not until the 1930s, under labor's New Deal, that an effective union was established for the iron, steel, and tin workers.

See also Homestead Lockout.

Amalgamated Clothing Workers of America (ACWA)

ACWA was a spin-off from the United Garment Workers, which was not meeting the demands of the immigrant work force in the men's garment industry. Formed in 1915, the ACWA was an independent union until 1934, when it joined the American Federation of Labor (AFL). In 1936 the AFL expelled the ACWA after its leader, Sidney Hillman, became one of labor's insurgents in the formation of the Committee on Industrial Organization, the forerunner of the Congress of Industrial Organizations. The ACWA was important because it successfully organized immigrant workers in the men's garment industry, was politically and socially conscious, embraced the concept of the new unionism, and became, in the twentieth century, one of organized labor's most militant unions. The ACWA, now known as the Amalgamated Clothing and Textile Workers Union, is today a key union for textile workers.

See also Hillman, Sidney; Textile Workers Organizing Committee; United Garment Workers of America.

American Communications Association v. Douds (U.S., 1950)

In *American Communications Association*, the Supreme Court upheld the provision of the 1948 Taft-Hartley Act that required labor union officials to certify that they were not members of the Communist Party. The association, which had been infiltrated by communists, challenged the law on the grounds that it violated freedom of speech as protected by the First Amendment. In a majority opinion, Chief Justice Fred Vinson declared that requiring labor union officials to file affidavits stating they were not communists was within the constitutional exercise of federal commerce power. The importance of this decision was that labor unions could require noncommunist oaths and affidavits from their officials.

See also Taft-Hartley Act.

American Federation of Labor (AFL)

The American Federation of Labor (AFL) is one of American labor's most important unions and the principal nineteenth-century labor union that survived into the twentieth century. Steps leading to its organization began at a Pittsburgh meeting in 1881. There Knights of Labor chief Terence V. Powderly and Samuel Gompers of the Cigar Makers, along with delegates representing the Noble and Holy Order and the trades unions, gathered to organize a union that would include all workers. Skilled workers wanted autonomy within their respective trades, while the unskilled remained under the authority of the Knights of Labor. For about five years, while the controversy continued, efforts toward federation floundered. Finally, following additional conclaves at Philadelphia and at Columbus, Ohio, the Federation of Organized Trades and Labor Unions became the American Federation of Labor in December 1886.

The new union recognized the autonomy of each trade. It also emphasized bread-and-butter issues, that is, a shorter workday and higher wages. The AFL was one of the first labor organizations to advocate collective bargaining between employer and employees as an instrument to determine conditions of employment.

CIO President George Meany, left, and AFL President Walter Reuther celebrate the merger of their unions in 1955.

In the beginning the AFL chiefly represented skilled, white, male workers.

The AFL experienced long-term stable leadership. Its first president was Samuel Gompers, whose term extended from 1881 to 1924, except for the year 1895. Gompers was followed by William Green, who led the AFL from 1924 into the World War II era. Other significant AFL leaders were George Meany and presently Lane Kirkland.

In the post–World War II era AFL president William Green and CIO leader Philip Murray died. Green's place was taken by the vocal George Meany while Murray was followed by UAW chief Walter Reuther. During the tenure of the Meany-Reuther regime, the AFL and CIO (Congress of Industrial Organizations) merged. The first convention of the AFL-CIO was held in December 1955. At that historic meeting George Meany was elected chief executive of American labor's largest union. A significant difference in the two bodies was that for decades the AFL was aloof in political matters while the CIO was a very political organization. With their merger, organized labor now had a union with outstanding political clout. From the days of the late eighteenth century when organized labor had little political power to the mid-nineteenth century, labor had gained the status of a new, powerful interest group in the United States.

See also Congress of Industrial Organizations; Gompers, Samuel; Kirkland, Joseph Lane; Meany, George.

American Federation of State, County, and Municipal Employees (AFSCME)

In the late nineteenth century and to a certain extent well into the twentieth century, American labor unions organized and represented the blue-collar class, or the "nuts and bolts" workers. In the post–World War II era, however, white-collar employees, dissatisfied with on-the-job conditions and unhappy with their bosses and employers, began to organize.

At first these workers formed associations, which later became labor unions. One such union is the American Federation of State, County, and Municipal Employees (AFSCME), which represents government employees on the federal, state, county, and municipal levels. AFSCME grew rapidly during the 1960s and 1970s, and by the end of the 1970s boasted a membership of over two million nationwide. In some cases when collective bargaining with employers did not produce a satisfactory contract, government workers resorted to strikes. For the most part such strikes were considered illegal, although the state of Minnesota and certain California metropolitan communities sanctioned the walkouts. AFSCME is today one of the largest unions in the country representing white-collar workers.

American Federation of Teachers (AFT)

The largest and most prominent labor union for public schoolteachers is the American Federation of Teachers (AFT). In Midwestern and Northern states teachers belonging to the American Federation of Teachers enjoy collective bargaining rights as well as the right to strike.

Like the blue-collar class, AFT members have input in contracts. On many occasions teacher strikes after Labor Day have delayed school openings. Recently the AFT has experienced phenomenal growth as teachers have become more politically conscious and active.

In most Southern states, educational associations or teachers' unions have taken the form of local countywide groups or larger statewide educational organizations. These groups, except recently, have not been political and have had little or no political clout. Outside Southern states the nation's public schoolteachers have been activists, joining the AFT and in many cases striking over salaries and working conditions. In higher education, university faculty are represented by the

American Association of University Professors (AAUP). Another organization, the National Education Association (NEA), represents teachers nationally and is a lobbying instrument on behalf of educators.

American Plan

After World War I, management decided to thwart labor unionism by supporting the principle of the open shop. Before and during the war, labor unions were quite prevalent. By adopting the open shop concept, big business hoped to take collective bargaining rights away from employees. As a result, in key industrial states (both in the Northeast phalanx and in the Midwest), employer associations, chambers of commerce, and the powerful National Association of Manufacturers (NAM) embraced the American Plan (open shop). Technically, the open shop meant that employers could fire workers without regard to union affiliation and could operate on a strictly nonunion basis. The latter principle was subscribed to by a majority of employers during the 1920s, an era referred to as labor's "lean years" by Irving Bernstein.

American Railway Union (ARU)

Organized by socialist Eugene V. Debs of Terre Haute, Indiana, the American Railway Union (ARU) grew rapidly. By 1894 it had a total membership of over 150,000 workers, including employees of the Pullman Palace Car Company, headed by George M. Pullman. Before Debs put the ARU together, from the 1860s, to the 1880s railway employees banded together mainly in four brotherhoods: Locomotive Engineers, Railway Conductors, Trainmen, and Firemen. Compared to the ARU the brotherhoods were more conservative groups. In 1894 when George M. Pullman, owner of the Pullman Palace Car Company, drastically cut wages but did not cut rents on com-

pany houses or prices at the company store, Pullman workers walked out. When the American Railway Union supported the strike, all the railroads in the Chicago area (west of the city), in addition to the Pullman operation, ground to a standstill. The ARU, under the leadership of Debs, was a formidable industrial union. Although the union eventually lost the Pullman Strike, it became a model for future organizations of industrial, assembly-line employees.

See also Debs, Eugene Victor; Pullman Strike.

American Steel Foundries v. Tri-City Central Trades Council (U.S., 1921)

One of the most important weapons in the hands of employees seeking union recognition is the strike. When workers strike, they often resort to picketing, walking up and down near company premises carrying signs or placards to publicize their grievances. Companies frowned on picketing; the courts leaned toward the employers. Earlier in the twentieth century the courts mandated that picketing must be peaceful. In 1921 in a New Jersey case, *American Steel Foundries v. Tri-City Central Trades Council*, Chief Justice William Howard Taft, speaking for the Supreme Court, severely curtailed peaceful picketing. In his opinion, Taft referred to picketing as a "militant" and "intimidating" activity by groups of workers that may be properly enjoined by the courts. Taft's opinions limited the right of workers to picket into the era of World War II.

See also Picketing.

Anderson, Mary (d. 1964)

An immigrant from Sweden, Mary Anderson was a women's labor leader in the early twentieth century. On 14 January 1910, after a strike against Hart Schaffner and Marx by the United Garment Workers, the Chicago Federation of Labor, and the Chicago Women's Trade Union League, she commented that the right of the workers to organize and to set up an arbitration board were two of the most important gains achieved. Anderson stressed the solidarity of workers during and after the strike and criticized favoritism shown to male workers over female employees. As a member of the union board, she was the only delegate not on the union's payroll, a classic example of the preference shown to men.

Baer, George (1842–1914)

George Baer was the strongly anti-union spokesman for coal operators in the anthracite coal strike in eastern Pennsylvania in 1902. When the coal miners walked out, the operators responded by dispatching 4,000 mine guards and bringing in strikebreakers (scabs). Determined not to negotiate with the United Mine Workers of America (led by John Mitchell) and to break the union, Baer imposed the "divine right" principle on the conflict. God, said Baer, had entrusted the property rights of this country to godly businessmen who would take care of the laboring class. Rebuking outside agitators and the union, Baer refused to arbitrate the dispute.

The coal strike began in May and continued into October. As winter approached, President Theodore Roosevelt finally applied pressure on the operators, conceiving a plan to call out the U.S. Army to patrol the coalfield and to take over the mines. Roosevelt's policy forced the operators to the bargaining table, and after five months, the coal miners returned to work.

Baer's stance in the anthracite strike of 1902 would be repeated again and again by Appalachian coal operators during the next three decades.

Bahr, Morton (1926–)

As the third president of the Communication Workers of America (CWA), Morton Bahr represents over 650,000 members in 900 locals throughout the United States. CWA is the largest communications union in the world, and Bahr, who also has a degree in labor studies, is an enigmatic labor leader. He is, in many respects, comparable to labor leaders of the 1930s such as John L. Lewis, who approached labor relations with a hard-boiled, bombastic manner. Unlike some of labor's earlier captains, however, Bahr has demonstrated a moderate, compromising attitude.

The CWA has its roots in the National Federation of Telephone Workers, which was organized in 1938. For a time AT&T was the leading employer of CWA members, but the union did not achieve national collective bargaining rights with the company until 1974. Following the dissolution of AT&T, the CWA has mainly dealt with various "Ma Bells" and with attempting to organize workers in the telecommunications field.

In recent years when telephone strikes occurred, CWA effectively maintained discipline over its members so management had to fill the jobs of union workers.

Bailey v. Drexel Furniture Company (U.S., 1922)

Congress passed the first Child Labor Act, or Keating-Owen Act, in 1916. Two years later a conservative Supreme Court invalidated the law in *Hammer v. Dagenhart*. The more progressive Congress responded by passing the Child Labor Tax law of 1919. This law levied a 10 percent tax on the net profits of a business employing child labor (children under 14) or children between 14 and 16 more than eight hours per day, more than six days per week, or between 7:00 P.M. and 6:00 A.M.

The Child Labor Tax law was quickly challenged in the courts. In *Bailey*, Chief Justice William Howard Taft, delivering the opinion for a conservative majority, declared the law unconstitutional on the grounds that it abused the taxing power of Congress by imposing a penalty on corporations. The taxing power, the Court ruled, could not be used as a regulatory instrument. In this decision the Supreme Court disregarded the fact that from the days of the Washington administration, the federal government had used its taxing power to regulate businesses.

Child labor laws were enacted mainly by the states (except in the South) until 1938, when Congress passed the Fair Labor Standards Act.

See also Hammer v. Dagenhart; Keating-Owen Act.

Bakery and Confectionery Workers Union

The Bakery and Confectionery Workers Union was one of the organizations scrutinized by the 1957 Senate Select Committee on Improper Activities in the Labor or Management Field. More popularly known as the McClellan Committee, the Senate group was chaired by Democratic Senator John McClellan of Arkansas. Charges against the union included misuse of union funds, extortion, and collusion between employers and union officials. When the Bakery and Confectionery Workers Union refused to reform its activities, it was expelled by the AFL-CIO.

Barry, John J.

It was a tradition in the Barry family to belong to a labor union. The son of a union electrician, John Barry also became an electrician and developed an interest in union activities, in time becoming a member of the executive board of his local. Rising through the ranks, Barry became president of the International Brotherhood of Electrical Workers (IBEW) in 1986. Before becoming chief executive, he was international vice-president and international representative. Like John L. Lewis and other twentieth-century labor leaders, Barry worked his way from a menial capacity to a leadership role in his union.

Electrical workers organized unions in the mid-nineteenth century. In 1883 the National Brotherhood of Electrical Workers was established, from which the IBEW evolved.

Presently the IBEW boasts 1,500 locals representing nearly a million workers in the construction, utility, manufacturing, telecommunications, broadcasting, and railway industries. In contrast to other international unions, the IBEW has locals throughout the South. In sharp contrast to other labor leaders, Barry foresees a bright future for American labor unionism.

Beal, Fred

Fred Beal was a fiery organizer for the National Textile Workers Union (NTWU), a Communist Party affiliate and the only union responsive to the needs of the South's textile workers in the 1920s. Despite strong opposition from the anti-union Manville-Jenckes textile operation in Gastonia, North Carolina, Beal, upon receipt of a telegram from a fired union worker, went to Gastonia to lead a strike against the company in mid-March 1929.

At Gastonia, Beal made an hour-long, impassioned appeal to both male and female textile workers meeting in a company house. The workers were so stirred by Beal's speech that they began to shout "Strike!" One youngster of 16, who could not write, exclaimed he was going out to recruit new members.

Two weeks after the initial meeting, which was secret, an open meeting was held. At that gathering, Beal, along with Nellie Dawson, a Scot who had enjoyed success as an organizer in New England, addressed several thousand workers as company men watched and took names of those attending the meeting.

Local clergy tried to dissuade the workers from joining the NTWU and from striking, and the company began releasing workers who had attended the public rally. The decision by the workers was loud and clear: Strike. A picket line was set up, and as workers excitedly sang organized labor's theme song, "Solidarity Forever," the Gastonia strike became a reality.

The strike was short-lived. North Carolina Governor O. Max Gardner deployed National Guardsmen to Gastonia, and the Communist Party rushed in its representatives. Within ten days, as supplies to the strikers diminished and relief money ran out, strikebreakers moved in to take the jobs of the workers. With the withdrawal of the National Guard, violence ensued and soon claimed the life of Police Chief O. F. Aderholt. Fred Beal, who led a demonstration prior to the slaying of Aderholt, was charged with conspiracy to commit murder. Before the trial in Charlotte ended, more violence erupted in Gastonia. Beal was found guilty in his second trial and received a prison sentence. While his case was being appealed, Beal visited Russia, where he was ordained a proletarian hero.

Beal remained in Russia until 1933. Upon his return to the United States, he was apprehended and returned to prison. In 1942 he received a full pardon from Governor J. Melville Broughton. The remaining 12 years of his life were filled with illness and poverty.

It has been said that Beal, a radical, was out of step with the times. His life revealed "the incompatibility between trade unionism and Communism."

Beck, David

As president of the International Brotherhood of Teamsters in the 1950s, Dave Beck became a chief target of the investigation conducted by the McClellan Committee. Committee hearings disclosed evidence of corrupt leadership in locals, extortion, racketeering, and close ties with gangsters, along with violence and terrorism in the Teamsters.

When McClellan interrogated Dave Beck, the Teamster chief assumed a cocky, pompous, disrespectful attitude toward committee members. Committee findings, despite Beck's refusal to answer numerous questions, showed that he had used union funds for personal reasons, including the building of a swimming pool at his estate, and that he ran the union in a dictatorial fashion.

The committee uncovered enough evidence against Beck to force him to give up the union presidency. Later he was indicted and convicted on charges of income tax evasion and grand larceny.

As Beck departed, James R. "Jimmy" Hoffa became head of the Teamsters. Under Hoffa, Teamster corruption continued.

See also International Brotherhood of Teamsters, Chauffeurs, Warehousemen and Helpers of America; McClellan Committee.

Berkman, Alexander (1870–1936)

During the 1892 Homestead Lockout in Pittsburgh, Carnegie Steel, under general manager Henry Clay Frick, used Pinkerton detectives against the strikers. The workers attacked the Pinkertons and ran them out of town. Incensed by the use of the detectives, Alexander Berkman, an anarchist who was born in Russia, charged into Frick's office and shot and stabbed him. The attack had been planned by Berkman and fellow anarchist Emma Goldman. Frick recovered and Berkman was apprehended, tried, and convicted in connection with the attack. He received a 22-year prison term. He was released after serving 14 years.

In 1917 Berkman was convicted of obstructing the selective service law. After serving a two-year term, he was deported to Russia. He died in France by his own hand in 1936.

See also Frick, Henry Clay; Goldman, Emma; Homestead Lockout.

Bill of Grievances (1906)

Having experienced few gains for its efforts in the late nineteenth century, organized labor in the early twentieth century turned increasingly to political activism. A first step in that direction came in 1906, when the American Federation of Labor submitted its Bill of Grievances to President Theodore Roosevelt and Congress. Included in the list of demands were a shorter workday and work week, along with higher wages. A major grievance was that labor should not be prosecuted as a conspiracy to restrain interstate commerce under the Sherman Anti-Trust Act. The Sherman Act, passed by Congress in 1890, prohibited contracts, combinations, and trusts that restrained interstate trade. While the law was intended to apply to big business (as interpreted by the courts), notably in connection with the Pullman Strike of 1894, it was used to hinder labor unions. The Bill of Grievances also sought relief from the injunction, a key weapon in the hands of the employer. It was too easy, labor reasoned, for employers to go into both state and federal courts and enjoin employees from striking, picketing, and boycotting.

Since neither Congress nor Roosevelt endorsed the Bill of Grievances, organized labor entered into politics in 1906. However, the kind of relief unions sought did not come until the 1930s, with the passage of the Norris-LaGuardia Act, among other measures.

Black-Connery Bill (1933)

Sponsored by Alabama Senator Hugo Black, a former member of the Ku Klux Klan and later associate justice of the U.S. Supreme Court, and Congressman William P. Connery, Jr., of Massachusetts, the Black-Connery Bill, brought before Congress in 1933, provided for a 30-hour work week as a step toward relieving the unemployment occasioned by the depression of the late 1920s and early 1930s. Both President Franklin Delano Roosevelt and Secretary of Labor Frances Perkins were lukewarm in support of the measure, especially because it did not include a minimum wage provision. Business leaders vigorously opposed the bill. Labor leaders, including United Mine Workers President John L. Lewis, desired a law broader in scope. As a result, the Roosevelt administration and its key advisers substituted the National Industrial Recovery Act for the Black-Connery Bill during the Hundred Days period of the first New Deal.

See also Thirty-Hour Week.

Black International

Formally known as the International Working People's Association, the Black International was composed of a group of radicals and anarchists led by German immigrant Johann Most and American-born Albert Parsons. The Black International, drawing support mainly from ethnic workers, gained control of Chicago's Central Labor Union in the early 1880s. The philosophy of the Black International included revolution, anarchism, and nihilism. At McCormick's Harvester operation in Chicago in May 1886, following a clash between strikers and Chicago policemen that left four men dead, the Black International flooded the city with circulars calling for a mass rally at Haymarket Square. At the conclusion of the meeting, an altercation between workers and policemen took the lives of four additional workers and several policemen. In the aftermath of two days of violence the Black International was blamed for the deaths of eight police officers. Although the evidence did not show any connection between the organization and the rioting, several anarchists were rounded up, tried, convicted, and executed. In 1892, Illinois Governor John Peter Altgeld, of German immigrant ancestry, pardoned three of the surviving anarchists, gaining a reputation as a friend to labor and anarchism.

The Haymarket Square episode would not be the last incident in which labor was branded radical or anarchistic.

See also Haymarket Square Riots.

Black Lung Disease

Black lung disease, also known as coal miners' asthma, silicosis, and pneumoconiosis, is a frequent and fatal malady of coal miners. The disease did not become an occupational hazard of coal miners in modern times. It was known in both Great Britain and Europe in the nineteenth century, and autopsies performed on American miners early in the nineteenth century showed evidence of the disease at that time.

In the United States, poorly ventilated coal mines caused the disease to escalate among the nation's coal miners. After a day's work, coal dust covered a coal miner—it was in his hair, ears, nostrils, mouth, and teeth; his face was caked, his eyes mascaraed with coal dust. When he spat, his sputum was black; when he coughed, up came black coal dust. In time, coal dust coated a coal miner's lungs, causing shortness of breath and making the slightest physical activity virtually impossible.

In present times, especially under the administration of W. A. "Tony" Boyle, the black lung issue became a chief topic for discussion. In 1960 consumer protection advocate Ralph Nader called for legislation to protect miners from occupational hazards. In West Virginia, the West Virginia Black Lung Association was formed to seek black lung benefits under worker's compensation laws. In Pennsylvania the union leadership demanded legislation enabling miners to get black lung benefits. In Pike County, Kentucky, coal miners were able to receive black lung payments, but only after hiring attorneys to prove disability before worker's compensation boards. Even then, attorney Kelsey Friend, in helping miners get benefits, became affluent enough to build a two-story mansion, complete with swimming pool, in an elite Pikeville, Kentucky, subdivision that was appropriately nicknamed Silicosis Hill.

Boyle, president of the United Mine Workers of America (UMW), along with his vice-president, George Joy Titler, did not seem responsive to the demands of coal miners for improved health and safety measures. Their indifference caused

Pennsylvania UMW official Joseph "Jock" Yablonski to oppose Boyle for the union presidency in 1969.

The black lung movement in the Appalachian coalfields eventually led to improved health and safety standards in the region's coal mines. Coal operators were required to improve ventilation in their mines, and miners had masks available to wear underground.

Listening to tapes of coal miners who have black lung disease, one quickly notices labored, raspy breathing and frequent coughing. The men often seem old and well past their prime while still in their forties and fifties.

Black Mountain

The Black Mountain coal mine was located in Harlan County, Kentucky, which came to be known as "Bloody Harlan" during the conflict there in the 1930s, when the United Mine Workers of America (UMW) attempted to organize the coal miners in the face of strong opposition from the Harlan County Coal Operators Association, to which most of the county's coal operators belonged.

Coal was discovered in southeastern Kentucky in 1750 by English land surveyor Dr. Thomas Walker. It was not until the early years of the twentieth century, though, that Harlan County's coal

Kentucky coal miner Harry Fain in 1946

deposits were developed. Until 1911 Harlan remained a backwoods, agricultural area. That year the L&N Railroad reached Harlan County, and its transition from a rural agrarian economy to an industrialized region began.

During the World War I period, the first attempts were made to organize the coal miners of Harlan County in the tri-cities area by the UMW. Violence erupted and a fatality occurred as operators used gun thugs, yellow-dog contracts, and house evictions to repel the union. The UMW was able to unionize one significant mine, the absentee-owned Black Mountain Coal Corporation, located at Kenvir, in the post–World War I period. Overall, the county's coal operators maintained a solid wall of opposition against all unionization efforts into the 1930s.

In 1931 the first major effort to unionize coal miners came at the Black Mountain mine. At once the company used gun thugs and house evictions in an attempt to keep workers from joining the United Mine Workers of America. On 5 May 1931, when Black Mountain tried to bring in a scab, violence flared about three miles from the mine. The skirmish, known as the Battle of Evarts, left four known casualties, including Jim Daniels, Black Mountain's most feared thug. Mass indictments and convictions of local union officials brought a sudden end to the union's efforts by 1932. After Congress passed the National Industrial Recovery Act (NIRA) in 1933, the UMW launched a serious union campaign. Union organizers suffered numerous ambushes, twin dynamitings of an organizer's apartment in Pineville, Kentucky, and other forms of harassment at the hands of Harlan County deputy sheriffs or gun thugs. To keep the union out of Harlan County, operators paid over 300 deputy sheriffs to intimidate miners and union organizers. Organizers were constantly shadowed or rough shadowed by deputies. Two thug gangs—one under the leadership of chief thug Ben Unthank, the other supervised by Merle H. Middleton—roamed the county, ha-

rassing organizers, abusing miners, and breaking up union meetings, so the UMW experienced little success in organizing the coal miners under the authority of NIRA. The union found it necessary to establish headquarters in Pineville, the county seat of Bell County, and journey into Harlan County by day. Even then they encountered Ben Unthank and other deputies at the county line and were turned back or chased.

The National Labor Relations Act, or Wagner Act, was passed by Congress in 1935. This prompted the union to reenter Harlan County. On 7 July 1935 an open air rally was held at Evarts to apprise the miners of their benefits under the Wagner Act. Once again deputies broke up the meeting by blowing automobile horns to drown out the union speakers, and several deputies waded into the large crowd brandishing pistols and shouting threats. After an elderly miner was pistol-whipped and a woman bystander was cursed, the crowd scattered.

The Harlan County Coal Operators Association controlled the county courthouse, including the powerful sheriff's office. Grand juries, staffed by friends and relatives of coal operators and county officials, failed to indict deputy sheriffs. The state's attorney received retainers from several coal companies. The circuit judge complained that his hands were tied. A lone exception to the operators' dominance of the county administration was County Attorney Elmon Middleton. In September 1935 Middleton's car exploded, killing the only friend the miners had in the county courthouse.

When the union planned to hold a mass rally in 1935, the county health department imposed a countywide meningitis quarantine, effectively banning union meetings. With the lifting of the quarantine late in the year, the UMW, in January 1937, sent a large contingent of organizers into the county; they established headquarters at one of the town's hotels. For two months organizers were threatened, ambushed, and tear-gassed out of the hotel. Their cars were bombed, and an organizer and his wife were shot at as they made a church visit on a peaceful Sunday afternoon. On 8 February three carloads of night riders shot into the house of UMW organizer Marshall A. Musick, killing his son Bennett.

The Bennett Musick murder led to an in-depth probe of Harlan County officials and coal operators by the La Follette Civil Liberties Committee. Following its inquiry the committee charged the operators with using industrial munitions, industrial policemen, and industrial espionage to keep the UMW out of Harlan County.

Subsequent to the La Follette investigation, a federal grand jury in Lexington, Kentucky, indicted 69 Harlan County coal operators, coal companies, and deputy sheriffs for conspiring to keep the union out of Harlan County. In federal court at London, Kentucky, May–August 1938, the Harlan County defendants were put on trial, witnessed by the entire nation through the pages of the *New York Times* and the *Christian Science Monitor*. The trial was filled with charges and countercharges, conflicting testimony, evidence of several perjury mills, and at least one attempt to influence the jury. At trial's end a mistrial was declared when the mountain jury could not agree on a verdict. Before a new trial could be scheduled, Harlan County operators, in late 1938, agreed to a closed shop contract covering the county's 12,000 coal miners.

The union's first countywide contract expired early in 1939. Turbulence renewed as the county's union miners picketed to prevent operators from using scabs to break another strike. The Battle of Stanfill in July 1939, like the previous Battle of Evarts, resulted in further bloodshed in Bloody Harlan. To restore order and keep the roads open, Governor A. B. "Happy" Chandler dispatched National Guardsmen to Harlan County. The federal government sent mediators to resolve the dispute. Finally, after days of tense negotiations, the union and the coal operators agreed to the county's first two-year closed shop contract, and the decade-long conflict came to an end.

There were further incidents of violence and bloodshed in the 1940s and again in 1974, when a second Bloody Harlan focused the eyes of the nation once more on the mountainous coal county. Today as coal mines still hum with productivity in Harlan County, there is only one major union mine—the operation at Lynch managed by ARCOL Minerals, subsidiary of Ashland Oil Company. Lynch, in the 1930s the site of United States Coal and Coke, an affiliate of United States Steel, employed 3,000 miners.

The legacy of coal on Harlan County: run-down company towns and houses, ramshackle, abandoned coal tipples, old pensioners who are rabid union men, and young men who no longer see any benefits from union membership.

See also Duke Power Company; Harlan County Coal Operators Association; United Mine Workers of America.

Blacklist

The blacklist was a key weapon of employers against organized labor. As workers attempted to organize and join unions, employers used elaborate espionage systems composed of Pinkerton detectives and deputy sheriffs to ferret out those they considered troublemakers. When company spies found that a worker had been seen talking to a union organizer or attending a union meeting, or when it was discovered that an employee had joined the union, the company dismissed and blacklisted the worker. The worker's name was actively placed on a blacklist that was circulated among employers locally, regionally, and nationally. Once blacklisted, it became virtually impossible for a worker to get a job. Being a union man was equated with being a radical, an anarchist, or a rabble-rouser.

Bloody Harlan

See Black Mountain; Duke Power Company; Harlan County Coal Operators Association.

Bloody Mingo

Mingo County is located the southwestern corner of Virginia just across the border from the eastern Kentucky coalfields. Mingo, Logan, McDowell, and Mercer counties comprise what is known as West Virginia's million-dollar coalfield. Mingo was a nonunion coal county in 1920 when the United Mine Workers of America (UMW) entered on an organizing campaign. As in nearby Harlan County, Kentucky, Mingo operators were strongly anti-union, and had the support of most local officials, with the notable exception of Matewan Police Chief Sid Hatfield of the feuding Hatfield clan. As miners enrolled in the United Mine Workers of America, the coal companies, principally Consolidated Coal Company and Island Creek Company, imported Baldwin-Felts detectives to evict union men from company houses. Matewan Police Chief Hatfield became a local folk hero among the miners when, in a gun battle with detectives, he gunned down seven thugs (and also two bystanders) in what is referred to as the Matewan Massacre.

The Matewan shoot-out signaled the beginning of civil war in West Virginia. In that state, as in Kentucky and other mining regions, nonunion operators used house evictions, yellow-dog contracts, scabs, and thugs to break the union. Union men and organizers fought back with their own weapons. Between May 1920 and July 1921 there were over 100 casualties in the West Virginia coal mine war.

On 1 August 1921, as Sid Hatfield and his bodyguard, Ed Chambers, mounted the steps of the McDowell County courthouse in Welch in the company of their wives, Baldwin-Felts agents opened fire, killing both Hatfield and Chambers. The slaying of the Matewan police chief pre-

UMW members march through Logan, West Virginia.

cipitated a month of full-scale war in West Virginia. Involved in the conflict was Mary "Mother" Jones, who at age 91 called on the union miners to fight for their rights. On the other side of the conflict was Logan County Sheriff Don Chafin, who, like counterpart Sheriff Theodore Roosevelt Middleton of Bloody Harlan, was a tool of the operators. The miners gathered 5,000 strong to march on Logan. Widespread strife and bloodshed seemed imminent. UMW District 17 President Frank Keeney finally urged the miners to disperse. At that moment, however, West Virginia state police shot into a group of miners, killing two, and the battle was forged. From 31 August to 3 September 1921 what became known as the Battle of Blair Mountain raged along a 30-mile front. Involved were between 5,000 and 7,000 miners and some 1,200 to 3,000 Logan defenders led by Sheriff Chafin, who used planes to drop handmade bombs. On 1 September a bombing squadron commanded by

Brigadier-General Billy Mitchell flew into the region, followed by 2,100 federal troops, a chemical warfare unit, and eight trench mortars. With the federal force on the scene, the firing ended, and the miners made their way homeward. In the week-long battle, over one million rounds were fired, and four people were confirmed dead.

In post-battle trials that tied up the courts until 1924, UMW officials were charged with murder and treason. There were two murder convictions and one for treason in the Charleston courthouse where John Brown was tried in 1859. Charges against other union members were dropped. The West Virginia coal mine war broke the efforts of the UMW to organize miners in the region until the New Deal days of the 1930s.

See also Hatfield, Sid; United Mine Workers of America.

Bloody Williamson

The coalfields of Williamson County, Illinois, became a battleground for striking miners of the United Mine Workers of America (UMW) and strikebreakers. In 1922 John L. Lewis, president of the UMW, opened negotiations with coal operators in the Central Competitive Field, which included southern Illinois, Indiana, and Ohio. The operators balked, preferring district negotiations. A generally peaceful strike followed. The Southern Illinois Company reopened, bringing in Chicago Steam Shovel employees as scabs. Hostilities broke out as strikers machine-gunned and attacked a company stockade in the town of Herrin, killing 19 men, mostly strikebreakers. The so-called Herrin Massacre turned public opinion against the miners. The union was successful in negotiating contracts with operators in Illinois, Indiana, and Ohio, but it lost western Pennsylvania, Maryland, Virginia, West Virginia, Alabama, Texas, Utah, and Colorado. Union successes in those states did not materialize until the New Deal era of the 1930s.

See also United Mine Workers of America.

Boston Mechanics' and Laborers' Association

In 1845 in Boston, Massachusetts, a cooperative called the Boston Mechanics' and Laborers' Association was formed. The organization drafted a platform that criticized monopolies and money-power in the United States. Because workers were oppressed by what they called the "idle few," the association called for labor to own shops, factories, and all tools of production so that labor could derive benefits from its toil rather than have most of the wealth go to the owners. The group further advocated the union of farmers, manufacturers, and merchants into a single organization so all the producers of wealth could share in the wealth each produced.

The Boston Mechanics' and Laborers' Association looked ahead to the cooperatives favored by the People's Party in the late nineteenth century.

Boston Police Strike (1919)

In 1919, the Boston police force, dissatisfied with low wages and poor working conditions, formed the Boston Social Club. The club requested affiliation with the American Federation of Labor. The Boston police commissioner condemned the action and warned policemen that they would not be allowed to join a labor union. Outraged by the commissioner's action, the policemen called a strike, and Boston was without police protection, especially at night. There was some vandalism in the city but no widespread lawlessness, and order was restored by state patrolmen and local volunteers.

Settling the strike was not an easy matter. The police commissioner was in no mood to yield to the policemen's grievances. The mayor was somewhat sympathetic to their demands, but public opinion condemned the policemen for failing to provide public safety to the city.

Calvin Coolidge, governor of the state, refused to fire the police commissioner and bring back the strikers. "There is no right to strike against the public safety by anybody, anywhere, anytime," Coolidge remonstrated. The public solidly backed Coolidge. The strike ended, the policemen lost their jobs, and Governor Coolidge was on a course for the White House.

The 1919 Boston police strike set a national precedent—firemen and policemen do not have a right to strike and leave a municipality, town, or village without protection.

Boyle, William Anthony (1904–1985)

William Anthony "Tony" Boyle was born in Bald Butte, Montana, in 1901. Like his father, who was a miner in England at age nine, Tony Boyle began his career in the mines of Montana. As a union man, Boyle was a United Mine Workers of America (UMW) district president in Montana. Ultimately, as UMW chief John L. Lewis had done before him, Boyle worked his way up to the international office in Washington by 1948. There Boyle remained in the background, serving as Lewis's assistant. In 1960 upon the retirement of the 80-year-old Lewis, Thomas Kennedy became president of the union. When Kennedy died in 1963, heir-apparent was Tony Boyle, who was Lewis's handpicked successor to the presidency. In 1964 Boyle won a union election to a full five-year term.

As president of the UMW, Boyle, like his predecessor Lewis, maintained a tight grip on the union. He did this by keeping in office men loyal to him, notably UMW District 19 officials William Turnblazer and Albert Pass in southeastern Kentucky and eastern Tennessee. Boyle also increased miners' wages and added paid holidays for the workers. Pensioners received modest increases. On the surface it seemed that Boyle was a miners' president.

So tightly did he control the union that few miners knew Boyle was misusing union funds. For example, the international secretary-treasurer was housed in a

Tony Boyle

two-room suite at Washington's Sheraton-Carlton Hotel at a cost to the union of nearly $69,000 over a five-year period. Three Cadillac limousines were purchased for top UMW officials. The miners had two-week vacations with pay while union hierarchy got four-week vacations with pay. Boyle also convened union members in such faraway resorts as Miami Beach, Florida, far removed from the Appalachian coalfields. Boyle loyalists attended the convention at union expense while dissidents had to pay their way.

Boyle's administration also rigidly controlled the pages of the *United Mine Workers Journal*. Article after article, picture after picture heaped praise on the union leader, while critical viewpoints sent in by the membership were excluded. At union conventions Boyle's lieutenants wore white hard hats that easily distinguished them from the rank-and-file members. When a dissident tried to speak from the convention floor, the microphone was cut off as men wearing white hard hats forcibly ejected the maverick from the hall.

The administration of John L. Lewis had negotiated "sweetheart" contracts, apart from the national agreement, with certain companies. Boyle continued the practice. The Boyle regime showed disregard for the health, welfare, and safety of the miners. In the wake of the Farmington, West Virginia, mine disaster in November 1968, Boyle flew down to the Consolidated operation and patted the company on the back. Grief-stricken widows and families of the 78 men who perished in the explosion were appalled by Boyle's words.

Because Boyle abused union leadership and did not respond to the miners' problems, Joseph "Jock" Yablonski of Clarksville, Pennsylvania, announced his opposition to Boyle in the union presidential election of 1969. Faced with Yablonski's opposition, Boyle contacted UMW District 19 president William Turnblazer and the district's secretary-treasurer, Albert Pass. The union officials huddled and decided that the Yablonski should be killed. Working through District 19 representative William Prater and pensioner Silous Huddleston, and collecting from 40 District 19 pensioners, Pass hired three hit men—Paul Gilly (married to Huddleston's daughter Annette), Claude Vealey, and Aubran "Buddy" Martin—to murder Yablonski. The trio trailed Yablonski in Washington, D.C., Clarksville, Pennsylvania, and in other locales for weeks. Finally, on New Year's Eve 1969, the killers slipped into Yablonski's Clarksville home and murdered Jock, his wife Margaret, and their daughter Charlotte as they slept in their beds.

In Pennsylvania, Prosecutor Richard Sprague, using an Ohio license tag number scrawled on a pad by Yablonski, traced the killers to Cleveland, Ohio. Annette Gilly and Silous Huddleston confessed to their roles in the murder plot, leading to the arrest of the killers and ultimately Prater, Pass, Turnblazer, and Boyle. In successive trials that lasted into 1975, all the defendants were found guilty. On 11 April 1974 Tony Boyle was convicted for his role in the Yablonski slayings, after a trial delay resulting from his overdosing on more than 100 sleeping pills. A year later the 73-year-old defendant was sentenced to three life terms.

To the end Boyle maintained his innocence. He died in 1985.

See also Pass, Albert Edward; Turnblazer, William Jenkins, Jr.; United Mine Workers of America; Yablonski, Joseph.

Brandeis, Louis Dembitz (1856–1941)

Kentucky-born and Harvard-educated, Louis D. Brandeis began practicing law in Boston. He was known as the peoples' attorney because he opposed big business and big government. On most issues and in most cases, Brandeis represented the people. In 1916 he was appointed associate justice of the U.S. Supreme Court after advising President Wilson on labor problems. Until 1939 he served on the Court and became one of its chief dissenters, along with Justices Oliver Wendell Holmes, Benjamin Cardozo, and Harlan Fiske Stone.

Brandeis established himself as a champion of labor in the landmark *Muller v. Oregon* case in 1908. Oregon passed a law in 1903 limiting the number of hours women could work in a laundry to ten hours per day. When the law was challenged, the state hired Brandeis to defend the constitutionality of the statute in the courts. In his elaborate and lengthy brief, the Boston attorney wrote only two pages regarding constitutional precedents and over 100 pages citing statistics in an effort to prove that long hours of labor was detrimental to the health, welfare, morale, and physique of women.

The "Brandeis brief" swayed the court to uphold the Oregon ten-hour law for women workers. The *Muller* opinion established a precedent for the Court to rule favorably in other cases involving the efforts of states to pass maximum hours laws for its workers under the police power of the state.

After his appointment to the Supreme Court, Brandeis, for more than two decades, ruled in favor of government regulation of business. He also favored social legislation passed by the states as well as laws designed to protect the activities of organized labor. In the New Deal era, Brandeis held that picketing was a form of free speech protected by the First Amendment.

See also Muller v. Oregon.

Bridges, Harry

Harry Bridges was president of the West Coast Longshoremen's Union and then the International Longshoremen's Association before and during the post–World War II period. Both unions were charged with having Bolshevik or communist tendencies. Bridges was accused of being a communist sympathizer. In the 1930s he formed the International Longshoremen and Warehousemen's Union (ILWU), which did not affiliate with the American Federation of Labor. On the West Coast in particular the union won several strikes, achieving major gains for the workers.

In the 1949 convention of the Congress of Industrial Organizations (CIO), which convened in Cleveland, Ohio, intense debate took place regarding the expulsion of communistic unions. At that gathering Michael Quill, head of the Transport Workers Union, and Joseph Curran, chief of the National Maritime Union, argued for expulsion of such unions as the ILWU. In rebuttal Bridges defended his union by suggesting that its main purpose was hours, wages, and working conditions, not political partisanship. He chided the CIO for desiring to expel members for political reasons when the ILWU claimed it was not political.

Since no noncommunist union adherents supported Bridges or other allegedly communist union officials, the CIO in 1949 removed the ILWU from its membership rolls. Bridges continued to lead the union effectively and successfully on the West Coast despite the charges of communism.

Broad Form Deed

In the early days of the twentieth century, capitalists entered the southern Appalachians in search of the coal deposits of the region. Upon the discovery of coal, three entrepreneurs approached the hill country folk and induced them to sign broad form deeds conveying to the coal companies the mineral rights on their land. The mountaineers were paid a nominal fee for the mineral rights, and most were glad to receive the money since they were barely making ends meet. Little did the highlanders realize the impact the broad form deed would make upon their lives.

Serene mountain valleys were transformed almost overnight. To get at the rich deposits of bituminous coal, the coal companies brought in bulldozers and heavy machinery to build roads, rip down virginal forests, erect company towns, and construct coal tipples. The original landowners were appalled, even incensed, at the uprooting of their lands and homes. They did not understand that to get at the mineral deposits they had signed away, it was necessary for the coal corporations to invade their private domains. With the coming of the coal industry, mountain life-styles were completely altered. As one old white-haired mountaineer put it, "They ran a concrete road through my hollow, and now I must live to see my grandchildren racing up and down in automobiles." In later years coal trucks rumbled up and down the roads cut in the valleys.

Brophy, John (1883–1963)

An immigrant from England in the late nineteenth century, John Brophy came from a family whose life-style centered around unions. As a coal miner, he became a union man, actively involved in the United Mine Workers of America (UMW). As president of UMW District 2, headquartered in central Pennsylvania, Brophy, a devout Roman Catholic, initiated a Save-the-Union crusade against the leadership of John L. Lewis in 1926. Emphasizing "a militant organizing drive, a labor party, nationalization of the mines, [and] close cooperation between bituminous and anthracite districts," Brophy challenged Lewis's presidency. His supporters included Alex Howat (the deposed president of Kansas's District 14), A. J. Muste (a minister who founded Brookwood Labor College), communists, and others from leftist-oriented union ranks.

In the hotly contested UMW presidential election of 1926, Brophy was defeated by Lewis in a landslide. He became persona non grata in the union, and like many others who opposed Lewis, was ousted. In the 1930s Brophy became a prime mover behind the formation of the Congress of Industrial Organizations (CIO).

As a coal miner working alongside his father, Brophy was well aware of the dangers, pitfalls, and poor working conditions in the mines. However, he entered into the coal pits with enthusiasm, developing a great sense of camaraderie both with his fellow workers and those who lived in the company towns. Commenting on his livelihood in his memoirs, Brophy proudly remembered his days as a coal miner and the four generations of his family who toiled underground.

Brotherhood of Locomotive Engineers (BLE)

Distressed over their low wages and long work hours, 13 engineers on the Michigan Central Railroad organized in 1863 to form the Brotherhood of the Footboard (BOF), the forerunner to the Brotherhood of Locomotive Engineers (BLE).

From the outset, the BLE was an independent organization that chose to remain apart from both the National Labor Union and the Knights of Labor. By 1873 the BLE included some 9,500 members.

Along came the difficult nationwide rail strike of 1877. Although the BLE was not greatly involved in the dispute, it was weakened by the walkout. Within a decade, however, the BLE recovered, building a membership of 20,000.

Again a strike on the Burlington line and the use of scabs undermined the union. Still it held a steady course as an independent union, rejecting overtures from the Knights of Labor, the American Federation of Labor, and Eugene V. Debs's American Railway Union, which was established for all railroad employees.

In the early years of the twentieth century the BLE threw its support behind the Adamson Act, which established an eight-hour day for railroad workers. With 80,000 members by 1920, the BLE was instrumental in developing work rules covering the entire industry. The union became politically active in the 1920s, and in 1924 supported Progressive candidate "Fighting Bob" La Follette for the presidency.

With the technological advances of the post–World War II era combined with increased competition from long-distance trucking lines, the BLE began a steady decline. In the 1960s its membership dropped to 68,000, and more recently it could count only 37,000 members. Headquartered in Cleveland, Ohio, the BLE consists of over 800 local unions dispersed throughout the United States.

Brotherhood of Locomotive Firemen and Enginemen (BLFE)

The Brotherhood of Locomotive Firemen and Enginemen was conceived at Port Jervis, New York, in 1873 when 11 firemen from the Erie Railroad system established the Brotherhood of Locomotive Firemen (BLF). Nearly three decades later enginemen were admitted, creating the BLFE.

In the beginning the BLF concentrated on funeral and sickness benefits. It grew steadily until 1877, when it was weakened by the railroad strike. Following a short period of decline the BLF revived in the early 1880s, and after a merger with the International Firemen's Union, membership jumped dramatically to 26,000 by 1894. During the 1880s the BLF concentrated mainly on improved working conditions and wages.

The Pullman Strike, along with the depression of 1894, temporarily halted the progress of the BLF. With the admission of enginemen, improved wages, an eight-hour day, and access to collective bargaining, the BLFE, by 1920, counted 126,000 workers. Its growth continued into the World War II era as it successfully gained further wage hikes and a five-day week for railroad yardmen. During this same period, the BLFE succeeded in keeping firemen on diesels, which led to a controversy over "featherbedding," or keeping certain classes of railway employees on the job when there was little or no work for them to do.

Merger talks between the BLFE and other types of railroad employees—including conductors, brakemen, trainmen, and switchmen—led to the creation of the United Transportation Union (UTU) in 1969. The dream of Eugene V. Debs, who in the 1890s attempted to combine all railway workers into one union, became a reality with the UTU.

The era of the railroad has passed, but as late as the 1970s UTU membership was around 67,750.

See also Brotherhood of Railroad Trainmen.

Brotherhood of Railroad Brakemen
See Brotherhood of Railroad Trainmen.

Brotherhood of Railroad Trainmen (BRT)
The Brotherhood of Railroad Trainmen (BRT) actually had its inception as the Brotherhood of Railroad Brakemen (BRB). Decrying wages of just over a dollar a day, a workday of 12 to 18 hours, blacklisting, and unsafe working conditions, the BRB was organized in 1883 in Albany, New York. The same year a na-

tional assembly gathered at Oneonta, New York, where the Grand Lodge of the BRB was conceived. It grew rapidly and by 1885 had enrolled 4,500 members.

The amazing success of the BRB led to the organization of conductors, roadmen, yardmen, dining car stewards, yardmasters, switch tenders, and baggage handlers. Since the BRB included diverse types of railroad workers, the name was changed to the Brotherhood of Railroad Trainmen in 1890.

Internal discord between Eastern and Western railroad trainmen and rivalry with the American Railway Union hampered the BRT at first. In the early years of the twentieth century BRT President William G. Lee was accused of running an autocratic operation by a rival BRT faction headed by Alexander F. Whitney. That imbroglio ended with Lee defeating Whitney in 1928.

During World War I the BRT grew rapidly, only to decline during the 1920s. With recovery from the depression in the late 1930s, BRT membership expanded to an all-time high of 217,000 members by 1956.

The AFL-CIO admitted the BRT to full membership in 1957 after it had dropped its racial exclusiveness. Over a decade later the BRT joined with the Brotherhood of Locomotive Firemen and Enginemen (BLFE) and the Order of Railroad Conductors (ORC) to form the United Transportation Union (UTU).

See also Brotherhood of Locomotive Firemen and Enginemen.

Browder, Earl (1891–1973)
A Socialist Party member who joined the American Communist Party during the World War I era, Earl Browder was a native of Wichita, Kansas. He dropped out of school when he was nine years old but later learned law. Through his association with farm cooperatives, he became a socialist at age 15.

Antiwar during the World War I, Browder was sentenced to prison for conspiracy against the U.S. government. In prison he became a convert to communism. Elected as secretary of the American Communist Party in 1930, Browder ran for U.S. president as a communist in 1936 and again in 1940.

During World War II Browder again was sent to federal prison on an illegal passport charge. Before the prison sentence he was militantly procommunist, pro-Russian, and anti-Nazi.

In the 1940s, following his release from prison, Browder edited *The Daily Worker*, the official organ of the American Communist Party. In 1946 Browder was replaced as American leader of the Communist Party by William Z. Foster and expelled from the party.

The American Communist Party supported and was allied to the U.S. labor movement in the twentieth century. In fact, several U.S. unions were Communist Party affiliates. Browder traveled extensively throughout Europe studying the labor movement and briefly acted as secretary of the Pan-Pacific trade union headquartered in Shanghai, China.

Browder, like Eugene V. Debs, spent time in prison in connection with the radical causes he advocated and also was pro-labor during a time when the toiling masses did not have many spokesmen.

Buck's Stove and Range Company

The Buck's Stove and Range Company was a St. Louis firm that manufactured stoves and ranges in the early twentieth century. In 1906 metal polishers employed by the company called a strike in support of a nine-hour day. The American Federation of Labor (AFL) supported the strikers by calling for a boycott of all Buck's stove products. J. W. Van Cleave, company president and head of the National Association of Manufacturers, obtained an injunction against the AFL, charging the union with violation of the Sherman Anti-Trust Act (1890) by instituting the secondary boycott against Buck's products.

Samuel Gompers and the AFL ignored the injunction. Gompers, cited for contempt of court, was sentenced to a year in prison. Other AFL officials received lesser sentences. While the sentences were never served and the cases were subsequently dismissed by the Supreme Court, company action sent shock waves throughout organized labor. Government by injunction under the Sherman Act, which was passed by Congress to curtail trusts and monopolies, became a chief concern of the working class and labor unions. It meant the injunction could be used extensively to repel the unionization of workers, and since violations of the court order could land both union leaders and workers in jail, the injunction was a key weapon in the hands of employers to thwart unionism. In the late nineteenth and early twentieth centuries, injunctions were employed to stop strikes, picketing, and secondary boycotts, which were widely used by labor in its attempt to gain recognition.

See also Loewe v. Lawlor.

Bunting v. Oregon (U.S., 1917)

The state of Oregon, which earlier had passed a ten-hour statute regulating the hours of women workers, added a law that established a ten-hour day for both women and men employees. The new law also contained a provision that stipulated that workers could not work more than three hours overtime per day at wages of time and one-half. Seemingly, the new statute regulated wages as well as hours. In its 1917 decision, the Supreme Court denied that the law denied due process by regulating wages. The Court, in a majority opinion, ruled that states could set maximum hours for both women and men employees following the 1908 *Muller v. Oregon* decision, which upheld a maximum hours law for women workers. Both Oregon maximum hours laws, upheld by the Supreme Court, were victories for progressives on the state level during the Progressive period, 1900 to 1917.

See also Muller v. Oregon.

Bureau of Labor Statistics

In the late nineteenth century, as the strength of labor unions diminished, feeble beginnings of labor legislation on both the national and state levels took place. One of the first agencies set up on the federal level was the Bureau of Labor Statistics. Likewise at the turn of the century, 32 states had set up similar organizations. For approximately 100 years the Bureau of Labor Statistics has existed as a significant department of the federal government.

Originally the Bureau of Labor Statistics was housed in the Interior Department. In 1913 it was relocated in the U.S. Department of Labor. The organization from 1884 to the present "collects and publishes data relating to wages and hours, employment, payrolls, and labor unions." It also circulates information "relating to the activities, welfare, and position of labor." It keeps the public and the government abreast of all issues affecting labor, including the transmission of monthly reports on unemployment as well as other pertinent information.

The Bureau of Labor Statistics performs an invaluable service by continually updating the status of labor conditions in the United States. As of 1950 it was one of eight main divisions of the U.S. Department of Labor along with the Women's Bureau, the Bureau of Labor Standards, the Wage and Hour and Public Contracts Division, the Bureau of Apprenticeship, the Bureau of Veterans' Re-employment Rights, the Children's Bureau, and the Office of International Labor Affairs.

Carey, Ronald

In December 1991, in a first for the Teamsters over its 90-year history, the rank and file elected a president, Ron Carey, to head the union of 1.6 million members. The largest U.S. labor union in the private sector, the Teamsters agreed to conduct a democratic election in a compromise with the Justice Department to settle a long-standing racketeering lawsuit.

In taking the helm, Carey talked of rebuilding the union and giving it back to the membership. He also pledged to rid the union of corruption and to sever all ties with organized crime. In an unprecedented move, Carey agreed to reduce his salary from $225,000 to $175,000 annually. Since his 1991 election was held on a democratic basis, he promised to restore the union to democratic principles and to guide it in the best interests of the workers.

If Carey succeeds in his prescribed goals, it will mark a significant change in Teamster leadership from the days of former union presidents Dave Beck and the late Jimmy Hoffa.

See also Hoffa, James Riddle; International Brotherhood of Teamsters, Chauffeurs, Warehousemen and Helpers of America.

Carpenters and Joiners Union v. Ritter's Cafe (U.S., 1942)

In several cases during the late 1930s and early 1940s, the Supreme Court ruled on the right of organized labor to picket during a labor dispute. In a 1940 Alabama case, the Court upheld the right of labor to picket as a form of free expression guaranteed in the Bill of Rights and extended to the states by the Fourteenth Amendment. Historically labor used picketing to publicize its goals and call attention to unfair labor practices on the part of employers. Workers believed the Wagner Act of 1935 gave them the right to engage in peaceful picketing. During strikes workers at times used roving squadrons of pickets to threaten and intimidate scabs (strikebreakers) who tried to work. Altercations followed in which strikers and scabs suffered serious injuries.

The Roosevelt Court—so-called because even though FDR's court-packing attempt was unsuccessful, several conservative justices retired, enabling the president to appoint activist justices—handed down several decisions that restricted the right of labor to picket. In *Carpenters and Joiners Union v. Ritter's Cafe*, a majority of the Court ruled that a state could legally restrain picketing of an employer not engaged in a labor controversy in order to coerce another employer who was involved. Four Roosevelt appointees, Justices Hugo Black, William O. Douglas, Frank Murphy, and Stanley Reed, dissented on the grounds that peaceful picketing was simply communication not to be enjoined.

The Supreme Court at this time disagreed on labor's right to picket. Peaceful picketing, it seems, was allowable, while picketing used to intimidate, harass, or coerce, or picketing that led to violence, was to be curtailed.

Carpenters and Joiners, United Brotherhood of

See United Brotherhood of Carpenters and Joiners.

Carter v. Carter Coal Company (U.S., 1936)

In 1935, after the Supreme Court had struck down the National Industrial

Recovery Act in *Schechter v. United States*, Congress passed the Bituminous Coal Act, commonly known as the Guffey Act. According to the new law, since the coal industry served the public, it should be federally regulated. A Bituminous Coal Commission was set up to negotiate a Bituminous Coal Code for the entire industry. The commission had authority to set coal prices in coal-producing states and tax coal 15 percent at the mouth of the mine. In addition to guaranteeing collective bargaining, the Guffey Act provided that contracts covering at least one-half of the coal miners and coal operations producing two-thirds of the nation's tonnage should bind the entire industry. In effect the Guffey Act attempted to establish a coal code in the absence of the codes of fair competition provided by the National Industrial Recovery Act.

The coal industry challenged the new law in the 1936 case *Carter v. Carter Coal Company*. In a fragmented decision the Supreme Court invalidated the entire Guffey Act, decreeing that the taxing provision of the law penalized the industry, and the labor provisions only indirectly related to interstate commerce. Thus attempts by Congress to legislate a code for the coal industry, on which the public depended for fuel and heat, was not allowed by the Supreme Court. Issues raised by the National Industrial Recovery Act and the Guffey-Snyder Act were not effectively addressed by Congress until passage of the National Labor Relations Act in 1935. *Carter v. Carter Coal Company* was another anti–New Deal decision by a conservative Supreme Court, which caused President Franklin Delano Roosevelt, following his 1936 landslide reelection over Republican opponent Alfred M. Landon, to attempt to pack the high court.

Case Bill (1946)

A forerunner to the Taft-Hartley Act of 1947, the Case Bill, sponsored by Democratic Congressman Francis Case of New Jersey, passed Congress in 1946 as part of the anti-labor sentiment of the post–World War II period. The measure established the Federal Mediation Board to arbitrate labor disputes, a 60-day cooling-off period before strikes could be enforced, a ban on secondary boycotts and jurisdictional strikes, and injunctions to restrict rough-and-tumble picketing. Workers who walked out during the cooling-off periods could lose their jobs, according to the Case Bill.

The Case Bill hailed back to the nineteenth century when workers generally did not have the right to strike and picket. President Harry S Truman vetoed the bill, and Congress could not muster enough votes to override the presidential veto.

In the midterm elections of 1946, the Republicans won control of both houses of Congress. Since anti-labor sentiment was strongest in the Republican Party, the mood in Congress became one of legislating prohibitions on organized labor. The result was the Taft-Hartley Act (1947), which was passed over Truman's veto. Within a decade after the New Deal, labor, which had gained the right to strike, engage in collective bargaining, and picket, now faced serious limitations imposed by a conservative Republican-dominated Congress.

Chafin, Don

Don Chafin was sheriff of Logan County, West Virginia, in 1921. At the beck and call of the coal operators, Chafin employed a legion of deputy sheriffs whose mission was to keep the union—principally the United Mine Workers of America (UMW)—out of the West Virginia coalfields. Chafin appointed deputies, many of whom were Baldwin-Felts detectives. They were then approved by the local courts and placed on the payrolls of local coal corporations. The coal operators backed Chafin with both money and supplies, including arms, ammunitions, and authority to use against union coal miners and organizers.

Chafin did his work well. During West Virginia's long, hot summer of 1921, a summer in which Matewan Police Chief Sid Hatfield was gunned down in Welch and the week-long Battle of Blair's Mountain was fought, Chafin and his army of deputies rounded up and detained in the Logan County jail over 200 miners whose only sin was joining the union.

Chafin was both feared and hated by the coal miners. On the other side of the controversy, Police Chief Hatfield was their hero. When Hatfield was murdered on 1 August 1921, the coal miners were aroused into action. Throughout the month of August violence surged back and forth across the mountainous West Virginia terrain.

During this time a mass march of over 5,000 miners was urged to disperse by Chafin. On request of Governor Ephraim Morgan of West Virginia, federal observers rushed to the scene. After meeting with UMW District 17 President Frank Keeney, the miners agreed to call off the march. Lack of transportation to take the men home and an incident in which state policemen attacked the miners led to renewed and uncontrollable warfare. President Harding urged the miners to disperse as did UMW International President John L. Lewis. Despite their plan, hostilities raged from August 31 to September 3. To complement Chafin's army of about 3,000 deputies, over 2,000 federal troops converged on the scene, and the situation came to an end with the beaten miners returning home. Sheriff Don Chafin had accomplished the task assigned to him by West Virginia coal operators—to keep the union out of their million dollar coalfield.

Chaikin, Sol Chick (1918–1991)

Born in New York in 1918, Sol Chaikin was educated at the City College of New York and at Brooklyn Law School. On completing law school, he went to work as an organizer for the International Ladies' Garment Workers' Union (ILGWU). For the next four decades the ILGWU became Chaikin's consuming interest. He had held nearly every office in the union by 1975, when he was elected president. From 1975 to 1986 Chaikin presided over the union, and on his retirement in 1986, he was made president emeritus. After his retirement, he was invited to lecture at Fordham Law School, Harvard Graduate School of Business, University of Minnesota, and Columbia University Graduate School of Business.

A devout union leader, Chaikin opposed American reliance on exports from abroad. While he favored human rights, he steadfastly was against affirmative action quotas. His motto: Where there are no free trade unions, there are no human rights. Chaikin supported the union movement and label in the United States but always resisted any shifting toward the left by the ILGWU.

As ILGWU membership declined in the 1970s and 1980s, Chaikin advocated strong federal action against competition from foreign garment and textile producers. His agenda included "federal enforcement of anti-dumping provisions, retaliation against countries that subsidize exports, and revision of U.S. tax laws that encourage overseas production of American business."

Chandler, Albert Benjamin (1898–1991)

As baseball commissioner in the 1940s, A. B. "Happy" Chandler presided over the desegregation of major league baseball by the Brooklyn Dodgers, who signed Jackie Robinson, a UCLA football star, to play second base. Prior to becoming baseball commissioner, Chandler was governor of Kentucky from 1935 to 1939. In Chandler's victory in both the primary and primary runoff, and in his win in the November general election, he received staggering vote totals from the coal mining company towns of Harlan County,

Kentucky, indicating widespread support from coal miners. Chandler, then, was Kentucky's governor during part of Bloody Harlan's labor warfare in the 1930s.

Once in office Chandler displayed a vacillating attitude toward Harlan's labor controversy. When he was inaugurated in December 1935, his escort for the day was coal-operator-controlled Sheriff Theodore R. Middleton of Harlan County. As governor, Chandler dismissed ouster proceedings against Middleton begun by his predecessor, Governor Ruby Laffoon, with the comment that the Harlan sheriff was a high-class and efficient government official.

During Chandler's administration and at his urging, the Kentucky General Assembly passed laws abolishing Kentucky's mine guard system and the compulsory scrip system used in company stores. The passage of those two bills triggered a Chandler Appreciation Day in downtown Harlan by the United Mine Workers of America (UMW) led by District 19 President William Turnblazer, Sr.

The UMW's support of Chandler, however, quickly vanished. During the 1939 strike, which turned violent in the Battle of Stanfill, Chandler dispatched National Guardsmen to Harlan County. With troops on the scene to patrol the roads and stop picketing of the mines by roving bands of union miners, scabs appeared at several mines. The UMW then referred to Chandler as a strikebreaker.

Following the bloodbath at Stanfill in July 1939, Turnblazer and George Joy Titler, who headed the organizing campaign in Harlan, were lodged in jail on charges of conspiring to incite a riot. Though indicted, they were never brought to trial. Before trials could be scheduled, a conference between UMW officials, coal operator representatives, and Kentucky leaders brought an end to a decade-long conflict in Harlan. Charges against Titler and Turnblazer were dismissed, and the UMW secured its first standard two-year

agreement with Harlan County's coal mining operators.

Chandler's role in Harlan's labor troubles was somewhat enigmatic. While he appeared to be on the side of labor, his sending of National Guardsmen to Harlan offended the UMW. On the other hand, the bills ending Kentucky's mine guard and scrip systems were hailed by organized labor. This, in fact, removed two formidable obstacles that stood in the way of unionization of the county's coal mines.

See also Black Mountain.

Chavez, Cesar (1927–1993)

Cesar Chavez began his work as an organizer of farm workers and migrant laborers without a dollar in his pocket. He was born in 1927 in Yuma, Arizona, and since his grandfather was a farmer, he grew up in a farming environment. During the depression of the 1930s, Chavez, at age ten, began toiling as a migrant farm worker. He met his wife while working in the California vineyards at age 21.

Through working as a migrant laborer in the grape-growing industry, Chavez saw the problems of migrant workers firsthand. He began his farmers' union activities with the Community Service Organization, but when that establishment refused to organize farm workers, Chavez, in 1962, founded the National Farm Workers Association (NFWA). Three years later 1,200 members of the NFWA collaborated with the AFL-CIO Agricultural Workers Organizing Committee (AWOC) in a five-year strike against California grape growers. The next year the NFWA and the AWOC became the United Farm Workers (UFW).

The boycott led by the farmers' union proved to be successful. In 1970 the grape growers signed contracts with the UFW. When California vegetable growers signed "sweetheart contracts" with the Teamsters, 10,000 farm workers quit in protest. When the grape contracts expired, most growers negotiated contracts

Cesar Chavez

Chavez was the most successful leader of an agricultural union in the United States. Through the use of boycotts and strikes, he gained contracts for the farm workers, especially in the prolific California fruit and vegetable fields.

See also United Farm Workers of America.

CIO
See Congress of Industrial Organizations.

CIO-PAC
See Congress of Industrial Organizations Political Action Committee.

Civil Rights Act of 1964, Title VII
The Civil Rights Act of 1964, passed during the administration of President Lyndon Baines Johnson, outlawed segregation in a variety of public settings. It also put in place the Equal Employment Opportunity Commission (EEOC). Title VII of the Civil Rights Act of 1964 was designed to keep labor unions from discriminating against workers because of race and/or sex.

Before the law was enacted, the National Association for the Advancement of Colored People (NAACP) charged the International Ladies Garment Workers Union (ILGWU) with discrimination against African American and Puerto Rican workers by paying minorities lower wages than whites, even though they were union members.

With the passage of the Civil Rights Act of 1964, both employers and labor unions were restricted from engaging in discriminatory actions against ethnic minorities and women.

Clayton Anti-Trust Act (1914)
Passed in 1914 as a significant part of President Woodrow Wilson's New Freedom platform, the Clayton Anti-Trust Act accomplished two major purposes.

with the Teamsters. Chavez then called what proved to be the largest and most successful farm strike in history. The walkout included an international boycott of grapes, lettuce, and Gallo Wines.

The strike, which lasted for about four years, was honored by many Americans. In the end the UFW became the exclusive bargaining agent for farm workers. In implementing the boycotts and strikes, Chavez followed the principles of nonviolence practiced by India's Mohandas K. Gandhi. Part of his personal involvement in the passive resistance movement included a 25-day fast. Chavez was called "one of the heroic figures of our time" by Senator Robert Kennedy, who joined the farm union leader at the end of his 1968 fasting.

In 1984 Chavez again directed a worldwide grape boycott using the slogan The Wrath of Grapes. The new boycott was geared toward publicizing the dangers of pesticides to farmers and consumers alike.

Aimed at J. Pierpont Morgan and John D. Rockefeller, Sr., it outlawed the interlocking directorate. Morgan and Rockefeller, through the buying of stock and controlling the boards of directors of over 300 corporations, had put together a business combination not explicitly covered by the Sherman Anti-Trust Act of 1890.

The Clayton Act was also referred to as Labor's Magna Carta. It attempted to exempt labor unions from the Sherman Anti-Trust Act stipulating that "the labor of a human being is not a commodity or article of commerce." Further, the Clayton Anti-Trust Act outlawed the use of injunctions in labor disputes "unless necessary to prevent irreparable injury to property, or to a property right ... for which there is no adequate remedy at law."

Labor leaders, including Samuel Gompers, applauded the statute. As labor saw it, workers now had the right to organize, strike, picket, boycott, and engage in collective bargaining with management. Alas, the hopes of organized labor were short-lived. Judicial interpretation severely crippled the application of the law to labor. An unfriendly and conservative Supreme Court in *Duplex Printing Press Company v. Deering* (1921) effectively emasculated the Clayton Act by denying labor's right to institute a secondary boycott. In effect, organized labor was still regarded as a conspiracy that restrains trade, and such conspiracies were prohibited by the Sherman Anti-Trust Act.

See also Duplex Printing Company v. Deering.

Closed Shop

A closed shop is one in which all the employees are union members, and being a member of a union is a condition of employment. The employer is required to hire only union members except in cases where a union member is not available. In such situations a nonunion worker may be hired with the requirement that he/she become a union member once employed.

The closed shop became a fact of life in the world of organized labor during the New Deal years of the 1930s. In 1935 Congress passed the National Labor Relations Act, more popularly known as the Wagner Act, which made it possible for the American blue-collar worker to join a labor union for the first time without employer recrimination. In the aftermath of that law, unions were established in major American industries, and with that type of union, the closed shop became a reality for workers.

The closed shop remained until the post–World War II era when the Taft-Hartley Act, passed by the Eightieth Congress during the Truman administration, limited union membership as a prerequisite for employment.

See also Open Shop.

Coalition of Labor Union Women (CLUW)

The Coalition of Labor Union Women (CLUW), an organization consisting of over 20,000 members, is a support group for women in the workplace. Its national president is Joyce Miller, who is also vice-president of the Amalgamated Clothing and Textile Workers of America (ACTWA) and a vice-president of the Executive Council of the AFL-CIO. A pioneer in the women's trade union movement, Miller earned a bachelor of philosophy and a master of arts degree at the University of Chicago. She has been active in promoting social services and addressing social issues for women workers.

Among the social issues addressed by Miller and the CLUW are equal economic opportunity for women, equal pay for equal work, and higher safety standards in the workplace. Additional social issues include drug testing, alcohol abuse, and an AIDS educational program. In the area of social services, the CLUW has worked through several labor unions such as the United Auto Workers to work for pay equity and sexual harassment policies. The CLUW has also been responsible for playing a leading role in the establishment of child care centers for working women.

Miller points with pride to the inclusion of other women as labor union leaders. Among them are Lenore Miller, president of the Retail, Wholesale and Department Store Workers Union; Susan Bianchi-Sand, head of the Flight Attendants; Patty Duke, president of the Screen Actors Guild; Colleen Dewhurst of Actors Equity; and Barbara Esterling, who is executive vice-president of the Communications Workers of America (CWA).

Considering the fact that the modern feminist movement only began in the 1960s, women have made considerable progress as union leaders and toward achieving equal opportunity in the workplace. There is still a long way to go before women reach the levels of men as executives and workers with equal pay, but certainly Joyce Miller and the CLUW have been responsible for the rapid progress women workers have made in the last three decades.

Collective Bargaining

The principle of collective bargaining was first introduced in the late eighteenth century by societies of workmen in New York and other Eastern industrial states. Collective bargaining in the early days consisted of negotiating sessions between the employer and employee with regard to hours, wages, and working conditions. Once a compromise was reached, committees of workers would go from shop to shop to ensure that the conditions of employment were followed.

When the first nationwide labor unions were established in the post–Civil War era, collective bargaining between the representatives of management and labor was not always allowed. Subsequently it was not until the organization of the American Federation of Labor by Samuel Gompers and others in the late nineteenth century that collective bargaining was emphasized. Still, organized labor

achieved little for its efforts until the New Deal era of the twentieth century.

In 1933 Congress passed the National Industrial Recovery Act, and Section 7a of the law guaranteed collective bargaining rights. When the Supreme Court declared NIRA unconstitutional in 1935, Section 7a was left intact. The National Labor Relations Act of 1935 included Section 7a, and after the Supreme Court upheld that law in 1937, American workers gained the right to collective bargaining guaranteed by federal law and enforced by federal courts.

In the post–World War II period Congress passed the Taft-Hartley Act. The provisions of that legislation, which included Section 14b or the right-to-work law and the union shop, somewhat diminished the entire principle of collective bargaining. Hours, wages, and conditions of employment were still chief topics for negotiation between management and labor while union recognition was not as much an issue.

Presently collective bargaining still exists where there are unions in the workplace. In recent years collective bargaining has also been used by the National Football League Players Association and in the player associations of the National Basketball Association and the National and American Leagues in baseball.

Colorado Fuel and Iron Company

The Colorado Fuel and Iron Company was one of the enterprises in the Rockefeller empire in 1913. The company practiced the open shop principle and displayed a vigorous anti-union policy. When employees called a strike for recognition by the United Mine Workers of America (UMW), the company used thugs, special deputies, and state militia to repel union organizers and union men.

For months bloody warfare raged between thugs and strikers. The bloodiest episode occurred at Ludlow, where state troops fired machine guns into a tent city erected by the union after the miners

Armed strikers at Ludlow, Colorado, in 1913

were evicted from company houses. Tent fires set by company thugs and state militia killed 11 children and two women. The company still refused to grant recognition to the UMW.

When Congress investigated the Ludlow Massacre, John D. Rockefeller, Jr., appeared as a witness before the House Committee. Rockefeller shocked Congress and the nation by suggesting that the company would never capitulate to the union and that Colorado Fuel and Iron would use whatever means necessary to keep out the UMW. He also criticized union organizers who came into the Colorado coal mining region to cause trouble by provoking the miners. Rockefeller, in his testimony, stood firmly on the principle of the open shop.

The hostile attitude of Rockefeller toward the union was indicative of management's stance toward organized labor well into the New Deal era of the twentieth century and beyond. In most labor situations corporations used thugs, scabs, spies, house evictions, and all types of munitions to keep the American worker from joining a labor union, and it was open season on labor organizers nearly everywhere.

See also Ludlow Massacre.

Committee on Political Education (COPE)

With union membership on the decline following the passage by Congress of the Taft-Hartley Act (1947), which included Section 14(b)'s right-to-work provision, the American Federation of Labor-Congress of Industrial Organizations (AFL-CIO) established the Committee on Political Education (COPE). The purpose of COPE was to get out the labor vote in support of congressional, senatorial, and presidential candidates who had demonstrated a pro-labor proclivity.

Practically, COPE's strategy meant down-the-line endorsement of Democratic candidates. In 1956 it threw its support behind Democrat Adlai Stevenson for president. Four years later COPE energetically campaigned for John F. Kennedy against Richard M. Nixon. In both presidential contests, COPE also backed Democratic candidates for the House and the Senate. While Stevenson lost in 1956, Democrats did pick up a substantial number of seats in Congress. With Kennedy's narrow victory in 1960, Democrats again were in the driver's seat in Congress.

Despite its electoral successes, COPE failed in the final analysis because it could not muster enough votes in Congress to repeal the Taft-Hartley Act and to enact new pro-labor measures. Compared to the Congress of Industrial Organizations Political Action Committee (CIO-PAC), which was remarkably successful in FDR's reelection campaign in 1944, COPE was unsuccessful. Its major credit came when it blocked additional right-to-work laws on the state level. In only two states did COPE fail to stop nascent right-to-work laws. In five others—California, Ohio, Colorado, Idaho, and Washington—it vanquished antiunion foes.

See also Congress of Industrial Organizations Political Action Committee.

Commonwealth v. Hunt (Massachusetts, 1842)

In 1842 in Boston, the Journeymen Bootmakers' Society had in effect established a closed shop because its members vowed to boycott an employer who hired a bootmaker who did not belong to their society. In a historic decision rendered by Chief Justice Lemuel Shaw of the Massachusetts Supreme Court, the action of the bootmakers was upheld. The impact of the decision was that labor unions were lawful. Bootmakers and workers had a legal right, according to the court, to require union membership as a condition of employment. Employers were put in a position of having to accept the union, a situation that looked ahead to the twentieth century when the U.S. Supreme Court, by upholding the National Labor Relations Act (Wagner Act),

legalized labor unions throughout the United States. Justice Shaw's 1842 opinion in *Commonwealth v. Hunt* was a forerunner to *National Labor Relations Board v. Jones-Laughlin Steel Corporation* in 1937.

See also *National Labor Relations Board v. Jones-Laughlin Steel Corporation.*

Company Stores

In industrial areas, when a company erected a company town for its workers, a company store was built as a matter of convenience. Since many of the company towns in the southern Appalachian coalfields were located in remote areas, and since transportation was not always available to employees, the company store was vital, supplying workers with everything they needed.

Company stores sold everything from bubble gum and licorice candy to appliances. They ranged from one-story buildings to multi-storied edifices. In the early 1900s in Lynch, Kentucky, United States Coal and Coke Company, a subsidiary of United States Steel Corporation, built a three-story company store, United Supply Company, for its 3,000 coal miners and a local population of about 12,000.

Company employees nearly always received credit at the company store. Charges were deducted from their bi-monthly or monthly payroll checks along with other costs levied by the company. In coal mining areas especially, employees in time could identify with the song, "Sixteen Tons"—"You load sixteen tons, and whatta you get? Another day older and deeper in debt; St. Peter, dontcha call me, I ain't ready to go, I owe my soul to the company store."

With the passage of time and with the coming of labor unions, company executives took steps to ensure that workers bought all their necessities at the company store. One of the most important and dramatic methods was the issuance of scrip or company money in various denominations. Scrip was metallic money engraved with the company logo and redeemable at the company store. If workers tried to use the scrip at a chain store, it was discounted. The scrip system, which in some areas remained in place until the World War II period, tied workers to the company store. If employees received payments after cuts for such items as rent, water, lights, hospital, doctor, or burial funds, they were paid in scrip.

An ever-present fact of the company store was inflated prices. A perusal of prices charged for canned goods, meat, and staples showed prices above those of the supermarket chains and comparable to those of convenience stores. Since workers were forced to trade at the company store, they had to pay higher prices. During the depression of the 1920s and 1930s, there were companies who not only kept their workers on the payroll but allowed them credit at the company store. In some instances the companies never recovered what was owed them by employees who received credit.

The company store system survived into the 1970s. As labor unions were established in the New Deal era of the 1930s, most company stores vanished. As union members, workers no longer were compelled to shop at company stores. Then with the abandonment of the scrip system and the payment of workers in cash, employees were free to frequent chain supermarkets and independent stores, where prices were basically lower. A few relics, with the company name emblazoned on the facade, remain. Workers use the last of the company stores to pick up necessary items in an emergency, but they use supermarkets to make most of their purchases.

See also Scrip.

Company Towns

As the United States became industrialized in the late nineteenth and early twentieth centuries, many employers built self-contained, self-sufficient company towns for their workers. In the 1890s, George Pullman erected Pullman, Illinois, for the employees of the Pullman Palace Car Company. In the early years of the twentieth century, United States Steel constructed the town of Lynch, Kentucky, where the workers of United States Coal and Coke, a subsidiary of the parent company, resided. In both instances, company employees were required to live in the company town.

In the development of company towns, employers first moved in heavy equipment to knock down trees and excavate the land. Then row upon row of company houses were built. These houses were simply constructed, designed the same, and looked alike. Employers thrust many of these houses upon the least amount of available land. Called shotgun houses, they were long and narrow and located extremely close to each other. The company rented the houses to the workers with rents based on the number of rooms. The employees were charged extra for indoor plumbing and, in the twentieth century, electric lights. The houses were painted the same color—a dull gray or a drab green. If one had a porch, each one did. Before indoor plumbing, sanitation facilities were furnished by an outdoor privy behind the house. Houses were separated by lanes or streets, usually dirt, that filled with water during rainy seasons. At times stock roamed at large in the streets. Some companies kept the streets barricaded or chained so workers had to get permission to exit and then reenter the town. In some instances, the towns were enclosed by fences so company officials could keep employees under strict surveillance.

The company town, as mentioned earlier, was a self-sufficient entity in which every service was made available to the employees. There was a company store, a company doctor, a company clinic, a school, a church, a tavern or pub, a jail, and, of course, company policemen to keep law and order. In the town of Lynch, United States Steel built a hotel, a golf course, and an athletic field. Later,

Wheelwright, Kentucky, built by Inland Steel

companies included a movie theater. Many companies sponsored athletic teams, where the competition between rival organizations was keen indeed.

Lynch, Kentucky, was a modern company town of about 12,000 inhabitants. Near Lynch, however, were camps that were quite primitive, with dilapidated houses perched on the banks of creeks. Residents in those camps often pitched garbage out the back door into the creek, and when the flivver would run no more, it too went down the bank and into the creek.

While company towns were necessary at the beginning of industrialization to afford employees a place to live, work, and trade, with the passage of time, the employer used the company town as a mechanism to control workers and to keep out labor unions. Employers became paternalistic, much like slavemasters in the antebellum South. With the coming of unions in the twentieth century, workers had freedom of choice with regard to living arrangements, and company towns passed into history.

Company Unions

With industrial unionism on the rise during the New Deal years, many employers resorted to the formation of company unions to circumvent recognition of the larger, powerful international and national organizations. As the term suggests, the companies sponsored the unions, which were largely staffed by company foremen and/or supervisors, as well as those workers who were deeply loyal to the company. As time passed employees who held membership in a union whose leadership came from the rank and file referred to the leaders of company unions as company "sucks" or "stoolies."

In Harlan County, Kentucky, as the United Mine Workers of America attempted to organize coal miners in the 1930s, several operators established company unions. At Lynch, site of the United

States Coal and Coke operation (a subsidiary of United States Steel), the Union of Lynch Employees (ULE) was set up. At Yancey, home of the strongly anti-union Harlan Fuel Company headed by Charles S. Guthrie, the Yancey Workmen's Association was organized. At Poor Fork, the location of the Harlan Central Coal Corporation presided over by C. Vester Bennett, the Poor Fork Employees Association was established. In each case these company unions tried to head off the coal miners' membership in the United Mine Workers of America. Corporations also implemented the company union format in other industrial areas.

With the passage of the Wagner Act in 1935 and subsequent inquiries by the National Labor Relations Board into company union practices, the company unions declined for the most part. Employers, after federal intervention, then agreed to negotiate with the national or international organization. After all, since they were directly mandated by the employer, the company unions could hardly expect to grant all the goals of the workers.

Conference for Progressive Political Action (CPPA)

Established in 1922 in Chicago, the Conference for Progressive Political Action (CPPA) was a forerunner of the Progressive Party of 1924. Made up mostly of labor union leaders, women's labor delegates, and socialists, the CPPA in 1924 backed Robert M. "Fighting Bob" La Follette, Sr., for president over conservative Republican Calvin Coolidge and conservative Democrat John W. Davis. The CPPA's platform included abolition of government by injunction, the rights of workers to organize and join unions, and the right of labor to bargain collectively with the union of their choice.

At first the American Federation of Labor (AFL) shunned the CPPA, but when both the Republican and Democratic parties failed to heed its objectives, AFL chief Gompers backed La Follette for president. Other AFL leaders supported Coolidge and Davis. In the election of 1924 La Follette received nearly five million votes, but carried only his home state of Wisconsin. While the AFL broke from its tradition of not endorsing a third-party candidate, it could not marshal the labor vote for La Follette.

With La Follette's defeat, the AFL resumed its traditional practice of refusing to support a third-party candidate for president. The CPPA—Progressive Party—collapsed. Not until the 1930s under Franklin Delano Roosevelt's New Deal did labor find a party and a platform responsive to its goals.

It must be emphasized, however, that the Progressive Party of 1924 was the link between the People's Party of 1892 and the Democratic Party of 1932 with regard to embracing organized labor and its platform. The vote of the working class became almost a bloc vote for the Democrats in the 1930s.

Congress of Industrial Organizations (CIO)

The demise of the Knights of Labor in the late nineteenth century left most industrial blue-collar workers without union representation by a national organization. That void was filled in the 1930s with the organization of the Congress of Industrial Organizations. The new union began in 1935 as labor czar John L. Lewis and colleagues Sidney Hillman, David Dubinsky, and other union heads came together to form the Committee on Industrial Organization. Despite strong opposition from the American Federation of Labor (AFL), led by President William Green, Lewis and his lieutenants moved ahead with organizing campaigns in the automobile, rubber, steel, and mining industries.

Armed with the Wagner Act, which was upheld by the Supreme Court in the 1937 *National Labor Relations Board v. Jones-Laughlin Steel Corporation* case, independent unions—members of the CIO—were established in major American industries. The United Automobile Workers (UAW) scored a major victory in 1936–1937 by staging a sit-down strike against the General Motors Corporation in Flint, Michigan. The steelworkers won union contracts with both Big Steel (United States Steel) and Little Steel (Youngstown Sheet and Tube and Republic Steel). Similar victories were gained by rubber workers and Appalachia's coal miners. In 1938, after almost a decade of conflict between the United Mine Workers of America and coal operators of Harlan County, Kentucky, the United Mine Workers realized its first contract in Kentucky's leading coal county.

Still, the American Federation of Labor looked upon the CIO as a disruptive force in the ranks of organized labor. Lewis was adamant in his plan to go ahead with the CIO's goal of unionizing the nuts-and-bolts workers, especially since the AFL had not really tried to include those workers. President Franklin D. Roosevelt tried unsuccessfully to get the two major unions together.

After World War II, CIO and UAW President Walter Reuther and AFL chief George Meany began a series of negotiations leading to the merger of the two unions. After more than two years of preliminary talks, 80 AFL affiliates and 33 CIO members accepted a plan for merger in 1955. On 9 February 1955 the marriage became official, and in December of the same year, the first joint AFL-CIO convention convened. At that historic conclave, Meany was elected president and Reuther became vice-president in charge of industrial unions.

The mammoth union included over 17 million members. The AFL added 9 million workers to the organization, while the CIO contributed 6 million, and an additional 2.5 million came from the UMW and the railway brotherhoods.

With the advent of the Congress of Industrial Organizations and its merger with the AFL, big labor had become a reality in the U.S. economy. For decades, dating back to the 1870s, labor had been striving for recognition. Finally, after a struggle that lasted for nearly three-quarters of a century, labor achieved its goal. Now the American employer had to bargain with the union; now the union had input into hours, wages, working conditions, and fringe benefits. John L. Lewis became the Moses who led the industrial workers out of the wilderness into the promised land of political activism. Today the AFL-CIO is a viable and significant organization that, in both national, state, and local elections, is a force with which candidates must reckon.

See also American Federation of Labor.

Congress of Industrial Organizations Political Action Committee (CIO-PAC)

The Congress of Industrial Organizations Political Action Committee (CIO-PAC) was organized in 1944 by CIO chief Sidney Hillman to get out the labor vote for President Franklin D. Roosevelt in his bid for a fourth term against Republican governor Thomas E. Dewey of New York. The PAC's strategy included a nationwide house-to-house campaign to encourage voters to register as well as to enlighten the public regarding the stance of members of Congress on issues affecting labor. The PAC had a significant effect on the Democratic platform in the 1944 election and supported the nomination of Harry S Truman over South Carolina's James F. Byrnes for vice-president.

The PAC did its work well. In addition to the house-to-house campaigning, the committee flooded the country with all kinds of pro-labor documents setting forth labor's agenda of "full employment, fair wages, adequate housing, and social security." The strategy worked. In the 1944 election FDR beat Dewey by a landslide, and the voters gave their assent to another Democratic Congress.

Big business and Republicans attacked the CIO-PAC. It was said to be radical, un-American, and dominated by communists. In the end it was responsible for gaining the almost unanimous support of organized labor for the Democratic Party. Its influence in the election of 1952 tailed off, but the PAC was an effective instrument in FDR's reelection in 1944 and Truman's victory over Dewey in 1948.

See also Committee on Political Education.

Contract Labor

During the Civil War, Congress passed a contract labor law. Supported by such luminaries as Senator Charles Sumner of Massachusetts, Supreme Court Chief Justice Samuel Chase, and clergyman Henry Ward Beecher, the law allowed immigrants from northern and western Europe passage to the United States in return for an assessment or a lien against their wages. Upon arrival in the United States, the immigrants were expected to comprise an important part of the labor force for the nation's burgeoning industries, including the railroads and manufacturing plants.

To implement the plan, the American Emigrant Company was formed. It recruited workers in cooperation with the railroads, steamship lines, and various factories. As a result a sort of indentured servitude, similar to what had existed in colonial America, was introduced.

Despite the efforts of the American Emigrant Company and its illustrious subscribers, very few immigrants came to the United States as contract laborers. Then immigration ebbed with the coming of the Civil War, accelerating again after the war's end. The new immigration from southern and eastern Europe and from China and Japan flowed unabated into the United States because there were no immigration quota laws. Western railroads, for example, used Chinese coolies until Congress intervened. Yet contract labor as a work force supplier for U.S. industry never really materialized—immigrants came by the thousands until restrictive quotas were imposed during the 1920s, but they did not come as contract laborers.

Cooling-Off Periods

Cooling-off periods in labor originated during World War II when strikes in defense industries would have seriously hampered the country's war effort. In 1941 cooling-off periods were suggested for 30 days, during which attempts were made to arbitrate labor disputes. After thirty days a majority vote of workers in elections supervised by the government was needed to call a strike.

Later a bill cosponsored by Congressman Howard Smith of Virginia and Senator Tom Connally of Texas included a 30-day cooling-off period. In the Smith-Connally Act a work stoppage would be averted for 30 days while the National Labor Relations Board conducted a strike vote of employees.

In the post–World War II era, Congressman Francis Case introduced a bill that called for a 60-day cooling-off period before a strike could be called. President Truman vetoed the bill because it was anti-labor and anti-union. When the Republicans gained complete control of Congress in the midterm elections of 1946, they were able to override presidential vetoes. Later Congress passed the Taft-Hartley Act, which included the 60-day cooling-off stipulation of the Case Bill. When Truman vetoed the measure, Congress promptly overrode the veto. The new law also allowed the president to secure an 80-day injunction against any strike that might jeopardize national health or safety.

Because of the possibility of strikes that might hamper the nation's war effort and national health and safety, cooling-off periods were enacted by law during and after World War II. While the cooling-off period was in effect, negotiations to deter a strike took place.

Coppage v. Kansas (U.S., 1915)

During the Progressive era the state of Kansas attempted to outlaw yellow-dog contracts, contracts in which the employer stipulated that the employee could not affiliate with a labor organization. In 1915 the U.S. Supreme Court ruled in *Coppage* that the state law prohibiting yellow-dog contracts was unconstitutional. In its decision the Court held that the employer should be able to hire an employee at whatever wage the two could decide without any third-party input, that is, input from a labor union. The Court also ruled in favor of freedom of contract between the employer and employee. Its decision reflected the stance of the judicial system in the early twentieth century, which favored the property rights of the owners over the human rights of the workers.

The state law outlawing yellow-dog contracts, according to the decision in *Coppage v. Kansas*, violated the due process clause of the Fourteenth Amendment. Justice John Marshall Harlan, in support of the Court's majority opinion, affirmed that the state statute had nothing whatsoever to do with the health, morals, and welfare of the state.

See also *Adair v. United States;* Yellow-Dog Contracts.

Coxey's Army (1894)

Jacob S. Coxey was an Ohio businessman who, in early 1894, organized and led a group of unemployed workers in what may have been the first march on Washington, D.C. As the walk kicked off, the country was in the throes of the panic of 1894, which was accentuated by widespread unemployment. Since the federal government was not providing relief measures, Coxey's army and demonstration was in support of a massive federal jobs program.

Coxey and his aides left Ohio with about 500 marchers. Other groups were to converge with the main column at the nation's capitol. When the motley crew reached Washington, Coxey and his coleaders were arrested for trespassing. With its leaders in custody, Washington policemen, using clubs and sticks, effectively scattered the ragtag demonstrators.

While no relief was forthcoming in the late nineteenth century, the march of Coxey and his cohorts was but a prelude to other demonstrations and to various types of work relief programs, such as the Civilian Conservation Corps of the New Deal years and the Job Corps of Lyndon Johnson's 1960s Great Society agenda.

Jacob Coxey

Daily Worker

The *Daily Worker* was an official publication of the Communist Party. During the labor strife of the depression years, copies of the leftist organ were circulated among workers in an attempt both to inform them about the party's labor philosophy and to solicit them as party members.

One notable area in which the *Daily Worker* appeared was the Harlan County, Kentucky, coalfield. The editor of the *Daily Worker*, Harry Gannes, showed up in eastern Kentucky as a member of Theodore Dreiser's National Committee for the Defense of Political Prisoners (NCDPP). The *Daily Worker* also dispatched reporter Vern Smith to cover the aborted National Miners' Union Strike in Bell and Harlan counties on 1 January 1932.

The newspaper and its representatives were successful in converting a handful of workers to the Communist Party. On the whole, however, there were only a few depressed employees who abandoned the stars and stripes for the hammer and sickle.

Dale, Charles

Charles Dale, who was born in Nova Scotia and studied at Victoria University in Wellington, New Zealand, was a major labor leader who helped bring unions into the newspaper business in Canada. As president of the Federation of Guild Representatives, he was the chief bargaining operative for the Newspaper Guild's staff. Before being elected to head the Newspaper Guild in the United States, Dale successfully organized the Canadian Wire Service Guild's unit of the Canadian Broadcasting Corporation.

While the Newspaper Guild is a relatively small union, numbering around 40,000 members in the mid-1980s, under Dale's leadership it represented newspaper reporters as well as clerical personnel, photographers, janitors, and key punch and computer operators. Established in the 1930s, the guild was the first industrial union in the newspaper industry.

Charles Dale is quite critical of the Deep South's attitude toward organized labor. He also opposes the right-to-work laws put into effect by Section 14(b) of the 1947 Taft-Hartley Act. To Dale, labor unions are vital to keep employers from underpaying, overworking, and generally harassing their employees. Labor unions, he believes, are necessary to provide job security for the work force. Further, Dale does not subscribe to the notion that it is degrading to enroll in a labor union. A prototype of a 1920s or 1930s union boss, Dale is most at home out in the field addressing the workers on the benefits of belonging to a labor organization and signing them up as members. The union needs the workers and, in turn, they need the union. Succinctly, that is Charles Dale's motto as a modern labor leader.

Danbury Hatters Case
See Loewe v. Lawlor.

Darrow, Clarence (1857–1938)

A distinguished and famous defense attorney for several decades, Clarence Darrow was a native of Chicago, Illinois. He began his career as a law partner of the famous John Peter Altgeld, who gained stature as a friend of labor by pardoning three Haymarket rioters in 1893 during his term as Illinois governor.

Darrow's real claim to fame came in 1894 when he defended Eugene Victor

Debs and the American Railway Union against the George M. Pullman Company. From that point Darrow became a champion of labor, a defender of the down and the outcast, literally an attorney for the damned. More often than not the Chicago barrister could be found in a courtroom defending minority rights and clients involved in unpopular causes such as strikes and labor unions.

Darrow, in fact, became a labor attorney. In the nationwide anthracite strike of 1902, which occurred during the administration of President Theodore Roosevelt, Darrow represented the union and the coal miners. Later he defended William D. "Big Bill" Haywood, president of the Industrial Workers of the World, and two other Wobbly leaders accused of the murder of former Idaho governor Frank Steunenberg.

A Democrat all his life, Darrow's fame increased as a defense lawyer during the famous Monkey Trial of 1925 in Dayton, Tennessee. While that case had nothing to do with organized labor, the publicity given the trial by the national media added to Darrow's reputation as a people's lawyer.

When it was unpopular to take the side of organized labor and to represent labor leaders, Clarence Darrow went against the grain to become one of the nation's first and famous labor lawyers.

Debs, Eugene Victor (1855–1926)

A native of Terre Haute, Indiana, Eugene V. Debs became the country's foremost socialist and a dedicated labor leader in the late nineteenth and early twentieth centuries. A railroad worker, Debs emerged as a leader of a railroad craft union. From that position, especially after the railroad brotherhoods failed to improve conditions, Debs organized the American Railway Union (ARU) in 1893.

In 1894 when the Pullman Palace Car Company imposed a wage cut on Pullman workers, Debs led a strike of ARU workers against the company. Despite a federal court injunction against the strike, Debs and the ARU stood firm. Finally he was sent to jail for six months in Woodstock, Illinois, for violating the antistrike court order. While in prison Debs came to the conclusion that the plight of the working class would never be improved within the capitalist system. Once out of confinement, Debs became a socialist and a leading mover and shaker within the Socialist Party. Five times Debs was the party's presidential candidate.

When the United States entered World War I, Debs opposed both the war and the draft. His opposition to the war effort landed him back in jail, this time in federal prison in Atlanta, Georgia. While in prison Debs ran for president, receiving nearly a million votes. He was released in 1921 after receiving a pardon from President Harding.

Out of prison, Debs tried unsuccessfully to reenergize the Socialist Party. Failing in that effort, he endorsed Senator Robert M. "Fighting Bob" La Follette, Sr., for president on the Progressive Party ticket in 1924.

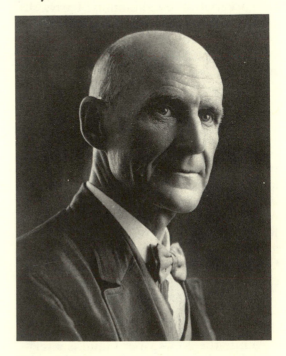

Eugene V. Debs

Debs was one of American labor's most committed leaders during his lifetime. On one occasion he said, "While there is a lower class, I am in it. While there is a criminal element, I am of it. While there is a soul in prison, I am not free." Despite his socialistic tendencies, Debs was not looked upon by his contemporaries as a criminal syndicalist. Clarence Darrow once remarked of Debs: "There may have lived sometime, somewhere, a kindlier, gentler, more generous man than Eugene Debs, but I have not known him."

DeFee, John M.

A union veteran of nearly half a century, John M. DeFee became international secretary-treasurer of the United Paperworkers International Union (UPIU) in 1983. The union presently has over a quarter million members in both the United States and Canada.

DeFee came up through the ranks as a labor leader. First he served as secretary of his local, then treasurer, vice-president, and president. Then in the 1960s he was an international representative (organizer).

Initial attempts to organize workers in the paper industry began in 1876 in Stroudsburg, Maine. Following a strike in which workers' grievances went unaddressed, the workers torched the paper mill. Papermakers later organized in Holyoke, Massachusetts, and from that point, paper mill workers joined such unions as the United Paperworkers of America, the International Brotherhood of Paperworkers, and the International Brotherhood of Pulp, Sulfite, and Paper-mill Workers. The UPIU was born in 1972.

As one of the UPIU's leading representatives, DeFee, like Charles Dale, was a rabid union adherent. He simply could not understand why workers refused to participate in the union movement, especially when they lived in company shacks with few or no amenities. The union, he believed, was responsible for improving the conditions of the workers. DeFee also firmly believed that the union should organize workers in the South. His motto, I love my union, was a throwback to the days of William H. Sylvis in the mid-nineteenth century.

DeLeon, Daniel

A socialist leader in the early twentieth century, Daniel DeLeon represented a radical faction at a Chicago convention that led to the formation of the Industrial Workers of the World (IWW). A dominating leader and outstanding speaker and writer, DeLeon waged a long-standing feud against the American Federation of Labor (AFL). Known as the socialist Pope, DeLeon referred to AFL President Samuel Gompers as "a labor joker," "an entrapped swindler," and "a greasy tool of Wall Street."

Other socialists opposed DeLeon's iron-fisted rule and revolutionary philosophy. They were led by Eugene Debs, who was more tolerant of the trade union movement. Both socialist leaders attended the IWW convention in Chicago in 1905. While they promised to resolve their differences, in the final analysis, DeLeon and his followers broke with the AFL.

Daniel DeLeon favored political action by the workers. His philosophy included revolution, the overthrow of capitalism, and the replacement of the capitalistic government with a government of, by, and for the workers. DeLeon's goal was one big union and one big strike, a class struggle until the workers gained control of the tools of production and set up a state controlled by the working class. One big strike, he believed, would lead to utopia, to the power of the working class.

Obviously DeLeon's approach was in opposition to the policies of Debs and Gompers. His was a minority voice, and the IWW enjoyed successes on a limited scale as the American working class generally refused to embrace the doctrines of radicalism espoused by DeLeon through the union.

Department of Labor

In 1903 President Theodore Roosevelt submitted a bill to Congress establishing a Department of Commerce and Labor with a Bureau of Corporations empowered to probe monopolies and trusts. When Congress dragged its feet, Roosevelt called a press conference and charged John D. Rockefeller with opposing the measure. The ruse worked. Congress speedily enacted the bill, setting up a Department of Commerce and Labor.

A decade later, during the administration of President Woodrow Wilson, the two departments were separated and an independent Department of Labor was established. To head the department, Wilson chose William B. Wilson, an esteemed official of the United Mine Workers of America. The new labor department included a Division of Conciliation with authority to step in and help arbitrate labor disputes and strikes.

In 1933 President Franklin D. Roosevelt appointed the first woman to a presidential cabinet when he named Frances Perkins secretary of labor. Famous as Madam Secretary, Perkins was vitally involved in the 1930s and 1940s in enforcing labor legislation passed by Congress as well as attempting to settle disputes between management and labor. Her department's Federal Mediation and Conciliation Service directly intervened in the labor strife of the New Deal years to bring about settlements.

Years later, when Congress passed the Taft-Hartley Act during the administration of President Harry S Truman, an independent Federal Mediation and Conciliation Service was established. Its authority largely consisted of intervening in labor disputes that could disrupt interstate commerce and the economy. In recent years federal mediators have presided over nonstop talks in efforts to end long-standing labor disputes that jeopardized the economy.

Dos Passos, John (1896–1970)

Following World War I and during the second American renaissance, several American writers, referred to by Gertrude Stein as the Lost Generation, were so disillusioned with American society and culture they authored works that emphasized individualism. Weary of the war and President Woodrow Wilson's Great Crusade, John Dos Passos and his colleagues took a somewhat cynical attitude toward the United States and its institutions.

A radical, Dos Passos was most famous for his trilogy, *U.S.A.*, published in 1939. Before the publication of that monumental work, Dos Passos joined the leftist National Committee for the Defense of Political Prisoners (NCDPP). Headquartered in New York and led by another radical author, Theodore Dreiser, the NCDPP in 1931 made a foray into the eastern Kentucky coalfields to investigate an alleged reign of terror in the troubled coal counties of Bell and Harlan. As part of the Dreiser troupe, Dos Passos from the outset was greeted by local authorities with suspicion and resentment. Foreign meddlers from the East, and especially liberals, were personae non grata in the twin coal counties. Despite attempts by local governmental structure to head off the inquiry, committee members, including Dos Passos, toured the area interrogating miners, their wives, and other local residents.

Despite attempts by the local political establishment to harass and impugn the integrity of Dos Passos and his colleagues, the NCDPP stayed in the area to complete its work. As a result of the NCDPP probe, *Harlan Miners Speak* was published. The thrust of that tome was that despite denials by the locals, there was indeed a reign of terror among the coal miners and their families in the Bell-Harlan area. According to Dos Passos and others, it was perpetrated by local law enforcement and judicial systems aided and abetted by the coal operators.

A preliminary inquiry into conditions in the coalfield was then made by a U.S.

Senate subcommittee of the Committee on Manufactures in May 1932. Following testimony by miners and their families, along with that offered by writers, journalists, and the clergy, the Senate subcommittee decided not to conduct a full-scale inquiry.

It must be noted that the junket and investigation of Dos Passos and the NCDPP in 1931 paved the way for subsequent inquiries into conditions in the coalfields, which in time led to federal intervention (1938–1939) to secure for the coal miners their right to join the United Mine Workers of America.

Dreiser, Theodore (1871–1945)

A native of Terre Haute, Indiana, Theodore Dreiser was a member of a family who experienced extreme poverty. Growing up in the Hoosier state he briefly attended Indiana University and was a reporter in Chicago, St. Louis, and Pittsburgh. In the 1890s he moved to New York, where he became an editor, editor-in-chief, and free-lance writer. In the twentieth century Dreiser became an important American novelist of the schools of realism and naturalism. His first novel, *Sister Carrie*, was so filled with realism and frank discussions of sex that the publisher decided against its issue. Later it was published, leading to other novels by Dreiser.

In the post–World War I era Dreiser converted to socialism. In the 1920s he visited Russia, returning to the United States to view the impact of the depression. Seeing bread lines and the unemployed queued up for soup made from tomato ketchup and water, Dreiser commented that he saw no such lines in Russia. That, he said, meant communism was a better system than capitalism. Near the end of his life Dreiser converted to Catholicism and received communion.

As mentioned, most of Dreiser's works were filled with realism and naturalism. A socialist and a limousine liberal, Dreiser in November 1931 headed the National Committee for the Defense of Political Prisoners, which went to Kentucky to investigate conditions among the coal miners. Against the advice of John Dos Passos, Dreiser took along a comely secretary named Marie Pergain. While stopping at the Continental Hotel in Pineville, Kentucky, one evening, some local citizens, upon seeing the scantily clad Marie enter the famous author's room, crept up to the door and placed a row of toothpicks along the bottom. When the toothpicks were still intact the next morning, Dreiser was charged with adultery in a warrant issued by Bell County authorities. Before the author could be arraigned, he agreed to leave the area. The case against Dreiser was dropped, but from Bristol, Tennessee, he issued a statement that while he enjoyed the ladies and was fond of their companionship, he was not guilty of adultery because he was "completely and finally impotent." The local newspaper warned the New York writer next time "to reach for a toothpick instead of a sweetie."

In *Harlan Miners Speak*, Dreiser revealed the denial of civil rights to Kentucky coal miners by the local sheriffs and their thug gangs. Lack of free speech, free assembly, and free press, he attested, were effective deterrents to the unionization of coal miners. As a result of his pilgrimage into the coalfields and the publicity given to conditions there, the federal government finally intervened in the decade-long conflict among the miners, operators, and law officers.

When he went to the Kentucky coalfields in 1931, Dreiser may have had in mind additional publicity or the gathering of material for another book. He was charged on both counts by local officials. Whatever Harlan-Bell citizens thought about the author and his trip to Kentucky, it is clear that while no immediate benefits came to the miners in the wake of his journey, in the long run additional publicity by other investigative agencies did result in the emancipation of coal miners from long hours, low wages, and unsafe working conditions. A liberal, a radical, a socialist, a communist, a Christian, yes, at one time in his life—Dreiser was all of these things. Impacting his writings was a social conscience that led to improved conditions for toiling miners in the first three decades of the twentieth century.

Dubinsky, David (1892–1982)

An effective trade union leader and president of the International Ladies Garment Workers Union (ILGWU), David Dubinsky was one of the founding fathers of the Congress of Industrial Organizations (CIO) in the 1930s.

Born in Poland, Dubinsky as a youth was exiled to Siberia for involvement in socialist activities. After escaping from a Russian prison, he migrated to the United States and took a job in a New York sweatshop. Following the tragic Triangle Shirtwaist fire, in which 146 workers either were burned to death or jumped to their deaths to escape raging flames, Dubinsky became active in the social justice movement.

Along with his post with the ILGWU and his role in the formation of the CIO, Dubinsky was also instrumental in welding together the CIO and the American Federation of Labor after two decades of intensive warfare.

As one of the country's stalwart labor leaders, Dubinsky built the ILGWU into a union of nearly half a million members. He stood firmly for better wages and working conditions, fringe benefits, and improved health and safety conditions for workers. As an ILGWU hero, Dubinsky made his union a model for organized labor. It accumulated a half billion dollars in pension, welfare, and treasury funds; developed cooperative housing, health centers, and a vacation resort in the Poconos of Pennsylvania; and ventured into the theater and movies. Attesting to Dubinsky's concern for humanity, the ILGWU dispensed over $40 million to labor and charitable causes.

Dubinsky remained loyal and true to capitalism. Often he was invited by U.S. presidents to the White House as a guest. To him labor needed capitalism as a fish needs water. He also fought against racketeering and corruption in labor, not stopping until labor miscreants like Jimmy Hoffa were ousted and Dave Beck and other labor racketeers were behind bars.

Following his retirement as ILGWU president, Dubinsky looked with horror upon declining wage standards triggered by the movement of garment makers to the south to take advantage of nonunion labor and lower wages. He also decried parcelling out to foreign locales work formerly done in the United States as the garment industry sought to circumvent ILGWU labor by paying a lower wage scale.

David Dubinsky's autobiography, published in 1977, is appropriately entitled *A Life with Labor*. While he stood only five-feet-five-inches tall, Dubinsky was a clarion voice for labor for virtually a lifetime. Truly he championed the rights of the working class, giving little thought to his own safety and comfort. A modest little man, he did not seek personal acclaim; instead his efforts were expended in behalf of the working class. He never forgot his roots, the days he spent in a New York sweatshop. His burning desire was to provide thousands of garment workers a workplace and a life-style befitting the dignity of the working class. In that, as a true champion of labor, he succeeded.

DuBois, William Edward Burghardt (1868–1963)

The first African American to receive a Ph.D. from Harvard University, W. E. B. DuBois was born in Great Barrington, Massachusetts. DuBois joined the faculty of Atlanta University, where he authored *The Souls of Black Folk* in 1903. In that book he severely criticized Booker T.

W. E. B. DuBois

Washington for failing to embrace full rights of citizenship for African Americans.

DuBois was one of the leading organizers of the Niagara Movement, established in 1905 to work for the end of racial discrimination in America. The Niagara Movement gave rise to the establishment of the National Association for the Advancement of Colored People (NAACP) in 1909. The NAACP, under DuBois's leadership, called for the end of segregation in the workplace and in hiring, and for equal opportunity for African Americans on the job and in supervisory capacities. As an early leader of the NAACP, DuBois advocated integration. During the Depression he became disenchanted with integration, turning to black nationalism and separatism. Subsequently, he was relieved of his NAACP duties.

A civil rights leader without an organization to implement his program, DuBois embraced socialism. After World War II he was accused of being a Soviet agent, charges that were later dropped. In his early 90s, DuBois, completely at odds with the United States, joined the Communist Party. He gave up his U.S. citizenship and moved to Ghana, where he died in 1963.

DuBois's emphasis on the full rights of citizenship for all Americans earned for him a place as one of the country's greatest African American leaders. Both black nationalists and black integrationists hailed him as one of their greatest champions.

Duke Power Company

A North Carolina corporation, Duke Power Company in 1970 acquired the coal mine formerly known as Harlan Collieries at Brookside, in Harlan County, Kentucky, from the Bryan Whitfield family of Alabama. Duke changed the name of the mine to Eastover Mining Company. It also bought other mines in neighboring Bell County and across the mountain in Lee County, Virginia. The Eastover mine was located on Clover Fork, one of Harlan's richest coal-producing areas in the 1930s. Duke Power also acquired the nearby High Splint mine.

Within a week after purchasing Eastover, Duke Power agreed to a contract with the Southern Labor Union (SLU), regarded by many miners in Harlan as a scab outfit. The miners at Eastover did not get to vote on representation by the SLU; the company simply told them, "here is your union."

Three years later the Brookside miners called for an election before Eastover's contract with the SLU expired. The men wanted the United Mine Workers of America (UMW) to represent them, and although the company terminated several UMW men, the miners nevertheless voted 113 to 55 to change unions. When negotiations between the UMW and Eastover broke down, the miners walked out, beginning a yearlong strike at the Brookside operation.

The 1973 strike at Brookside and High Splint was similar to the labor controversy of the 1930s in Harlan County. The UMW set up a picket line, Eastover brought in scabs, the company asked Circuit Judge Byrd Hogg, a former coal operator, to limit the pickets to three per mine, and the judge granted the company's request.

There was one significant difference in the Brookside strike of 1973 and Bloody Harlan of the 1930s. Harlan women, many of whom were wives and relatives of the strikers, went to mines armed with switches to use against scabs, and the judge's order applied only to strikers, not women. Finally, Judge Hogg extended his order to include women, and when they refused to obey the injunction, they were taken to the Harlan County jail. Several women took their children with them. The media circulated pictures of jailed women and children, arousing sympathy for the strikers and their families all across the nation.

The Brookside conflict raged into 1974. Eastover began to fire strikers and evict them from company houses. A picket line went up on Kentucky Highway 38 at the High Splint mine. In the summer of 1974 a scab was shot at High Splint, and the home of UMW local President Mickey Messer was the target of gunfire in the night. Meanwhile, UMW miners and their supporters picketed Duke Power Company on Wall Street.

Then on the hot, sultry day of 24 August 1974, Lawrence Dean Jones, a Brookside UMW miner, met up with Billy Carroll Bruner, a company supervisor at Brookside and High Splint on Jones Creek in Harlan County. The two were friends before the strike, but found themselves on opposite sides of the dispute. Bruner pulled his pistol and shot Jones, who died in the Harlan hospital, leaving his 16-year-old wife and three-month-old baby. Bruner was later acquitted of murder.

In the wake of the Jones killing, stockholders of Duke Power threatened to sue the company for gross mismanagement. The suit was never filed. In the meantime Duke Power CEO Carl Horn and Eastover President Norman Yarborough flew to Washington for negotiations with the UMW to end the strike. After a bloody, 13-month-long conflict, appropriately called the "second Bloody Harlan," the company agreed to a contract with the UMW.

See also Black Mountain.

Duplex Printing Company v. Deering (U.S., 1921)

Congress, in 1914, passed the Clayton Anti-Trust Act. The law, which was designed to restrict trusts, was also referred to as Labor's Magna Carta. The Clayton Act suggested that the Sherman Anti-Trust Act (1890) should not regard labor unions as conspiracies that restrained interstate commerce. It also prohibited injunctions in labor disputes "unless necessary to prevent irreparable injury to property, or to a property right . . . for which injury there is no adequate remedy at law."

In the midst of labor's lean years of the 1920s, with Chief Justice William Howard Taft (the "injunction judge") presiding, the Supreme Court effectively weakened the Clayton Act in *Duplex Printing Company.* In its decision the Court ruled that the Clayton Act did not make secondary boycotts lawful or protect unions from injunctions.

With this decision, management continued to use injunctions against organized labor until the 1932 passage of the Norris-LaGuardia Act. Unions and labor achieved effective relief from the injunction law with the rise of big labor during the New Deal years.

See also Clayton Anti-Trust Act.

Eastover Mining Company
See Duke Power Company.

Eight-Hour Day
The eight-hour day crusade in American labor began in the 1860s when the National Labor Union, headed by William H. Sylvis, called for a shorter workday. Chief spokesman for the eight-hour day was Ira Steward, a Boston machinist and a member of the National Labor Union. Steward took his message to union meetings, published many tracts, and spoke to the Massachusetts legislature in support of the eight-hour day. He also established the Grand Eight Hour League of Massachusetts.

Alas, the efforts of Steward and others immediately resulted only in the adoption of an eight-hour day by the federal government for its workers and by six states for state employees.

In the twentieth century, the Adamson Act (1916) established an eight-hour day for the nation's railroad workers. Further attempts to regulate the hours of workers during the Progressive period were unsuccessful, except for women laundry employees in Oregon.

Maximum hours laws for most workers were not legislated by Congress until the 1930s. As part of the New Deal, in 1938 Congress passed the Fair Labor Standards Act, which authorized an eight-hour day for most employees. It was not until the passage of that law that the nine-to-five workday became a reality for a majority of the nation's workers.
See also Ten-Hour Day.

Employer's Associations
Associations of employers, or employers' unions, in essence, were set up early in the twentieth century to circumvent the organization of employees into labor unions. The basic premise of employer's associations was the open or nonunion shop. The Industrial Alliances and the Citizens' Industrial Association were two early employers' associations. The National Association of Manufacturers (NAM) openly assailed organized labor and the closed shop.

The 1920s saw a profusion of employers' groups that supported the open shop principle, particularly in the key industrial states of the Northeast and Midwest. Those groups had allies in chambers of commerce and the National Association of Manufacturers, among other organizations. As a result, the American Plan—the name given to the open shop—became the watchword of employers' groups around the country.

With the advent of big labor in the 1930s, employers continued to form associations to combat national labor unions and the closed shop. Following World War II the NAM and its sister alliances joined in concert to support the passage of the Taft-Hartley Act (1947). That law, which was passed over President Truman's veto, dealt a severe blow to the closed shop. Into the 1970s the NAM as well as other employers' associations continued to band together both to oppose labor unions and the closed shop.

Erdman Act (1898)
The Erdman Act, passed by Congress in 1898, outlawed discrimination against the nation's railway workers, specifically employees of interstate railroads, because of union membership. Although this provision of the law was later set aside by the Supreme Court in *Adair v. United States*, the Erdman Act was one of the first federal laws designed to protect

the right of workers to join a labor organization.

See also Adair v. United States.

Ethical Practices Committee

The Ethical Practices Committee of the AFL-CIO was set up soon after the merger of the American Federation of Labor (AFL) and Congress of Industrial Organizations (CIO). The purpose of the committee was to ferret out corruption in labor and to impose on labor leaders a code of conduct in an effort to combat racketeering and corruption by union officials.

The Ethical Practices Committee was organized as a voluntary effort by labor to cleanse itself of corrupt practices. The fact that labor leaders were identified with gangsterism and the mafia caused a great deal of concern in the AFL-CIO leadership. Charges of corruption were lodged principally against the Teamsters and the International Longshoremen's Association.

Labor's attempt to rid its ranks of racketeers, gangsters, hoodlums, and the mafia did not head off a federal investigation of crime in labor by the McClellan Committee (1957). Headed by Arkansas Senator John McClellan, it probed deeply into alleged criminal activities of the Teamsters, along with several smaller unions.

Disclosures to the McClellan Committee pressed the Ethical Practices Committee into action. It placed a number of unions, including the Teamsters, on probation. When these unions failed to reform leadership and practices, they were expelled from the AFL-CIO.

To deal with corruption in labor unions, and as a direct outgrowth of the McClellan inquiry, Congress in 1959 passed the Landrum-Griffin Act, aimed toward cleaning up union corruption.

Fair Labor Standards Act (1938)

Legislated by Congress in 1938 as part of Franklin D. Roosevelt's second New Deal, the Fair Labor Standards Act (FLSA) enacted a minimum wage of 25 cents per hour and a work week of 44 hours. The law provided that minimum wages would rise to 40 cents per hour by the end of World War II and that the work week would be cut back to a 40 hours within three years. Another important stipulation of the law restricted firms from shipping products in interstate commerce if children under the age of 16 were employed.

The FLSA was challenged in the courts, and in 1941 the Supreme Court upheld the act in *United States v. Darby Lumber Company*.

The Fair Labor Standards Act was the culmination of a goal sought by labor in both the nineteenth and early twentieth centuries. Ira Steward, the high priest of the eight-hour day movement, had called for a nine-to-five workday in the late nineteenth century. In the first two decades of the twentieth century the Progressives had tried to legislate maximum hours, minimum wages, and a national child labor law. They enjoyed limited success on the state level, especially

"Breaker boys" sort slate from anthracite coal in the 1900s before the passage of the Fair Labor Standards Act.

in Western states, but a federal child labor law, enacted under President Woodrow Wilson, was struck down by a conservative court. Now came a liberal Roosevelt Court, made by Roosevelt's appointments after the court-packing episode of his second term, to approve the FLSA. U.S. policies toward maximum hours, minimum wages, and an effective child labor law had come full circle.

As amended, the law's provisions remain in effect to the present. The FLSA set up a minimum wage scale that is still followed, as is the maximum hours stipulation. Some employers circumvent the child labor law through the hiring of both part-time help and laborers engaged in seasonal work.

See also United States v. Darby Lumber Company.

Federal Laboratories

According to the investigation of the La Follette Civil Liberties Committee into the trouble in the Harlan County, Kentucky, coalfield in the 1930s, Federal Laboratories was an operation that furnished all kinds and types of weapons and ammunition to the coal operators to use against the United Mine Workers of America. Several coal companies, on request, produced invoices that showed purchases of revolvers, shotguns, rifles, tear gas grenades, sickening gas grenades, riot guns, both long- and short-range projectiles, and Thompson submachine guns. In short, several coal companies maintained well-stocked company arsenals during labor's civil war in the 1930s.

Federal Laboratories, in addition to being a supplier of weapons to Kentucky coal corporations, also shipped sizable amounts of armaments to other corporate interests in the United States. In fact, when the La Follette Committee subpoenaed company executives, attempts were made by the companies to destroy their records. Not to be outdone, the committee sent its agents to incinerators to procure fragments of invoices, which were transported to Washington where the records were pieced together laboriously. In that manner the La Follette inquirers successfully linked Federal Laboratories to a blue book of corporations who bought arms and ammunitions in an attempt to prevent the American working class from joining labor unions.

Federal Mediation and Conciliation Service

In 1947 the U.S. Congress passed the Taft-Hartley Act, cosponsored by Republican Senator Robert A. Taft of Ohio and Michigan Congressman Fred Hartley. President Harry S Truman vetoed the law, but a Republican-controlled Congress easily passed the bill over presidential veto.

Title II of the law, which was designed both to curb the power and excesses of organized labor as well as to put in place machinery for dealing with strikes that impaired a national emergency, also set up the Federal Mediation and Conciliation Service. The new federal agency was an independent body with power to intervene into any labor controversy that could seriously disrupt interstate trade or commerce.

The new board provided federal mediators and conciliators, whose principal function was to arbitrate long-standing labor disputes that were detrimental to the national economy. For example, federal arbitrators could and did involve themselves in coal and steel strikes along with rail and trucking lines work stoppages. By bringing labor and management together in what often were nonstop, round-the-clock bargaining sessions, solutions were found and disputes resolved more or less amicably. The idea behind the intense negotiations was to seek an end to disputes so workers could return to their jobs to keep the economy moving.

The Federal Mediation and Conciliation Service is an important agency that today is still used to arbitrate labor-management disputes.

Federated Press

During the Harlan County, Kentucky, coal mine war of 1931–1932, the Federated Press sent at least two of its reporters to relate alleged acts of terrorism against the coal miners by the Harlan County Coal Operators Association. The county's sole newspaper, the *Harlan Daily Enterprise*, was pro-operator. Except for its staff writers and possible Associated Press reporters, outside correspondents and writers were personae non grata in Kentucky's Home of Good Coal.

The treatment received by Winnetka, Illinois, writers Boris Israel and Mrs. Harvey O'Connor at the hands of Harlan County officials was not totally unexpected. On 17 August 1931, Israel was abducted at the Harlan County courthouse, taken to the hills for a "little mountain air," dumped out at the county line, and shot in the leg by deputy sheriffs who warned him to hit the road and never return to Harlan County.

Following the unceremonious departure of Israel, Mrs. O'Connor was sent to Harlan by Federated Press. She was in the county only a short while before she received a note telling her she had been in the county too long already and that she should not let the sun go down on her in Harlan County. The threatening note was signed "100 per cent Americans." Undeterred, Mrs. O'Connor said she would stay, saying, "I am not afraid anything will happen to me."

Both Israel and O'Connor were abused by Harlan County authorities because they represented what was reputed to be a radical newspaper. In 1931–1932, outsiders, whether they came as writers, clergymen or students, were anathemic in the Harlan County coalfields. When outsiders entered the county, they often received the kind of harassment extended to Israel and O'Connor.

Fitzsimmons, Frank (1908–1981)

James R. Hoffa, president of the International Brotherhood of Teamsters, went to jail in 1967 on charges of corruption and gangsterism. His handpicked successor, Frank Fitzsimmons, assumed leadership of the Teamsters upon Hoffa's departure. Instead of a change in Teamster affairs, the union traveled down the same corrupt road under Fitzsimmons's leadership. Because the new Teamsters president was a devout Republican, President Richard M. Nixon tolerated him and his abuses of union power.

After serving only four years in federal prison, Hoffa was pardoned by Nixon in 1971 on the condition he would separate himself from involvement in Teamster affairs and elections. In 1974, however, he apparently planned to challenge Frank Fitzsimmons for the presidency of the Teamsters. Before this could happen, Hoffa disappeared, and his disappearance and probable death are still a mystery.

Meanwhile, throughout the 1970s and into the 1980s the Teamsters continued to be a target of federal inquiry. Fitzsimmons was replaced by Roy Williams as president of the Teamsters. In 1982 Williams was convicted of attempting to bribe a U.S. senator.

Under presidents Hoffa, Fitzsimmons, and Williams, the Teamsters was one of the nation's most corrupt unions. It also was connected to the mafia and organized crime in the United States.

Flint Sit-Down Strike (1936)

From 30 December 1936, when a group of unionists shut down the Chevrolet I plant in Flint, Michigan, to 11 February 1937, a massive sit-down strike paralyzed General Motors Corporation (GMC), idling 112,000 of the corporation's

150,000 employees. The auto workers refused to vacate the GMC premises at Flint; instead they sat down, refused to work, and in some cases reclined on automobile seats. In effect the sit-in became a "lie-in." GMC representatives criticized the strike and the strikers; United Automobile Workers' (UAW) head Homer Martin assailed the company for refusing to bargain with the union, and Congress of Industrial Organizations (CIO) chief John L. Lewis stood squarely behind the workers.

Company officials dealt with the crisis by cutting off heat in the plant in the midst of a Michigan winter. The workers stood fast. When company policemen attempted to invade the factory, they were met by a fusillade of nuts, bolts, automobile hinges, and other car parts. When company guards threatened to use tear gas on the workers, the employees turned the plant's fire hoses on the policemen, who retreated in what was referred to as the Battle of the Running Bulls.

As the strike became prolonged, workers remained firm as food and other supplies were brought through the picket lines. Inside the plant the workers enforced a special brand of rigid discipline. No smoking was allowed, no liquor tolerated, and a special patrol of 45 men kept everything under control.

Governor Frank Murphy of Michigan, friendly toward organized labor, refused to send state militia into the affray. The company did obtain a court order setting 3 February as the deadline for the workers to evacuate the plant, however,

United Auto Workers stage a sit-down strike in Flint, Michigan, in January 1937.

Murphy hastily summoned a conference between John L. Lewis and company president William S. Knudsen. The conference ended in a stalemate, and the 3 February deadline passed. Workers continued their sit-down strike as supporters sang labor's theme song, "Solidarity Forever," outside the plant. When President Roosevelt urged a settlement, Governor Murphy, Knudsen, and Lewis, with input from other representatives of the company and the UAW, resumed what amounted to nonstop deliberations. Finally, after a solid week of negotiations, the Great Sit-down Strike was over. The union, while not realizing all of its demands, did wring the concession from the company that it would not bargain with any other union. GMC also agreed to end the injunction against the workers, to not discriminate against union members, and to institute a grievance procedure.

After six weeks of turmoil at Flint, the union had gone head-to-head with one of the nation's largest corporations and had emerged a winner. What had been entirely an open-shop operation was now union country. With the unionization of the Flint workers a fait accompli, the door was now open for the organization of workers throughout the auto industry as well as in steel and related industries.

See also United Automobile Workers.

Flynn, Elizabeth Gurley (1890–1964)

The original rebel girl, Elizabeth Gurley Flynn was born in Boston, Massachusetts, in 1890. Coming from a background that included six generations of Irish rebels and claiming kinship to author George Bernard Shaw on her mother's side, she spoke from a soapbox in New York as a teenager. After affiliation with the Industrial Workers of the World (IWW), Flynn gained fame in the tradition of Mother Jones as the red flame and the Joan of Arc of the working class.

Like other IWW leaders, Flynn spent her share of time in jail. A fighter for free speech, even for alleged radicals or suppressives, she publicized that female inmates were prostitutes for policemen and jailers in the Spokane, Washington, jail.

Flynn participated in the Lawrence, Massachusetts, textile strike in 1906 and the Paterson, New Jersey, silk workers strike in 1913. She was one of the leaders in trying to get IWW colleague Joe Hill out of jail, causing Hill to dedicate the song "The Rebel Girl" to her. In 1916 during the Mesabi strike, Flynn was expelled from the IWW.

Two decades later, in 1937, Elizabeth Gurley Flynn—like Bill Haywood, head of the IWW, and John Reed, leader of the Communist Labor Party—joined the Communist Party. During the Korean War Flynn was back in jail for three years, charged with violation of the Smith Act. In the latter years of her life, she remained true to the principles of the IWW and the Communist Party, which she had advocated as a young girl.

Forty-Hour Week

The 40-hour work week, in essence, was established during the New Deal era of President Franklin Delano Roosevelt. In 1933 Congress passed the National Industrial Recovery Act (NIRA) and set up the National Recovery Administration (NRA) to implement the law. Codes of fair competition negotiated under the NRA generally called for a 40-hour week.

After the Supreme Court declared NIRA unconstitutional in the 1935 case *Schechter Poultry Corporation v. United States*, Roosevelt continued to press for the 40-hour work week. After his reelection in 1936, as part of the second New Deal Congress passed the Fair Labor Standards Act. The new law originally established a 44-hour week, which was to be cut back to 40 hours by the early 1940s. Since the New Deal years the normal work week has been 40 hours. If

Elizabeth Gurley Flynn inspired IWW leader Joe Hill to compose "The Rebel Girl" in 1915.

employees work longer than that, they generally receive overtime pay. This is in sharp contrast to a usual work week of 60 to 80 hours in the late nineteenth century.

See also Schechter Poultry Corporation v. United States.

Foster, William Z. (1881–1961)

William Z. Foster was a radical labor agitator who began his labor organizing in the Industrial Workers of the World and then became a leading member of the Communist Party. In 1918 Foster led a committee that attempted to organize the nation's steelworkers. He advocated strikes and was able to get most of the steelworkers to walk out in the great steel strike of 1919. When that strike failed because of the strong opposition of steel magnates such as Elbert H. Gary of United States Steel Corporation, Foster then established the Trade Union Educational League (TUEL) and the Trade Union Unity League (TUUL) to promote the unionization of all industrial workers apart from the American Federation of Labor.

Foster was a candidate of the Communist Party for president of the United States, running as a third-party candidate against Calvin Coolidge in 1924. He received only 33,361 votes. In 1928 Foster garnered 48,770 votes and in 1932 his vote total jumped to 102,991.

Toward the end of World War II the Communist Party of the United States disbanded. It was replaced by an organization called the Communist Political Association (CPA), allegedly a nonpartisan group. The year the war ended, 1945, saw the end of the CPA and the rebirth of the Communist Party. William Z. Foster was installed as president, replacing Earl Browder.

A radical, agitator, communist, and labor leader, William Z. Foster, in the tradition of Bill Haywood and others, advocated direct political action to improve the working conditions of the nation's toiling masses.

See also Trade Union Educational League; Trade Union Unity League.

Frankensteen, Richard

Richard Frankensteen was a United Automobile Workers (UAW) official who in May 1937 accompanied Walter Reuther to the Ford Motor Company's Dearborn plant near Detroit, Michigan. At what was called Ford Overpass near Gate 4 on company property, Frankensteen and Reuther were suddenly surrounded by between 25 and 150 Ford thugs. After warning the duo that they were on Ford property and to "get the hell out of here," company thugs began beating them. Frankensteen was struck on the back of the head, knocked down, and kicked in the stomach, head, and scrotum. The thugs stood him up and then knocked him down again. This was repeated several times while Dearborn police watched but did not intervene to stop the assault.

Blows kept coming as Frankensteen was knocked down the steps leading to the overpass and was bounced from one step to the other. On a landing more blows were rained on the union official. The carnage lasted until thugs had knocked their victim down to the cindered streetcar track. Then he was bounced on the cinders.

Finally, Frankensteen was allowed to retrieve his coat, and newspapermen at the scene hurriedly drove him to a physician's office.

The attack on Frankensteen came four years after the passage of the National Industrial Recovery Act (NIRA) and two years after the enactment of the Wagner Act. Meanwhile, Henry Ford criticized labor unions as being predatory, while refusing to engage in collective bargaining with the UAW. He also refused to sign a National Recovery Administration code, using his private army, called the Ford Service Department, to assault workers and union men alike.

It must be pointed out that during the late 1930s, well after the passage of NIRA and the Wagner Act, workers and unionists at Ford plants and elsewhere received much the same kind of treatment received by Frankensteen. In 1941, Henry Ford finally concluded an agreement with the UAW. Until then the Ford Overpass, at which Reuther and Frankensteen were attacked, was known to Ford employees as the "Doorway to Hell."

Fraser, Douglas (1916–)

As president of the United Automobile Workers (UAW) in the 1970s and 1980s, Douglas Fraser sought reforms in the

National Labor Relations Act, passed by Congress in 1935. Among the reforms desired by Fraser and the AFL-CIO were speedier handling of unfair labor practice cases and representation elections; additional penalties for employer violations of the law; no federal contracts to violators; and equal time for organizers to address workers in union elections.

When the labor reform law died in Congress (with President Jimmy Carter's blessing), Fraser resigned his post as a member of the AFL-CIO Labor-Management Group. His letter of resignation openly and severely criticized business and both the Republican and Democratic parties for assuming an anti-labor stance.

In 1979–1980 it became popular for auto workers to forego benefits in return for job security. When Chrysler Corporation was threatened by bankruptcy, the UAW gave up some gains as Fraser was appointed to the company's board of directors. Among the fringe benefits workers agreed to relinquish in the face of foreign competition were a decrease in paid holidays and vacation time.

Along with other blue-collar labor unions, the UAW under Fraser's recent leadership has remained intact by cooperating with management. These tactics have made labor a less militant special interest group within the past two or three decades.

See also United Automobile Workers.

Frick, Henry Clay (1849–1919)

Henry Clay Frick was a central figure in the tumultuous Homestead Lockout of 1892. As general manager of the Carnegie Steel Company's plant at Homestead, Pennsylvania, Frick closed the plant and ordered a lockout after workers refused to accept a reduction in wages.

Frick brought in company policemen to protect company property and to guard company gates. Workers promptly chased the company guards away. On the morning of 6 July 1892, Frick attempted to bring two barges of 300 armed Pinkerton detectives up the Monongahela River near the plant. Barricaded workers lining the river banks opened fire on the detectives, and the Battle of Homestead was on, raging from about 4:00 A.M. until 5:00 P.M. Late in the day the workers poured oil on the river and one tossed in a match. The river became a blazing inferno and, for the Pinkertons, troubled waters with no bridge. After the oil had burned out the detectives were allowed to come ashore. As they did, workers and their wives began to club and switch them. Fortunately the Pinkertons dashed to a railroad siding, where a passenger train pulled them to safety.

Six days later, on 12 July 1892, the governor of Pennsylvania dispatched 8,000 troops to Homestead and declared martial law. The company reopened its gates and brought in scabs, and the Homestead lockout was history. Only about 800 of the original 4,000 employees got their jobs back.

Frick had succeeded in breaking the strike and smashing the union. As the turbulence wound down at Homestead, Alexander Berkman, an anarchist of Russian extraction, burst into Frick's office to assassinate him. Although he shot and stabbed Frick, the Homestead official was not seriously wounded. Berkman was sentenced to a 22-year prison term.

Frick's handling of the Homestead strike was typical of how management responded to the demands of labor in the late nineteenth century. Using guards, Pinkertons, and state troops, the strike was broken, the union curbed, and the working class defeated. It was not until four decades later that the nation's steelworkers successfully organized a steelworkers' union.

Gannon, John A. (1923–)

John A. Gannon, a native of Ohio, spent more than 30 years of his life as a firefighter in Cleveland. He attended Miami University of Ohio and Glasgow University in Scotland. He was an active leader in Fire Fighters local no. 93 in Cleveland, holding nearly every office. A labor activist most of his adult life, Gannon was at one time vice-president of the Cleveland Federation of Labor and vice-president of the Ohio AFL-CIO.

In 1980 Gannon was elected president of the International Association of Fire Fighters (IAFF), and was reelected to that post in 1982, 1984, and 1986. The IAFF was organized in 1918 as local fire fighters' unions across the United States merged. During the early years of the twentieth century fire fighters' unions were believed to infringe upon the sovereignty of a city. With the passage of the National Industrial Recovery Act and the Wagner Act in the 1930s, the IAFF substantially increased its membership.

Gannon took a no-nonsense approach to the organization of fire fighters' unions. It was his idea that locals put no-lockout and no-strike clauses into contracts because fire fighters were engaged in the protection of public safety.

Today the IAFF boasts some 180,000 members in the United States and Canada. The union includes drivers, hosemen, tillermen, sergeants, lieutenants, and captains. In recent years the union has stressed occupational safety and health benefits for its members. Since fire fighting is such a hazardous occupation, Gannon and the IAFF have worked toward not only training fire fighters in proper safety techniques, but in promoting the best protective clothing and safest equipment.

Garland, Jim (1905–1978)

Mountain man Jim Garland was the son of a coal miner from deep in the hills of eastern Kentucky.

At age 13 he entered the mines, and for the next 14 years was a coal miner, like most men in the Kentucky mountains.

Garland worked in Harlan County and neighboring Bell County. More often than not he worked on his knees. Toiling daily, Garland experienced the low wages, long hours, and unsafe working conditions prevalent in the coal mines of the post–World War I era, and he became interested in attempts by the United Mine Workers of America (UMW) to organize the coal miners in the Bell-Harlan area after World War I. Garland attended UMW meetings in Pineville, Kentucky, where he was impressed by the speeches of UMW executive Phil Murray.

After the famous Battle of Evarts in May 1931, Garland became disenchanted with the UMW. Later that year he was attracted to the National Miners Union (NMU), which he joined and in which he worked as an organizer. Immediately he became a marked man as a communist. When NMU efforts to organize the coal miners failed, Garland left the area for New York City. There he, along with his sister Sarah Ogan Gunning and Aunt Molly Jackson composed and recorded numerous labor and protest songs. Garland, Gunning, and Jackson performed many of their songs on the radio and stage throughout the United States. Garland made recordings for the Library of Congress and even traveled back to the Kentucky mountains to record several songs. Among the compositions of the Garland-Gunning-Jackson trio were "Barbara Allen," "Casey Jones," "Cumberland Gap," "The Death of Harry

Simms," "Hard Times in Coleman's Mines," and "Which Side Are You On?"

After Garland became a songwriter and performer, he met and grew to be friends with the famous Woody Guthrie in the late 1930s. Garland occasionally returned to his roots in Kentucky, but he finally settled in Washington State, where he died in 1978.

Garrison, William Lloyd (1805–1829)

Abolitionist and newspaperman William Lloyd Garrison was born in Newburyport, Massachusetts. After attending school for a short time, he became an apprentice journalist in his home town, where he later became editor of the newspaper. The late 1820s found Garrison in Boston in the company of antislavery crusaders, especially Quaker abolitionist Benjamin Lundy.

In 1831, as a fierce abolitionist, Garrison began publishing *The Liberator*, which he edited for over three decades. While his principal claim to fame was as an antislavery author and crusader, Garrison also wrote some pointed editorials about the American working classes. In the first issue of *The Liberator*, he chastised workers for complaining about working conditions. While admitting that laborers had problems and grievances, Garrison took the position that all classes of society had grievances. He deplored the arousal of workingmen to violence and to the formation of a workingmen's party. Seemingly Garrison took the position that the working classes were not being exploited by employers; thus there was no need for organizations to "dump the bosses off their backs."

Ironically, while Garrison called for the abolition of slavery in *The Liberator*, he did not support the goals of workers to improve conditions of employment through labor organizations. Laborers, he suggested, were well off compared to slaves. While there were grievances to be redressed, Garrison was deeply concerned about the mode of redress work-

ers adopted. From his writings in *The Liberator* Garrison seemed to be taking an anti-labor position comparable to the media of the twentieth century.

General Manager's Association (GMA)

The General Manager's Association (GMA) was composed of 24 railway executives who essentially controlled all railroads in and out of Chicago—over 40,000 miles of track.

When the Pullman Strike erupted in 1894, the General Manager's Association, in an attempt to break the strike, ordered the firing of any worker that cut a Pullman car from a train. Workers of the American Railway Union were not intimidated by the GMA edict. When a Pullman worker was fired, an entire train crew quit in protest. Thus rail traffic in and out of Chicago was tied up, and the nation's railway system was on the verge of a complete standstill. The press supported the GMA position, while the union, led by Eugene Debs, backed the workers.

The strike grew violent when the GMA imported Canadian strikebreakers, who coupled mail cars to Pullman cars. Thus, when workers attempted to cut Pullman cars, they were actually interfering with the U.S. mail. Attorney General Richard Olney dispatched 3,400 special deputies to keep the trains moving. As violence broke out between workers and deputies, President Grover Cleveland dispatched to Chicago four companies of infantry over the protests of Illinois Governor John Peter Altgeld. The workers stood fast, however, and most of the railroads in and out of Chicago ground to a stop for a time.

However, the GMA position, supported by the U.S. government, eventually broke the strike. When it ended, organized labor had suffered a serious setback. For its strong efforts the working classes made few gains toward the improvement of working conditions in the late nineteenth century. Government by injunction was victorious in the Pullman Strike.

Giboney v. Empire Storage and Ice Company (U.S., 1949)

In 1949 the Supreme Court upheld a Missouri law that prohibited picketing. In his opinion, Justice Hugo Black wrote that the union was using picketing to coerce Empire Storage to "abide by the union rather than state regulation of trade."

According to the unanimous verdict of the Court in *Giboney*, a state could control picketing whenever it considered the practice unacceptable. Into the 1950s the Court sustained state statutes against picketing.

See also Picketing.

Girdler, Tom Mercer (1877–1965)

Tom M. Girdler was the vehemently anti-union president of the Republic Steel Corporation in 1937. One of several Little Steel companies, along with Youngstown Sheet and Tube, Inland Steel, and Bethlehem Steel, Republic was a holdout against the Steel Workers Organizing Committee (SWOC). In May 1937 SWOC issued a strike call against the Little Steel combine. The companies retaliated with scabs, thugs, tear gassings, assaults on pickets, and arrests of strike leaders.

As a result, violence erupted throughout the Little Steel industrial towns. The turbulence reached its zenith at the South Chicago operation of Girdler's Republic Steel on Memorial Day, 30 May 1937. There large crowds of workers and their families celebrated the holiday with a picnic. City police attempted to scatter the celebrants, opening fire on the throng, which refused to leave the area. Unarmed workers scurried from the scene to escape the barrage of bullets. In the massacre ten workers were slain and over a hundred workers were injured, as were 22 policemen.

While newsreel photos showed that workers had not instigated the assault and that fleeing workers were shot in the back, the violent episode did not help labor's cause at the time. In fact, the strike was lost.

Tom Girdler remained an outspoken and aggressive foe of unionism. Summoned to testify before the La Follette Civil Liberties Committee, he remained adamant against the union. Finally, in 1938, with the intervention of the federal government, the strongly anti-union ranks of Little Steel and Girdler's Republic Steel were broken as steelworkers flocked to join the CIO's Steel Workers of America.

Goldman, Emma (1869–1940)

Anarchist Emma Goldman helped plan the 23 July 1892 attack on Henry Clay Frick during the Homestead Lockout. In the assault, Frick was shot and stabbed by Alexander Berkman, Goldman's anarchist companion.

In 1919, during the country's first Red Scare, Goldman was deported as part of the "Palmer raids" conducted by Attorney General A. Mitchell Palmer. Goldman continued to travel and lecture on behalf of radical causes. She died in Toronto, Canada, in 1940.

See also Berkman, Alexander; Frick, Henry Clay; Homestead Lockout.

Goldsborough, Thomas Alan (1877–1951)

T. Alan Goldsborough was the federal district court judge in Washington, D.C., who, during the coal strike of 1946, upheld a government injunction against the strikers. The strike began on 1 April 1946 when over 400,000 miners left the pits in Pennsylvania, West Virginia, Kentucky, Alabama, Illinois, and Iowa. Chief John L. Lewis of the United Mine Workers of America (UMW) mocked the operators and the government by keeping the miners out. The government took over the mines under the provisions of the Smith-Connally Act.

Emma Goldman and Alexander Berkman in 1918

As the strike continued, the government took its case to the courts. Goldsborough, calling the work stoppage "an evil, demoniac, monstrous thing," authorized the injunction. Characteristically John L. Lewis disregarded the court's ruling; he was charged with contempt, tried, found guilty, and fined $10,000. The UMW was fined $3.5 million.

The case was appealed to the U.S. Supreme Court where, in a 5 to 4 vote, Judge Goldsborough's verdict was sustained. The Supreme Court ruled that despite the anti-injunction provision of the Norris-LaGuardia Act, the government could impose an injunction when a strike affected national security. Lewis ended the strike and ordered coal miners back into the pits. The Court decreased the fine against the union to $700,000, and in a subsequent contract with the coal operators, Lewis won an agreement that included nearly all his demands both with regard to wages and welfare fund contributions.

See also Injunctions; Lewis, John L.; Norris-LaGuardia Act.

Gompers, Samuel (1850–1924)

Born in England, Samuel Gompers served an apprenticeship as a cigar maker in London before migrating to the United States at the age of 13. In the United States, Gompers joined the International Union of Cigar Makers, rising to its presidency in a little over a decade. His career as the country's foremost labor leader had begun. One of the prime movers behind the establishment of the Federation of Organized Trades and Labor Unions of the United States and Canada, Gompers helped to reorganize that union into the American Federation of Labor (AFL) in 1886. Elected president of the AFL, Gompers served in that position, except for one year, until his death in 1924.

As chief of the American Federation of Labor, Gompers emphasized several significant principles: (1) craft unionism bringing together craftsmen as skilled workers in a single occupation, i.e. carpenters, electricians, bricklayers; (2) pure and simple (bread and butter) unionism, which stressed short range goals such as shorter hours and higher wages for workers; (3) opposition to radicalism in the labor movement; and (4) opposition to a workers' third party. Gompers preferred to work within the structure of the two-party system to help labor achieve its goals. He was always careful not to commit himself or his union to a certain political party. Rather his philosophy was to support candidates irrespective of political preference who favored labor's agenda. He rarely placed himself in the company of laborites who embraced socialistic or communistic dogma.

A prototype of a modern labor leader, Gompers was a cigar chewer. He also was one of the boys, preferring to go where the workers were to mingle in order to learn what their thoughts were as well as their grievances. As chief executive of the AFL, Gompers successfully led a union of approximately 500,000 craft members by the 1890s. Despite the turbulence in the American labor movement at that time, which dealt a death blow to most labor unions, the AFL survived to become the major union of the nineteenth century and extend its influence into the

Samuel Gompers

twentieth century. The standards set under the administration of Gompers remained those of the AFL in modern times. Today the AFL is a strong voice for American workers. A major change in AFL philosophy developed in recent years when the union openly endorsed political candidates favorable to labor's program, especially those running on the Democratic platform.

Green, William (1873–1952)

On the 1924 death of longtime American Federation of Labor President Samuel Gompers, William Green of the United Mine Workers of America succeeded to the AFL presidency. For the next 28 years Green headed one of the country's most powerful labor unions. He continued the AFL in the craft union tradition begun by Gompers.

During Green's presidency, the AFL became politically active and its membership grew to over 3 million nationwide. In 1935, the Committee on Industrial Organization was established within the AFL framework, but it was soon restructured as a separate organization, the Congress of Industrial Organizations, under the leadership of John L. Lewis.

Under Green's leadership and largely because of the pro-labor support of Congress, the Supreme Court, and the Roosevelt administration, the AFL increased to nearly 9 million members. It also became politically active, supporting Robert M. La Follette, Sr., as the Progressive Party candidate for president in 1924. The AFL also backed the Democratic Party during the 1930s, when a Democratic Congress legislated the National Industrial Recovery Act, the National Labor Relations Act, and the Fair Labor Standards Act.

In the post–World War II era, Green's AFL fought for the repeal of the Taft-Hartley Act (1947), passed by the Republican-controlled Eightieth Congress. In 1952 the union endorsed the candidacy of Democratic presidential hopeful Adlai E. Stevenson, who also supported repeal of the Taft-Hartley Act.

While William Green led the AFL for nearly three decades, it enjoyed outstanding success representing craft unionists throughout the United States. On Green's death in 1952, George Meany became the leader of the American Federation of Labor.

See also American Federation of Labor.

Greenback-Labor Movement

The Tompkins Square Riot (1874) in New York City, the Molly Maguires revolt in eastern Pennsylvania (1875), and the nationwide railroad strike (1877) led to the formation of the Greenback-Labor Party on 22 February 1878 in Toledo, Ohio. The first party convention was attended by 800 delegates from 28 states. The party's initial platform, in addition to calling for the free coinage of silver, demanded a reduction in hours for workers and the limitation of immigration, especially for the Chinese.

Entering its first candidates in the midterm elections of 1878, the Greenback-Labor Party won 14 seats in Congress. Iowa Congressman James B. Weaver, a former Civil War general for the Union, became the titular head of the party. Two years later the party's platform included women's suffrage, federal regulation of interstate commerce, and a graduated income tax.

In the 1880 presidential contest, the Greenback-Labor Party nominated James B. Weaver for president and B. J. Chambers of Texas for vice-president. Weaver's vote total of over 300,000 easily eclipsed that of another third party, the Prohibition party. In 1884 the Greenback-Labor Party convened in Indianapolis to nominate another former Civil War general, Benjamin F. Butler, for president and A. M. West from Mississippi for vice-president. Butler's vote total was a little more than half that of Weaver's four years earlier, and the year 1884 was the last time the Greenback-Labor movement offered a candidate for president. It must be pointed out, however, that many of the aims of the Greenback-Labor Party were adopted in 1892 by the Omaha Platform of the People's Party, the most important third party in U.S. history.

Griffith, Tom W.

A Colorado native, Tom Griffith is the son of a rural letter carrier from Eaton, Colorado. After a stint in the U.S. Navy, Griffith enrolled at Colorado State University. In time he followed in his father's footsteps by becoming a rural letter carrier, and for over four decades Griffith was with the U.S. Postal Service. During his tenure he was an officer in his local union, an executive board member of the National Rural Letter Carriers' Association (NRLCA), and the association's national vice-president from 1981 to 1983.

In 1983 Griffith was elected president of the 70,000-member union. As president from 1983 to 1986 he was the chief negotiator for NRLCA in its deliberations with the U.S. Postal Service. When his term expired in 1986, Griffith returned to his home state and retired as an NRLCA leader.

Established at the turn of the century, NRLCA today represents rural letter carriers who annually drive 2.4 million miles, covering 43,000 rural mail routes and distributing mail to 18 million rural families. Rural letter carriers, in essence, operate post offices on wheels, furnishing complete postal service to the country's rural areas. Rural letter carriers often are regarded as family by customers who get to know them personally, in marked contrast to the impersonal attitude of urban postal workers toward the public.

To his retirement in 1986, Griffith was a devout union leader who always strove to get the best working conditions for rural letter carriers. He loved the NRLCA, built up its membership, held union members together, and successfully dealt with the Postal Service to improve matters.

Griggs v. Duke Power Co. (U.S., 1971)

Thirteen black employees of the Draper, North Carolina, plant of Duke Power Company brought suit against the company in 1965, charging that they were denied their civil rights under the 1964 Civil Rights Act passed by Congress. The complaint of the black workers rested on the fact that they were not promoted because they did not hold high school diplomas and had not passed aptitude tests. They further claimed that neither a high school diploma nor the test affected their job performances.

In *Griggs v. Duke Power Company*, the Court ruled in a unanimous decision that texts, diplomas, and degrees could no longer be used as guidelines in hiring practices if they had nothing to do with the type of work an employee did. Chief Justice Warren Burger, speaking for the Court, applied the 1964 Civil Rights Act to the hiring and firing regulations of businesses, the ramifications of which affected most employers.

Grosscup, Peter Stenger (1852–1921)

During the 1894 Pullman Strike in Chicago, railroad barons were successful in convincing the U.S. attorney general to take action to end the strike. As a result, on 2 July 1894 Federal District Judge Peter J. Grosscup issued a blanket injunction against the American Railway Union directed by Eugene Victor Debs.

The injunction barred railroad and Pullman employees from interfering with the U.S. mails and railroad operations in interstate commerce, as well as from attempting to restrain railroad workers from doing their jobs.

When Debs refused the injunction because Pullman would not take back striking employees, Judge Grosscup empaneled a special grand jury to investigate reputed violations of the blanket injunction by union leaders. Debs and several of his associates were arrested, released on bond, and then arrested again for violation of Grosscup's court order. The second time around Debs went to jail in Woodstock, Illinois, for six months. The injunction was enforced with the arrests of several hundred strikers. With their leader in prison, the strike was broken by federal intervention.

Judge Grosscup's blanket injunction ironically was issued under the Sherman Anti-Trust Act (1890), which was passed to prevent conspiracies by big business in restraint of trade. In the Pullman Strike, Grosscup's order was used against a labor union for conspiring to restrain interstate commerce. The standard of government by injunction against labor unions was set, a standard that remained in place until the anti-injunction laws and court decisions of the 1930s.

Guffey-Snyder Act (1935)

Also known as the National Bituminous Coal Act of 1935, the Guffey-Snyder Act was shaped to regulate the coal industry after the Supreme Court, in 1935, struck down the National Industry Recovery Act (NIRA) in *Schechter Poultry Corporation v. United States*.

The Guffey-Snyder Act held that the coal industry was "affected by a national public interest." It also averred that since the production and distribution of coal directly involved interstate commerce, federal regulation was mandatory.

The law established a National Bituminous Coal Commission cloaked with authority to establish a coal code for the bituminous coal industry. The coal code governed coal prices in coal-producing states through district boards. A tax of 15 percent was set on all coal sold at mine heads, with nine-tenths of that rebated to coal operators who agreed to the coal code.

Significantly the Guffey Act guaranteed collective bargaining and stipulated that contracts agreed to by operators producing two-thirds of the entire coal output and employing more than half of the workers were binding for the entire industry.

The Guffey-Snyder Act was passed to replace the NIRA, but it was overturned by the Supreme Court in *Carter v. Carter Coal Company*. Meanwhile, Congress passed the National Labor Relations Act (1936), which was upheld by the Court in 1937. Under the new law, collective bargaining between employers and employees to determine hours, wages, and other important conditions of employment became a way of life in labor and industrial relations.

See also National Industrial Recovery Act.

Hague v. C.I.O. (U.S., 1939)

A 1939 Supreme Court case testing whether Jersey City, New Jersey, could invoke a city ordinance banning public assemblies without a permit from the municipality's director of public safety. The city statute was used by city policemen who resorted to violent methods to break up labor rallies, stop the circulation of union literature, and chase union organizers out of the city.

In a divided opinion, the Court ruled the ordinance unconstitutional. In the majority opinion of the Court, the right of a peaceful assembly was one of the privileges and immunities of citizens secured by the Fourteenth Amendment. The Court also ruled that the due process clause of the Fourteenth Amendment protected the right of citizens to convene in a peaceable manner. Chief Justice Hughes, voting with the majority, wrote that the right to meet for a discussion of the National Labor Relations Act was a privilege of U.S. citizens.

The Jersey City ordinance restricting public meetings by labor unionists was strikingly similar to laws prohibiting similar gatherings in many other industrial areas. In locations such as the southern Appalachian coalfields, company policemen and deputy sheriffs broke up labor rallies without the authority of a city or county ordinance.

The Court's opinion in *Hague v. C.I.O.* exemplified its changing views toward organized labor during the New Deal era.

Hammer v. Dagenhart (U.S., 1918)

A Supreme Court case that involved the constitutionality of the Keating-Owen Child Labor Act passed by Congress in 1916 as part of President Woodrow Wilson's New Freedom legislative program. Known as the first Child Labor Act, the law prohibited manufacturers from shipping in interstate commerce the products of mines, quarries, factories, canneries, and similar workshops in which children under 14 were employed within 30 days of shipment. The law also restricted manufacturers who employed children between the ages of 14 and 16 for more than eight hours a day or at night. Congress passed the law under its right to regulate interstate commerce.

In 1918 the Supreme Court invalidated the Keating-Owen Act by a 5 to 4 vote. In its majority opinion the Court ruled that the law was not a regulation of commerce but a direct restriction on the states. Earlier the Court had accepted the Pure Food and Drug Act and the Mann Act (white slave law) because those laws prohibited harmful activities. Now the Court held that child labor was harmless and the shipment in interstate commerce of products made by child labor was harmless. The Court also ruled that the Child Labor Act was an invasion of the reserved power clause of the Tenth Amendment.

With the Court's ruling in *Hammer v. Dagenhart*, attempts to regulate child labor by the Progressives were nullified. Effective federal regulation of child labor did not happen until the successful passage of the Fair Labor Standards Act in 1938 as part of Roosevelt's second New Deal.

See also Bailey v. Drexel Furniture Company; Keating-Owen Act.

Harlan County Coal Operators Association (HCCOA)

An association of nearly all the coal operators in Kentucky's number one coal county, which was established in 1916 soon after the Harlan County coalfield was opened up mostly by outside capitalism. United States Coal and Coke, a subsidiary of United States Steel, and Wisconsin Steel, owned by International Harvester at Benham, were the only nonmembers.

The Harlan County Coal Operators Association (HCCOA) was politically active in the 1920 and 1930s. Coal operator Silas J. Dickenson was county Democratic chairman, and association secretary George S. Ward was county Republican chairman. The HCCOA controlled county elections and figured prominently in statewide elections. In most instances candidates favored by operators won elections on the county level and received handsome majorities in statewide races. Through control of the county courthouse, the HCCOA was able to keep most county mines out of the union (United Mine Workers of America) until 1938.

The association's bylaws suggested that one of the premier purposes of the organization was to suppress the union in Harlan County. To achieve its stated goal, the HCCOA levied an assessment on tonnage produced by Harlan County coal operators who were association members. The slush fund was used by the HCCOA to hire over 300 mine guards, most of whom were deputized, to quell the union. Among the mine guards were ex-convicts and industrial policemen who had seen action in the Appalachian coalfields and steel mill areas. Leading the army of mine guards were Chief Deputy Ben F. Unthank and Merle H. Middleton. Unthank was on the sheriff's payroll, while Middleton was a cousin of Sheriff Theodore Roosevelt Middleton, a coal operator and tool of the HCCOA.

Throughout the 1930s the HCCOA was able to repulse the union because mine guards terrorized union organizers, broke up union rallies, restricted the distribution of union literature, dynamited organizers' vehicles, tear-gassed the hotel in which organizers resided, and shot into an organizer's home, killing his son.

Finally, in the late 1930s, after federal intervention by the La Follette Civil Liberties Committee, the U.S. Justice and Labor Departments, the Federal Bureau of Investigation, a federal district court in Kentucky, and the National Labor Relations Board, the death grip held by the HCCOA over Harlan County's more than 12,000 coal miners was broken. In 1938 the HCCOA accepted the first countywide contract with the United Mine Workers of America in its strife-torn history.

See also Black Mountain.

Harrington, Michael

An American author who in 1962 published *The Other America*, describing many American workers who toiled for low wages in what were identified as dead-end jobs. Harrington singled out three groups—nonwhites, women, and teenagers—who applied for nonunion jobs that were unstable and low paying. As a result, the socialist author stressed, many American workers in the lower strata of the laboring class were entrenched in poverty in the country's rural and urban areas.

Harrington's muckraking exposé in the early 1960s pricked the consciences of Congress and the presidency. As a result, President John F. Kennedy established a federal jobs program, and President Lyndon B. Johnson declared a war on poverty after jetting to remote Martin County, Kentucky, in the heart of poverty-stricken Appalachia in the mid-1960s.

Despite Harrington's tome and the efforts of the Johnson administration to end poverty in the United States, recent studies reveal extreme poverty not only in Appalachia but in urban areas across the country. Many teenagers and adults—both black and white, as well as people of other ethnic groups—are still trapped in low-paying jobs.

Hatfield, Sid (1892–1921)

Sid Hatfield was a member of the Appalachian mountain clan that engaged the McCoys in a legendary feud along the West Virginia–Kentucky state line in the latter decades of the nineteenth century. An ancestor of the famed patriarch, Devil Anse Hatfield, Sid Hatfield began his working years, like many of his friends and neighbors, as a coal miner. By the time he reached his mid-twenties, however, the lanky Hatfield was police chief of Matewan, West Virginia, situated along the Kentucky–West Virginia border in historic Mingo County.

In sharp contrast to most Appalachian lawmen, Hatfield positioned himself on the side of the coal miners. Adorned with a silver badge on his shirt and two six-shooters strapped to his waist, Hatfield became a miner's hero in May 1921 when he refused to permit Baldwin-Felts mine guards to evict union miners from company houses in Mingo County. When more detectives flooded into the area to impose company authority on the coal miners, Hatfield met the train and shot into a group of Baldwin-Felts detectives, killing seven of the hated thugs. Hatfield's role in what became known throughout the hills as the Matewan Massacre made him a living legend.

Ultimately the gritty police chief was indicted in connection with the deaths of the detectives. On the morning of 1 August 1921 in Welch, West Virginia, as he and his personal bodyguard, Ed Chambers, ascended the steps of the McDowell County Courthouse accompanied by their wives, three Baldwin-Felts agents opened fire on the redoubtable lawman, puncturing his head and chest with five bullet holes. Hatfield was scheduled to stand trial the morning he was gunned down.

Sid Hatfield

The slaying of Sid Hatfield signaled the beginning of the last phase of the West Virginia coal mine war during the summer of 1921. Because their champion had been murdered in cold blood, thousands of coal miners, many of whom were World War I veterans, armed themselves and trekked 70 miles into Logan and Bloody Mingo counties in support of union coal miners. During the month-long conflict, the Battle of Blair's Mountain raged for a week between miners and 2,000 deputy sheriffs and state militiamen. The bloody warfare finally ended when President Warren G. Harding sent in U.S. infantry supported by army aircraft.

In many southern Appalachian coal counties, sheriffs, deputy sheriffs, police chiefs, and policemen aligned themselves with coal operators to keep the United Mine Workers of America out of their private fiefdoms. In Matewan, West Virginia, fearless Police Chief Sid Hatfield stood out as a champion of the coal miners. For his courageous actions, Hatfield sacrificed his life and became a martyr to the coal miners and the union.

See also Bloody Mingo.

Haymarket Square Riots (1886)

The Haymarket Square Riots took place over the first four days of May 1886 in Chicago, Illinois. As a prelude to the riots, employees at the McCormick plant were on strike in support of a nationwide eight-hour day for industrial workers. The first two days of the strike passed by without incident as workers demonstrated and paraded around the city and the plant. On 3 May McCormick's attempted to bring in strikebreakers (scabs), and a battle between the strikers and scabs followed. Chicago policemen were called in to break up the disturbance, resulting in the deaths of four men. That evening a radical organization known as the Black International, established in the United States by the German radical Johann Most, circularized the city calling for the deaths of the four comrades to be avenged.

A protest rally was scheduled for 4 May in Haymarket Square. Over 3,000 people assembled to hear anarchists deliver fervent speeches in support of the labor movement. The meeting was calm, and as the afternoon wore on, the mayor went down, observed a tranquil scene, and went home. Suddenly a cold wind began to blow in from Lake Michigan and rain began to fall. The workers had begun to disperse when into their midst rode 200 Chicago policemen, who ordered the remaining workers to leave. The sight of the policemen, after the events of 3 May, incensed the crowd. Someone, the identity of whom was never established, hurled a homemade bomb in the direction of the policemen, killing one. Gunfire erupted between the policemen and the workers. When the shooting ended, seven more policemen and four workers were killed and over one hundred people were injured.

Chicago authorities, spurred on by the press and public opinion, arrested eight men, charging them in the deaths of the eight policemen. No policemen were apprehended in connection with the murders of the eight workers.

The trial of the eight workers was conducted in an atmosphere charged with emotion. All eight were found guilty; seven were given the death penalty, one received a 15-year prison term. All eight were convicted on the basis of circumstantial evidence to save the country from radical anarchist influence.

The Haymarket Riots caused public opinion to turn against labor; not until the third decade of the twentieth century did labor unions received recognition. The riots also hastened the decline of the Knights of Labor, although that union could not be identified with involvement in the disturbance.

Later a monument was erected in Haymarket Square in memory of the eight policemen who lost their lives in two days of fighting. That monument presided over the park until 1968, when rioting by protesters outside the Democratic National Convention scarred the edifice. Mayor Richard Daley of Chicago ordered the monument restored—a continual reminder of the tragic days of the Haymarket Square Riots.

Hays, Arthur Garfield (1881–1954)

A New York attorney, Arthur Garfield Hays was often found in the role of defense counsel for labor organizers and union men during the late 1920s and early 1930s. In a 1929 case involving Gastonia, North Carolina, strikers implicated in the murder of Gastonia Police Chief O. E. Aderholt and the wounding of three other officers, Hays appeared as counsel for the International Labor Defense (ILD), the legal affiliate of the Communist Party. Although Hays was replaced by the ILD during the trial, he continued his effort in behalf of the workers and strikers.

Earlier a member of the defense staff in the famous Sayers Monkey Trial in Dayton, Tennessee, Hays headed an American Civil Liberties Union (ACLU) delegation that attempted to enter the Bell-Harlan County, Kentucky, coalfields during the coal mine war of 1931–1932. Hays and his troupe, who made the trip presumably to test if civil and constitutional rights were being denied coal miners, were met at the Bell County line by local authorities and turned back.

Undaunted, Hays retraced his steps to London, seat of the federal district court for eastern Kentucky, to seek an injunction against Kentucky authorities allowing him to enter the strife-torn area. But Federal District Judge A. M. J. Cochran denied the injunction because he reasoned that, as well as the "freedom of" clauses contained in the First Amendment to the U.S. Constitution, persons also have "freedom from" self-styled, pestering investigators. The federal court order ended the ACLU's efforts to go into the Bell-Harlan coalfields in 1932. Hays and his companions comprised the last of six groups of outsiders who went to the turbulent Kentucky coalfields in the early 1930s to investigate charges that a reign of terror inspired by coal operators and their armed hirelings was denying coal miners freedom of speech, press, and assembly, and the right to join the United Mine Workers of America.

Haywood, William D. (1869–1928)

Born in Salt Lake City, Utah, in 1869, William D. Haywood, later known as Big Bill, was a miner at age nine. When his father died in a mining camp, Haywood, only three at the time, was reared by his mother. By the time he was seven, Haywood had seen a lot of violence and death, so much that he was inured to it. About the same time he stabbed himself in the right eye while working on a slingshot. (Permanently blinded in the right eye, Haywood always kept his good left eye to the camera while posing for pictures.) At age nine he worked in mining camps to support his widowed mother. He grew accustomed to the rough-and-tumble life in

the camps, and when peers ridiculed his blinded eye, Haywood dueled.

For a time he left the mining scene and tried cowboying in Nevada, but eventually returned to the mines where he began to rail against what he referred to as wage slavery.

In 1893 Haywood helped establish the Western Federation of Miners, and in a Chicago convention in 1905 he and Eugene Victor Debs brought into existence the Industrial Workers of the World (IWW), a radical, revolutionary organization.

Haywood was both an effective speaker and organizer. By September 1907, only two years after the IWW was founded, he had helped to establish over 200 local unions throughout the United States. The radical union, under Haywood's leadership, enjoyed its greatest success in the Western mining and lumbering fields and in the textile centers of the Northeast. In 1908 the Western Federation of Miners parted company with the IWW,

William Dudley Haywood

causing it to go into a rather serious decline. Some IWW locals, like the Stogie Workers of Cleveland, Ohio, the Hotel and Restaurant Workers of Goldfield, Nevada, and the Window Washers of Chicago, were temporary unions. Haywood also established, during a rodeo in Denver, the Bronco Busters and Range Riders Union (BBRR). After enjoying limited success in fixed wages for bronco busting and range riding, the BBRR was "soon headed for the last round up."

Haywood, despite his organizational abilities, was able to build up the IWW to a peak membership of only 25,000 nationwide by the time of World War I. Then, following his conviction on charges of sabotage and conspiracy to oppose World War I, and accused of misappropriating union funds, Haywood in 1921 fled to Russia. He hoped to find a home in the Communist Party and in the Bolshevik revolution in his adopted homeland. Ironically the Bolsheviks never really involved Haywood in their activities. Haywood never returned to the United States, dying in Russia in 1928.

Helvering v. Davis (U.S., 1937)
See Steward Machine Company v. Davis.

Herrin Massacre
See Bloody Williamson.

Hicks, Marshall M. (1931–)
Born in Claiborne County, Tennessee, in the shadow of the historic Cumberland Gap, Marshall M. Hicks migrated north to Michigan as a young man. He found employment with Consumers Power Company from 1952 to 1967. He became a local union official, serving in a variety of capacities. In the 1970s, Hicks became a state officer of the Michigan State Utility Workers Council, and from 1971 to 1989 he was national secretary-treasurer of the Utility Workers Union of America (UWUA).

Hicks' UWUA was formed in 1945 when a company union of Consolidated Edison combined with Congress of Industrial Organizations (CIO) members as the Utility Workers Organizing Committee. By 1990 the UWUA totalled 60,000 members in the electric and public utility industry. Union members include electrical utility linemen, nuclear power plant operators, water, gas, and sewerage workers, and clerical and professional employees. Today the national organization contains 230 local unions that are practically self-governing and represent members in about that number of collective bargaining negotiations.

Marshall M. Hicks is of the opinion that unions are necessary and that today's workers enjoy better pay, working conditions, and fringe benefits because of them. He also feels there is still a place for unions because so many workers are being shortchanged in today's workplace. Among the issues unions need to address today, according to Hicks, are job security, group insurance, and pension plans. The latter issue is extremely important, he believes, because most utility workers stay with the industry until retirement.

A committed union man, Hicks is at his best when he feels he is helping people improve conditions of employment and their quality of life.

Hill, Joe (1882–1915)
Joe Hill, who was born as Joel Emmanuel Haaglund in Jevla, Sweden, was regarded as the folk-poet, balladeer, and songwriter of the Industrial Workers of the World (IWW). In 1901 he came to the United States and drifted around the country searching for work. During that time he apparently assumed the name by which he became famous: Joe Hill. In 1910 Hill settled in San Pedro, California, and joined an IWW local union. Between 1910 and 1915 Hill, in addition to being an active member of the IWW, fought on the side of the rebels during the 1911 Mexican Revolution. In 1912, while par-

ticipating in a free speech fight in San Diego, Hill was badly beaten, suffering wounds that left scars on his face, neck, and body.

Hill organized workers in ports and agricultural areas across California. He was so active in industrial unionism that he found himself blacklisted by most employers. Finally he left the state and moved to Utah, settling in the Salt Lake City area. The problems he encountered in California followed him to Utah, where it became increasingly difficult for Hill to get a job. Meanwhile, Hill, who was tall, slim, blond, and blue-eyed, was living off holdups. The fact that he was a card-carrying member of the IWW also placed him in jeopardy with local authorities.

In January 1914, Joe Hill was arrested in connection with the holdup murder of grocer John Morrison and his 17-year-old son. In a trial that rivaled the famous Sacco-Vanzetti case of the mid-1920s, Hill was found guilty and sentenced to death. Nearly two years passed before he was executed, and during that period, pleas from many IWW colleagues and workers from around the world called on Utah Governor William Spry to free Hill. On the morning of 19 November 1915, Hill was executed by a five-man firing squad at the Utah State Penitentiary in Salt Lake City. His last words to his friends and workers everywhere: "Don't waste time in mourning. Organize."

Since Joe Hill was such a prominent labor leader, it is fitting to print some lines from one of his songs as well as his last will and testament:

The Preacher and the Slave

(Tune: "Sweet By and By")
Long-haired preachers come out every
  night
Try to tell you what's wrong and what's
  right;
But when asked how 'bout something
  to eat
They will answer with voices so sweet:

[chorus]:
You will eat, bye and bye,
In that glorious land above the sky;
Work and pray, live on hay,
You'll get pie in the sky when you die.

Hill's last will and testament:

My will is easy to decide
For there is nothing to divide,
My kin don't need to fuss and moan
"Moss does not cling to rolling stone."
My body? Oh! If I could choose,
I would to ashes it reduce;
And let the merry breezes blow
My dust to where some flowers grow.
Perhaps some fading flowers then
Would come to life and bloom again,
This is my last and final will
Good luck to all of you.

—*Joe Hill*

Hillman, Sidney (1887–1946)

One of the nation's most forceful and politically active labor leaders, Sidney Hillman, born in Lithuania, headed the Amalgamated Clothing Workers of America (ACWA) in the 1930s. He was instrumental in getting the ACWA into the American Federation of Labor, and in 1935 was an important member of the organizational group that breathed life into the Committee for Industrial Organizations. Hillman, along with John L. Lewis, Philip Murray, and David Dubinsky, transformed the committee into the Congress of Industrial Organizations (CIO), the country's most powerful industrial union.

Under Hillman's potent leadership, the Textile Workers Organizing Committee was formed. It was extremely successful in making inroads into the unionization of Southern textile mills in the 1930s. In Southern mill towns the ACWU won union victories where AFL organizers had not dared to tread.

During World War II, Hillman was one of the primary movers and shakers behind the organization of the CIO's

Sidney Hillman

apparent that FDR told his aides to "clear everything with Sidney."

To his death in 1946, Sidney Hillman was one of the country's most significant labor leaders. He always supported candidates favorable to the workers and always bargained for the best conditions of employment for the toiling masses.

See also Amalgamated Clothing Workers of America; Textile Workers Organizing Committee.

Hillquit, Morris (1869–1933)

Morris Hillquit was one of the founders of the Socialist Party of America (SPA) at the turn of the twentieth century. In 1898 he led malcontents in the Socialist Labor party, headed by Daniel DeLeon, to establish an independent socialist faction known as the Rochester or Kangaroo convention. Three years later Hillquit's socialists became the center of the Socialist Party of America.

Hillquit's SPA endorsed the concept that the successes of American socialism depended on the support of organized labor. He decried DeLeon and others for their hostile attitude toward labor and the American Federation of Labor (AFL). Hillquit and his followers reaffirmed that the AFL would never embrace socialism in the face of unfriendly socialistic opposition.

Hillquit espoused what was known as evolutionary socialism, in which socialists and labor united in order to support candidates and win elections for the betterment of the working classes. The party in which Hillquit played such a key role also included Eugene Victor Debs, five-time Socialist Party candidate for president. The vote-getting power of the SPA with Debs as its presidential candidate alarmed many Americans, as did its opposition to World War I. In contrast to DeLeon's Socialist Labor Party and the Industrial Workers of the World, however, Hillquit's brand of socialism was evolutionary, not revolutionary.

Political Action Committee (CIO-PAC). CIO-PAC, together with Hillman's ACWA, were among the most politically active of all labor organizations in the mid-1940s. A visionary, Hillman dreamed of the day when there would be no unemployment and of a utopia where workers would experience complete economic and political freedom.

Along with Lewis and Murray, Hillman was an anticommunist labor leader. At times, however, his PAC was accused of being radical and un-American. During World War II, Hillman and General Motors Vice-President William S. Knudsen were coexecutives of the Office of Production Management. After the war Hillman and other labor leaders effectively stymied the efforts of South Carolina's James F. Byrnes to be Roosevelt's running mate in the election of 1944; instead, the Democrats tapped Harry S Truman for second place on the ticket. Hillman's political activism was so

Hitchman Coal and Coke Company v. Mitchell (U.S., 1916)

This Supreme Court case involved the issue of whether or not an employer, in this instance a West Virginia coal company, could require coal miners to sign a yellow-dog contract stipulating they would never join the United Mine Workers of America. The Court ruled that employers could legally require employees to sign nonunion or yellow-dog contracts. In its decision the Court held that "the same liberty which enables men to form unions, and through the union to enter into agreements with employers willing to agree, entitles other men to remain independent of the union and other employers to agree with them to employ no man who owes any allegiance or obligation to the union."

In the aftermath of the *Hitchman* opinion, the use of yellow-dog contracts mushroomed. Within a decade, for example, more than a million workers had agreed to these contracts and the courts had enjoined labor unions from resisting them. In essence, union campaigns ground to a halt. Congress, in 1932, passed the Norris-LaGuardia Act, which attempted to put an end to yellow-dog contracts. Despite the law, some employers, professing ignorance about the Norris-LaGuardia Act, still required workers to sign yellow-dog contracts into the late 1930s.

See also Yellow-Dog Contracts.

Hoffa, James Riddle (1913–1975?)

James R. "Jimmy" Hoffa was the son of an Indiana coal miner. Born in Brazil, Indiana, Hoffa, like many children of coal miners, quit school to work. He did not project himself into the labor union picture until the New Deal years, when he was elected president of a local Teamsters union. As Hoffa became active in the Teamsters, a small core of political activists, headquartered in Minneapolis, laid plans to take over the long-distance trucking business in the United States. When that faction was ousted, Hoffa, ever the opportunist, used the occasion to forge his dominance within the Teamsters.

When Teamsters President Dave Beck was sent to prison for stealing union funds in 1957, Jimmy Hoffa was installed to lead the union. Hoffa did not stay out of trouble for long. Soon the activities of Hoffa and the Teamsters came under the scrutiny of the Select Committee on Improper Activities in the Labor and Management Field, chaired by Arkansas Senator John McClellan with Robert F. Kennedy as chief counsel. A bitter feud developed between Hoffa and Kennedy, who maintained that the Teamster chief had definite connections with hoodlums and gangsters and that the union was riddled with corruption. Despite Kennedy's accusations, Hoffa remained entrenched in power following his reelection to the Teamster presidency in 1961. Hoffa manifested his power by countering every Committee action against him. Finally in 1964 he was convicted on a charge of jury tampering. After exhausting all appeal avenues, he went to prison in 1967. Meanwhile, because of McClellan Committee allegations against Hoffa and his union, or as Kennedy put it, the "Hoodlum Empire," the AFL-CIO expelled the Teamsters.

President Richard M. Nixon paroled Hoffa in 1971 on the condition that he stay out of Teamster affairs. After his release from prison, however, Hoffa apparently plotted to regain control of the union from President Frank Fitzsimmons. Suddenly and without warning in July 1975, Jimmy Hoffa disappeared, leaving no hint with regard to his whereabouts. No clues as to his mysterious disappearance were uncovered. The likeliest scenario is that he was murdered by the "Hoodlum Empire" over which he presided for a decade. However, Joseph Franco, Hoffa's chief lieutenant in the Teamsters, in a book entitled *Hoffa's Man*

Jimmy Hoffa

(1987), claimed he saw Hoffa get into a car in a Detroit shopping center on the afternoon of 30 July 1975 with two "government" men. Franco theorizes that the two federal agents who drove off with Hoffa may have disposed of him under government orders.

See also International Brotherhood of Teamsters, Chauffeurs, Warehousemen and Helpers of America.

Holbrook, Douglas C. (1934–)

Douglas C. Holbrook, who was elected secretary-treasurer of the American Postal Workers Union (APWU) in 1983, has long been active in APWU affairs. He spent two years as an auto worker in Detroit before joining the post office as a part-time clerk in 1956. From that date to the present, Holbrook has worked in the postal service and has been an active member and officer of the APWU. Among the offices held by Holbrook are president of the Detroit district area APWU local and the National Postal

Union (predecessor of APWU); board member of the metro Detroit AFL-CIO; trustee of the Detroit local of APWU; editor of the *Detroit Postal Worker*; and vice-president of the Detroit area APWU.

Born in Colburn, Virginia, Holbrook was educated in a Virginia high school and attended Wayne State University, where he studied labor relations and administration.

The APWU, the largest postal workers union in the world, was created from the consolidation of five postal unions. For years the APWU could not engage in collective bargaining negotiations because it was an affiliate of the federal government. However, when 200,000 postal workers walked out in 1970, Congress legislated the Postal Reorganization Act, which made the Postal Service an independent and separate entity. Presently the APWU has a membership of 765,000, including clerks, maintenance workers, motor vehicle workers, special delivery employees, and mail handlers. While other unions representing federal workers cannot engage in collective bargaining, Holbrook's APWU can bargain with regard to hours, wages, and the like. More and more it seems the APWU is trying to join the ranks of the private sector.

Holbrook is a strong believer in the union and the principles for which it stands. It is his view that the APWU and other labor unions are to be credited with giving birth to middle-class America. He points out that the APWU, which is an open shop organization, has experienced tremendous growth and has been essential to improving the quality of life not only for its members but for all Americans.

Holbrook is a strong advocate of collective bargaining, because it is through that instrument that wages, hours, and conditions of employment for postal employees has improved.

Homestead, Pennsylvania, at the turn of the century

Homestead Lockout (1892)

The Homestead Lockout and strike, which took place at the Homestead, Pennsylvania, plant of Carnegie Steel Company near Pittsburgh in July 1892, was occasioned by a wage cut imposed by plant manager Henry Clay Frick. Following the wage cut, workers walked out and Frick ordered company gates locked. Company guards were called out to enforce the lockout, but employees attacked the guards and drove them away.

On 6 July 1892 the company brought 200 Pinkerton detectives up the river to protect company property. Scabs were hired to replace the striking workers. As the Pinkertons neared the plant at about dawn, armed workers lining the river bank opened fire on the two barges carrying the detectives. The Pinkertons answered with their own fire, and all day long the Battle of Homestead raged. Toward evening, as their ammunition ran low, the strikers poured oil on the water and lit it, turning the river into a blazing inferno. The detectives were in troubled waters, indeed.

After the oil burned out, the Pinkertons were allowed to come ashore. As they did, the workers, along with their spouses and families, used clubs to chase them to a nearby railroad siding, where the Pinkertons were pulled to safety on a passenger train. The battle resulted in the deaths of ten workers and guards.

Finally Carnegie Steel appealed to the governor of Pennsylvania, who sent 8,000 state troops to protect the scabs. In full battle dress, the state militia repulsed the strikers, protected the scabs, and made it possible for the company to reopen its gates and resume operations. The strike ended, and the union suffered a crushing defeat. The country's steel industry was not unionized until the New Deal years of the 1930s.

See also Frick, Henry Clay.

Hutcheson, William Lewis (1874–1953)

Head of the United Brotherhood of Carpenters and Joiners of America, William

Hutcheson was one of the two most powerful labor leaders in the United States during the Progressive Era. One of five children, Hutcheson, christened William Lewis, was born in a lumber town, Saginaw, Michigan. He grew up to be a husky young man over six feet tall, weighing somewhere between 225 and 300 pounds, and he loved to fight. Hutcheson attended school briefly, stopping at age 13 to become an apprentice to his father, who was a carpenter. At age 14 he heard Samuel Gompers speak and was impressed by his union philosophy. As a boy he also had heard messages on the eight-hour day and witnessed a strike by lumberjacks for a ten-hour day. All these incidents made a deep and lasting impression on young Hutcheson.

He soon grew dissatisfied with working conditions, and after an altercation with a fellow worker, Hutcheson quit his job and became a wanderer. In his wanderings he spent some time on a dairy farm, where he met his wife, who later bore him four children. Next he ventured into Western wheat fields and traveled to Coeur d'Alene, Idaho, in time to see a strike broken by government troops. Later his interest was aroused by Debs's leadership of the Pullman Strike.

At the turn of the century Hutcheson finally found his niche in the carpentering industry. By 1906 he had become an effective organizer, and back in his hometown of Saginaw, Michigan, he became involved in two local carpenters unions. Within a decade Hutcheson had risen to the presidency of the United Brotherhood of Carpenters and Joiners, a union of over 322,000 members by 1929. He had become the most powerful individual in the building trades industry.

Hutcheson also became politically active in the 1920s. The foremost Republican in labor, he supported Calvin Coolidge for the presidency in 1924. Coolidge, along with Presidents Warren G. Harding and Herbert Hoover, courted him as secretary of labor. He refused the cabinet position, content to be a labor confidante to Republican presidents.

In the 1930s Hutcheson resisted efforts to take the United Brotherhood of Carpenters into the AFL. When an attempt to include industrial workers in the AFL was defeated, Hutcheson and John L. Lewis got into an altercation. Reportedly, in some of the verbal wrangling that went on at the AFL convention, Hutcheson called Lewis a bastard, and Lewis responded by delivering a hard uppercut to Hutcheson's jaw. (Both men weighed well over 200 pounds.) Onlookers separated the antagonists, but the incident was symbolic of the intense feelings between craft unionists and industrial workers.

Two of Hutcheson's contemporaries held the man in awe. It was said that William Green, head of the AFL, "admires him, and fears him." John L. Lewis, Hutcheson's bitter rival, remarked: "He was a strong man. He was never an inconsistent man. He met his problems head-on."

See also United Brotherhood of Carpenters and Joiners of America.

Hutchinson, Barbara B. (1946–)

Sometimes referred to as a "feminist unionist," Barbara B. Hutchinson was born in Braddock, Pennsylvania, in 1946. She was educated at the University of Pittsburgh, where she was a political science major; she later obtained a law degree from Dickinson School of Law. Following her educational experience, Hutchinson became a trial attorney in many civil rights cases.

In 1980 Hutchinson was chosen as the second director of the Women's Department of the American Federation of Government Employees (AFGE). A year later she was selected as a vice-president of the AFL-CIO's executive board, the second woman to be a member of that important body. Before rising to such lofty positions on labor councils, Hutchinson was a steward and first vice-president of the Equal Employment Opportunity Commission, Local 3599, in Atlanta. Currently, she also is a board member of the A. Philip Randolph Institute and the Joint Council on Economic Education.

Under Hutchinson's guidance, the Women's Department of the AFGE sponsors a biennial training conference for women, awards an outstanding achievement certificate to AFGE women, and defrays legal costs in discrimination cases under the Equal Employment Opportunity Law.

There were unions of federal employees in the nineteenth century, but collective bargaining rights were nonexistent. All that changed in 1962 when President John F. Kennedy invoked Executive Order 10988, which gave AFGE collective bargaining rights but denied the right to strike. Collective bargaining rights do not include issues like wage levels, pensions, fringe benefits, and personnel actions.

Hutchinson's organization presently represents over 700,000 federal employees, making it the largest union of government workers.

Hutchinson has been somewhat of a pioneer as a labor leader in the modern women's labor movement and as a member of one of the highest labor councils in the country. She has become a model for other women who wish to become involved in labor as well as in the legal profession. She certainly has used her position in an attempt to break racial and sexual barriers in federal employment practices.

Industrial Workers of the World (IWW)

The Industrial Workers of the World (IWW) was established in Chicago, Illinois, in 1905. From its inception the IWW stood for the overthrow of the capitalist state. In fact, the preamble to the IWW constitution states, "It is the historic mission of the working class to do away with capitalism."

The revolutionary union, the basis of which was syndicalism, aimed to organize all American workers into one big industrial union. After the downfall of the capitalist class/system, a workers' government would be set up. The workers would also own the machinery of production. The IWW emphasized a series of strikes, culminating in a general strike and bringing an end to capitalism.

Members of the IWW were called "Wobblies." An apocryphal story suggests that the term was originally from a West Coast Chinese waiter, who one day at lunch inquired of a group of workers: "All loo eye wobble wobble?" From that salutation the members of the IWW began to call themselves "I wobbly wobbly." Perhaps a better explanation for the name is that it is based on the use of the wobblesaw, a circular saw, by lumberjacks in the Western lumbering area. The initials IWW were also construed to be "I won't work," "I want whiskey," "International Wonder Workers," and "Irresponsible Wholesale Wreckers."

The IWW was at its peak between the years 1905 to 1924. It was most successful in organizing Western lumberjacks and miners, immigrant textile workers on the East Coast, farmers in the Plains states, and coal miners in the southern Appalachians. During the dark days of the depression, the IWW attempted a comeback in the Harlan County, Kentucky, coalfields. The union flooded Kentucky's premier coal county with literature and organized at least one local. With the return of good times in the early 1940s, however, the IWW folded its tents.

In comparison to unions such as the American Federation of Labor and the Knights of Labor, the IWW enrolled far fewer members. Apparently its peak membership was around 100,000. On the other hand, one historian of the Wobblies has estimated that around one million workers at one time or another were card-carrying IWW members and were apprised of its ideology.

During the World War I era, the Wobblies opposed both the war and the draft. Many were imprisoned and fined for sabotaging and subverting the war effort. The IWW never fully recovered.

Basically, the philosophy of the IWW called for one union of industrial workers.

An Industrial Workers of the World poster

It drew no sexual or racial barriers. Among its leading organizers and adherents were Elizabeth Gurley Flynn, known as the rebel girl, and Mary Harris Jones, affectionately called Mother Jones. Among its other prominent leaders were President William D. "Big Bill" Haywood, who fled to and died in Russia, and Joe Hill, the famous writer of a number of Wobbly songs. The theme song of the Wobblies was "Solidarity Forever," performed to the tune of "John Brown's Body"—labor's martial song today.

The most revolutionary of all U.S. labor unions, the IWW never really made much headway into the ranks of the American working class; hence, it did not materially improve working conditions for the toiling masses.

Injunctions

Injunctions are court orders, and were one of management's most effective weapons against the rise of organized labor in the United States. Injunctions were used to restrain unions and workers from such activities as strikes, picketing, marches, demonstrations, and trespassing on company property. Injunctions were issued by both federal and state courts to restrain labor. In fact, in the late nineteenth century, the injunction was so widely used that government by injunction was virtually a *fait accompli*.

Once granted, the injunction was used by big business to break strikes (for example, the 1894 Pullman Strike in Chicago) and generally to keep workers from joining labor unions. When a labor leader or a union violated the court order, the union head was sent to jail, as was Eugene V. Debs during the Pullman Strike, and the union was fined.

With the injunction, companies and corporations successfully thwarted labor's right to organize the working class from the late nineteenth century to the 1930s.

In 1932 Congress passed the Norris-La-Guardia Act, cosponsored by Republican Senator George W. Norris of Nebraska and Democratic Congressman Fiorello LaGuardia of New York. Known as the anti-injunction law, the Norris-LaGuardia Act limited the use of federal injunctions in labor disputes except in cases in which "substantial and irreparable injury" to company property for which there was "no adequate remedy at law" occurred. In other words, the company, before obtaining an injunction against a labor union, had to prove that the labor dispute would irretrievably damage company property and that there was no recourse for the company in the courts.

The anti-injunction statute, of course, was left open for interpretation by the federal courts. While the courts generally had sustained injunctions from the late nineteenth century into the third decade of the twentieth century, the Roosevelt Court after World War II denied injunctions in labor disputes. More recent court cases favored organized labor. Government by injunction became a thing of the past and big labor had finally gained recognition in the United States.

International Brotherhood of Teamsters, Chauffeurs, Warehousemen and Helpers of America (IBT)

At the turn of the century a handful of Midwestern laborers met with Samuel Gompers to explore the possibility of organizing unskilled team drivers. Out of that historic meeting evolved one of the country's largest and perhaps most corrupt labor unions, popularly known as the Teamsters.

At first the International Brotherhood of Teamsters (IBT) consisted of numerous locals supervised by powerful bosses. It grew steadily, and in 1899 was chartered by the American Federation of Labor (AFL) as the Team Driver International (TDI) with 1,700 members. Workers at that time had to put in a 14-hour day, a six-day week plus a half-day Sunday, and had to groom their own teams—all for $10 to $12 weekly.

Chicago locals assumed leadership in forming the TDI. In 1902, however, Chicago unionists seceded from TDI to form the Teamsters National Union. In 1903, the Chicago union rejoined TDI, and the IBT was established.

Collective bargaining on a coordinated scale was impossible at the outset because of the local market concept, which emphasized local autonomy. It was not until the presidency of Dave Beck that local autonomy gave way to national organization as long-distance trucking lines developed.

Collusion and corruption existed early in the IBT. While the union was relatively free of these elements during the presidency of Daniel J. Tobin (1907–1952), corruption was prevalent in the trucking industry. Tobin worked for stability in the IBT and rarely became involved in local affairs. He reduced IBT expenses and called for conventions at five-year intervals. He was an AFL officer during most of his tenure as IBT president.

The IBT added stablemen and truckers in 1910 and dairy processors in 1918. Under Dave Beck the union grew rapidly, as did its corruption. After Beck was caught up on conspiracy and extortion charges, the IBT was ousted by the AFL.

Jimmy Hoffa succeeded Beck. During his reign the union expanded to include bakery, beverage, cannery, building and construction, laundry, produce, cold storage, warehouse, department store, wholesale optical, and agricultural workers. Workers engaged in general and local hauling also joined the IBT, as did one local of college professors. Hoffa secured a first national contract for the Teamsters in 1964; it was renewed in

1967. He also expanded health and medical programs for IBT employees.

Hoffa went the way of Beck. In 1963 he was convicted on similar counts and went to prison until pardoned by President Richard Nixon in 1967. He was succeeded by Frank Fitzsimmons.

In the 1970s the IBT warred with Chavez's United Farm Workers and the United Brewery, Flour, Cereal, Soft Drink and Distillery Workers. That conflict ended in 1972 when those two unions merged with the IBT. Membership in the IBT now hovers around the 1.6 million mark with nearly 800 locals.

Current IBT President Ron Carey was chosen by a direct election of union members. A far cry from the days of Beck and Hoffa, Carey has brought new and fresh leadership to the IBT by severing connections with organized crime.

See also Carey, Ronald; Hoffa, James Riddle.

International Brotherhood of Teamsters Local 695 v. Vogt (U.S., 1957)

Seven years after the Supreme Court's *Hanke* decision, it unreservedly abandoned its previous position on peaceful picketing. In the *Vogt* case, a majority of the Court upheld a Wisconsin law that disallowed peaceful picketing "against an employer in the absence of a labor dispute." Again, Justice Frankfurter wrote the majority opinion for the Court. In it he emphasized that a state could not legally pass a law enforcing "blanket regulations against picketing," but that it could oversee the reasons for picketing. If a state believed that the motives behind picketing needed to be limited, then it could enact legislation to do just that.

Without question, the Supreme Court in the *Vogt* case had gone "full circle," in the words of Justices Hugo Black and William O. Douglas, from its position in the late 1930s and early 1940s, when it upheld peaceful picketing. In the 1950s the Court's decisions reflected the view that states could limit picketing for specific reasons.

In the face of both the *Hanke* and *Vogt* cases, the highest court in the land dealt organized labor a serious blow by giving states the authority to limit picketing. It must be pointed out that picketing was/is one of the most effective instruments used by unions to publicize their aims. With the limitation of picketing in the *Hanke* and *Vogt* cases, labor organizations could not get their views before the public as effectively as before the Court's decisions.

See also International Brotherhood of Teamsters v. Hanke; Picketing.

International Brotherhood of Teamsters v. Hanke (U.S., 1950)

The Supreme Court ruled in *International Brotherhood of Teamsters v. Hanke*, that the state of California could restrain picketing by a labor union even though it was carried out through legal means. A California injunction had barred picketing to force the owner of a small automobile repair shop to embrace the union shop. Speaking for the Court's majority, Justice Felix Frankfurter stated that a state might limit picketing albeit peaceful and for a legitimate purpose. In this case the Court reversed an earlier position— expressed in *Senn v. Tile Layers Union* (1937), *Thornhill v. Alabama* (1940), and *American Federation v. Swing* (1941)— that peaceful picketing was an expression of free speech protected by the First Amendment to the U.S. Constitution.

See also International Brotherhood of Teamsters Local 695 v. Vogt; Picketing.

International Labor Defense (ILD)

A communistic and leftist-oriented agency, the International Labor Defense (ILD) offered legal assistance to union men and organizers who were apprehended and incarcerated in connection with the vio-

lence and turmoil in industrial areas during the labor warfare of the 1920s and 1930s. The ILD sent into the troubled textile mills of the Carolinas and into the southern Appalachian coalfields its legal counsel, both male and female, along with other representatives to lend support to workers accused of crimes against management. The ILD became a support agency to other Communist Party affiliates—Workers International Relief, Federated Press, the Young Communist League, and the National Committee for the Defense of Political Prisoners, among others. In the coalfields the ILD backed the National Miners Union, a Communist Party affiliate based in Pittsburgh. Among the ILD personnel who entered areas of labor conflict were Allan Taub, a New York attorney; J. Louis Engdahl, chairman of the ILD; Jessie Wakefield, a young female ILD representative; George Maurer, who influenced coal miners to strike and affiliate with the National Miners Union; attorney Dorothy Ross Weber; and attorney Leon Josephson.

Since ILD lawyers and representatives were avowed communists, they were not very welcome in both the coalfields and textile towns. Local authorities resented their intrusions; subsequently they were arrested, incarcerated, and released with a warning to leave the area and never return. Allan Taub received a special brand of mountain justice when he was driven to Cumberland Gap and beaten, allegedly by Kentucky officials, in 1932. In some instances, Kentucky coal miners refused legal counsel offered by the ILD, preferring the assistance of local attorneys. In other areas the ILD defended unionists and organizers after easing aside local defenders.

With the National Industrial Recovery Act of 1933 and the National Labor Relations Act of 1935, American workers began to join rank-and-file labor unions. As they did, the ILD and other Communist Party affiliates failed to function in industrial sections of the United States.

International Ladies Garment Workers Union (ILGWU)

In 1900 New York cloak makers issued a call for a convention of workers employed in the garment industry. On 3 June, 11 delegates representing seven locals with around 2000 members met and organized the International Ladies Garment Workers Union (ILGWU). Three weeks later the American Federation of Labor chartered the new union.

Between 1900 and 1904 the ILGWU supported boycotts and attempted to unionize firms by using the union label. In the meantime the Industrial Workers of the World (IWW) tried unsuccessfully to bore into the ILGWU. By the end of World War I the ILGWU had developed into one of the country's strongest and best known unions.

Two strikes gave the union a sense of permanency. In 1909 the New York City shirtwaist makers won a strike, and in 1910 New York City cloak makers, who struck for a 6-day, 54-hour week, a union shop, and arbitration of grievances, were also successful.

Throughout its history the ILGWU resisted communism, and by 1938 it had expelled most communists from its ranks. The National Industrial Recovery Act of 1933 heralded expansion for the union, whose membership jumped to over 200,000 by 1934.

The ILGWU was always in the vanguard of American industrial unionism. Under the leadership of its most famous president, David Dubinsky, the union focused on economic and social reforms, including numerous fringe benefits such as employer-financed unemployment compensation, union health centers, and increased wage levels.

Women garment workers composed about 80 percent of the ILGWU mem-bership in the late 1930s. Headquartered in New York City, the ILGWU counts among its most prominent members in recent years New York City's African American and Hispanic workers and California's Mexican American and Chinese employees.

Presently the ILGWU has a membership of approximately 175,000 workers nationwide.

International Longshoreman's Association (ILA)

Although American dockworkers had developed the posture of militancy as early as the Jacksonian Era of the 1830s, the first formal union was not established until 1864. After the Civil War, dockworkers became more aggressive with strikes in New York and other port cities in the United States. In the 1870s,

An ILGWU member who works as a cutter

following strikes on the New York waterfront, the Knights of Labor organized that city's dockworkers. Toward the end of the nineteenth century a separate organization, the American Longshoremen's Union (ALU) emerged with a total membership of 15,000 dockworkers in 21 locals. When the ALU's general secretary fled with union funds, the union collapsed.

Meanwhile, in the 1890s, Great Lakes dockworkers founded the National Longshoremen's Association. When Canadian workers joined that union in 1895, the name was changed to the International Longshoremen's Association (ILA). The ILA remains the principal union for longshoremen to the present.

Additional associations for dockworkers appeared early in the twentieth century. In 1902 the International Longshoremen, Marine and Transport Workers Association was formed along with the International Seamen's Association to compete with the ILA.

A key leader of West Coast longshoremen in the 1930s was Harry Bridges, who became president of the San Francisco local. Bridges, a militant labor organizer, leaned to the left as did his local. Bridges led an ultra-successful strike of the West Coast Maritime Union, a Communist Party affiliate, in 1933–1934. At the end of the strike Bridges won far more concessions for his men than had any East Coast or Gulf Coast longshoremen's groups. In 1938 the National Labor Relations Board extended recognition to the ILA. The American Federation of Labor (AFL) had also recognized the ILA, but when Bridges was identified as a communist and as he pushed the West Coast strike of 1933–1934, the strikers established a separate union, the International Longshoremen and Warehousemen's Union, not recognized by the AFL.

By the 1950s two main longshoremen's unions—the ILA and the International Brotherhood of Longshoremen—courted the nation's dockworkers. Those two unions merged and were readmitted to the AFL-CIO. In 1953 charges of corruption and racketeering in the ILA led to its expulsion by the AFL-CIO.

Presently the ILA has a membership of about 110,000 workers.

International Printing Pressmen's Assistants Union
See International Typographical Union.

International Typographical Union (ITU)

The International Typographical Union (ITU) and its predecessors were considered the oldest national union in the U.S. labor movement. Before the Civil War a craft union of journeymen printers was established. For a time printers dominated the organization. With the technological innovations of the postwar period, printers soon were in competition and conflict with compositors and the pressmen. As commercial presses developed apart from newspaper printing, which was the principal aim of the ITU's earliest organizing campaigns, further strife surfaced. In a compromise effort, the ITU made concessions to job printers and power printers as typesetters dominated most local and national unions.

Born out of this internecine warfare in 1889 was the International Printing Pressmen's Assistants Union (IPPAU). Five years later the ITU and IPPAU reached an accord whereby the ITU represented compositors and IPPAU represented pressmen. Conflict resumed following a short-lived truce, and by 1901 the IPPAU became the chief representative of the printing trade.

Throughout the twentieth century the IPPAU has represented the printing profession. In 1973 it merged with the International Stereotypers, Electrotypers, and Platemakers Union of North America to form the International Printing and Graphic Communications Union (IPGCU).

Recent figures show that presently the IPGCU has a membership of nearly 128,000 workers in 711 locals throughout the United States and Canada.

International Union of Cigar Makers (CIU)

The first national union of American cigar makers was established before the Civil War. As the industry grew, two important changes took place: cigar making moved from one-man shops to large shops, and Canadian cigar makers joined, creating a true international union.

By 1869, 5,800 workers comprised 87 locals of the International Union of Cigar Makers (CIU) in the United States and Canada. Again dramatic changes appeared as women and children were hired and tobacco molds, breakers, and rollers were introduced. As technology enhanced manufacturing methods, wages declined.

In the 1870s, however, through the leadership of Adolph Strasser, the fortunes of the workers improved. Adopting a policy of what he termed "pure wage-conscious unionism," Strasser called for higher union dues and centralized control of locals. At the same time wages increased, and the union provided fringe benefits such as loans to members who had to relocate to get employment, and sickness, death, and jobless benefits. The 1890s were the CIU's golden years, as membership jumped to over 24,000.

A rival organization, the Tobacco Workers International Union (TWIU) was formed in 1895. Concentrating its efforts outside cigar making, the TWIU by 1940 had 18,000 members whereas enrollment in the CIU dropped to 7,000. The CIU struggled along for a while, finally merging with the Retail, Wholesale and Department Store Union in 1974.

All the while through the strong leadership of Strasser and Samuel Gompers, both of whom resisted machinery, the CIU maintained a solid position in the American Federation of Labor.

For cigar makers, the CIU was a very important vehicle that lost some of its power with the advent of technological advances, especially in the twentieth century.

See also Gompers, Samuel.

International Union of Mine, Mill, and Smelter Workers

See Western Federation of Miners.

International Working People's Association

See Black International.

International Workingmen's Association (IWA)

The International Workingmen's Association (IWA) had its roots in Europe. Associated with the First International and having a Marxist philosophy, the IWA especially appealed to immigrant workers who migrated to the United States in the late nineteenth century.

At first William H. Sylvis, head of the National Labor Union, sought ties with the IWA in the "war between poverty and wealth." In fact, when Sylvis died suddenly in 1869, Karl Marx eulogized the bold leader as one of the "tried champions in the bloom of life."

In time German immigrants who fled their homeland in the face of Otto Von Bismarck's antisocialist regime formed socialist groups in the United States. By the 1870s they had succeeded in transferring Marx's International Working Men's Association to New York City.

As radicals were scheduled to speak to workers in New York City in 1874, the authorities, upon learning that the IWA was involved in the proposed meeting, revoked a permit for the rally. The working classes, unaware of the change, gathered in Tompkins Square, where men, women, and children were struck and stampeded by the city's mounted policemen. The Tompkins Square Riot resulted in the injury of many workers and onlookers alike.

In the aftermath of the altercation in New York City, the IWA relocated in Philadelphia, where it drew its last breath in 1876. Once again, most American workers had refused allegiance to a leftist, radical labor movement that supported both violence and revolution and embraced anarchism, socialism, strikes, and labor unrest.

Iron Molders' Union

A forerunner to the National Labor Union, the National Molders' Union was organized by William H. Sylvis in 1859. At a Philadelphia convention 46 delegates from 18 locals breathed life into the national organization. With the coming of the Civil War, the new union languished as Sylvis went off to war for about two years. In 1863, as president of the Iron Molders Union, Sylvis revitalized the organization into a union of 53 locals with national membership of between 7,000 and 8,500 members. By the end of the Civil War, the Iron Molders' Union was a viable labor organization. The rise of the union was largely because of the untiring efforts of Sylvis, who ranged from one end of the country to the other. Sylvis advocated collective bargaining and a closed shop, and embraced strikes as a last resort.

The Iron Molders' Union grew slowly during the 1860s. Stove manufacturers and iron foundries, however, began to move strongly against the union by slashing wages and laying off union workers. The workers responded with a strike; the companies imposed a lockout. The strikers continued the action for several months, but when strike funds ran out, the union had to admit defeat. While Sylvis was able to salvage a remnant of the Iron Molders' Union, he shifted to a broader-based program of labor activity. The Iron Molders had given him a platform for a national labor movement; now he became the charismatic leader of one of the country's first nationwide labor organizations—the National Labor Union.

See also National Labor Union; Sylvis, William H.

Jackson, Molly Garland

Born the daughter of Oliver Perry and Deborah Robinson Garland in East Bernstadt, Kentucky, Molly Garland was the half-sister of Kentucky coal miner and National Miners' Union supporter Jim Garland. While quite young, Molly married John Mills, her first husband. She had two other husbands, Jim Stewart and Bill Jackson. From 1910 until 1932, Molly was a well-known midwife in the Kentucky hills, delivering or presiding over about 5,000 births.

From duties as a midwife in her early years, Aunt Molly Jackson by the 1930s had become a speaker, songwriter, and singer. In 1931–1932, when famous author Theodore Dreiser visited the Bell-Harlan County area to investigate an alleged reign of terror among Kentucky's poverty-stricken coal miners, Aunt Molly joined the New York liberal in support of the miners' cause. She separated from Jackson in 1932 to travel to New York City to seek aid for distressed Kentucky coal miners. By that time she had become known affectionately as Aunt Molly Jackson. In New York City she became an associate of author Sherwood Anderson, songwriter Woody Guthrie, and of course, her half-brother Jim Garland and his sister, Sarah Ogan Gunning. Seven of her compositions were recorded by artists Pete Seeger, Mike Seeger, and John Greenway.

Aunt Molly Jackson, between 1935 and 1940, made 31 commercial recordings and 171 field recordings, ranging from mountain ballads to protest songs that described conditions among Kentucky's impoverished coal miners. Among Aunt Molly's field recordings now contained in the Archive of Folk Song, Library of Congress, Washington, D.C., are these folk songs-hymns: "Ain't Nobody's Business But My Own," "Amazing Grace," "Autobiography of Aunt Molly Jackson" (sung and spoken), "Barbara Allen," "Casey Jones," "Come All You Fair and Tender Ladies," "Dry Bones," "How Firm a Foundation," "A Little Talk with Jesus," "Old Joe Clark," and "Skip to My Lou, My Darling."

Aunt Molly also recorded a number of union and protest songs, as well as compositions describing the lives and plight of Kentucky coal miners. These include "Hard Times in Coleman's Mines," "I Love Coal Miners, I Do," "I Am a Union Woman," "Death of Harry Simms," "Dreadful Memories," "Kentucky Miners' Dreadful Fate," "Hungry Disgusted Blues," "Coal Creek Disaster," and "Coal Miner's Child." Additional Aunt Molly's songs recorded by other artists include "Hard Working Miner," "I Am a Union Woman," "Join the CIO," "Join the NMU," and "Poor Miner's Farewell."

In the 1930s Aunt Molly Jackson became nationally famous for her songs and recordings. She was a fixture in New York City as a speaker and as a singer in support of the working class, especially Kentucky coal miners.

"The Ballad of Harry Simms," written by Aunt Molly's half-brother, Jim Garland, and recorded by Aunt Molly, is a good example of the type of music she recorded. The song concerns Harry Simms, an organizer for the National Miners' Union and a member of the Young Communist League, who was gunned down by thugs on Brush Creek in Knox County, Kentucky, in February 1932. After Simms' funeral in New York City, Garland penned this song in memory of his deceased comrade:

Comrades, listen to my story,
Comrades, listen to my song.

*I'll tell you of a hero that now—is dead
and gone.*
*I'll tell you of a young boy whose age
was just nineteen.*
*He was the strongest union man that I
have ever seen.*
*Harry Simms was a pal of mine, we
labored side by side,*
*Expecting to be shot on sight or taken
for a ride*
*By the dirty coal operator gun thugs
that roam from town to town*
*To shoot and kill our Comrades
wherever they may be found.*
*Harry Simms and I were parted at five
o'clock that day.*
*"Be careful, my dear Comrade," to
Harry I did say.*
*"I must do my duty," was his reply to
me.*
*"If I get killed by gun thugs, please
don't grieve over me."*
*Harry Simms was walking down the
track one bright sunshiny day.*
*He was a youth of courage. His step was
light and gay.*
*He did not know the gun thugs were
hiding on the way*
*To kill our dear young Comrade this
bright sunshiny day.*
*Harry Simms was killed on Brush
Creek in nineteen thirty-two.*
*He organized the miners into the
NMU.*
*He gave his life in struggle, that was
all that he could do.*
*He died for the union, also for me and
you.*

[final verse of the original]:

*Comrades, we must vow today, this one
thing we must do—*
*We must organize all the miners in the
good old NMU.*
*We'll get a million volunteers from
those who wish us well,*
*And sink this rotten system in the
deepest pits of hell.*

[final verse composed later]:

*Comrades, we must vow today, there's
one thing we must do—*
*We'll organize all the miners into the
good old NMU.*
*We'll get a million volunteers from
those who wish us well,*
*And travel over the country and
Harry's story tell.*

Jones, Mary Harris "Mother" (1830–1930)

Mary Harris Jones was born in Cork, Ireland, the daughter of a railroad construction worker. In 1835 she came to the United States. She tried teaching school in Michigan and then the dressmaking business in Chicago before settling in Memphis, Tennessee. There she married a member of the Iron Molders Union. After her husband and four children died in a yellow fever epidemic, she returned to dressmaking in Chicago. Soon she began to attend meetings of the Knights of Labor, and her course as a labor leader was set. She became involved in the Baltimore and Ohio national strike in 1877, but her real fame was gained as an organizer among the nation's coal miners.

In the 1890s and early years of the twentieth century, she helped unionize coal miners in the Fairmont and New River coalfields of West Virginia. In 1903–1904 Mary Jones, who became known as "Mother" Jones among her union comrades, traveled west to Colorado to support the striking coal miners in that area. In her early years as an organizer she was affiliated with the United Mine Workers of America (UMW), but left the organization after a dispute with UMW chief John Mitchell.

Still in the West, Mother Jones supported railroad machinists in a strike against Southern Pacific Railroad and agitated for the Western Federation of

Mother Jones

Miners in an Arizona copper strike in 1910.

Back East she rejoined the UMW in 1911 and was actively involved in the 1912–1913 West Virginia coal strike. When trouble flared anew in the Colorado coalfields in 1913–1914, Mother Jones returned to the West, where she was arrested and expelled three times. While in Colorado she witnessed the horrors of the Ludlow Massacre, which she publicized in speeches and testimony before a House Committee in 1914. In the 1910s Mother Jones was involved in a New York City streetcar and garment workers' strike, and in 1919 she was active in a nationwide steel strike.

Mother Jones was always deeply interested in the evils and abuses of child labor. Throughout her life as a labor leader she emphasized the exploitation of children. On one occasion she led a chil-

dren's march from a Kensington, Pennsylvania, textile mill to Oyster Bay, New York, the home of Theodore Roosevelt, to dramatize the horrors of children in the workplace. She also worked in the textile operations in Alabama and South Carolina, where she observed firsthand child labor conditions.

Regarded as a radical at times, Mother Jones helped found the Social Democratic Party in 1898 and was an organizer for the Industrial Workers of the World in 1905. After campaigning for the Democrats in 1916, she supported the Farmer-Labor Party in 1924.

Teacher, dressmaker, anti–child labor advocate, organizer, demonstrator, and speaker, Mary Harris "Mother" Jones was one of the country's most important labor leaders in the nineteenth and early twentieth centuries. The real measure of her devotion to the labor movement can be found in the West Virginia coal strike of 1920–1921. There she spoke to the miners, marched with them, and although in her nineties, picketed with them. Whenever and wherever they needed her, Mother Jones was always there supporting the nation's toiling masses. Throughout her life she was a devout union member and organizer in the interest of improving conditions for the working class. Coal miners were as special to her as children; in return, Mary Harris Jones was their mother. Following her death on 30 November 1930 as a centenarian, the following song, which places Mother Jones in proper historical context, was composed:

The Death of Mother Jones

*The world today is mourning the death
    of Mother Jones;
Grief and sorrow hover around the
    miners' homes.
This grand old champion of labor has
    gone to a better land,*

*But the hard-working miners, they
   miss her guiding hand.
Through the hills and over the valleys
   in every mining town,
Mother Jones was ready to help them;
   she never let them down.
In front with the striking miners she
   always could be found;
She fought for right and justice; she
   took a noble stand.*

*With a spirit strong and fearless, she
   hated that which was wrong;
She never gave up fighting until her
   breath was gone.
May the workers all get together to
   carry out her plan,
And bring back better conditions for
   every laboring man.*

Kaplan, Allen H.

A pioneer in the unionization of government employees, Allen H. Kaplan first began working in the Chicago Office of Economic Opportunity in 1967. There he joined in the formation of Local 2816 of the American Federation of Government Employers (AFGE). Quite active on the local front, Kaplan was treasurer and also chairman of the local's grievance committee. Before his career as a federal employee, he worked in Chicago's Cook County Department of Public Aid. As part of the municipal scene, he helped in unionizing the Independent Union of Public Aid Employees, which grew to over 2,000 members with Kaplan as president.

While employed by the city of Chicago, Kaplan was a prime mover in the organization of the National Federation of Social Service Employees (NFSSE). That organization expanded to a national membership exceeding 10,000 employees with chapters in Chicago, New York, Los Angeles, San Francisco, and other municipalities across the country. As executive board chairman of NFSSE, Kaplan led strikes in Los Angeles and Gary, Indiana.

Like a number of modern American labor leaders, Kaplan was professionally trained and educated. A graduate of the University of Wisconsin, where he majored in history and English, he also attended at night the Chicago-Kent College of Law. A veteran of the Marine Corps, Kaplan, on one occasion, ran as an independent for a seat on the Chicago City Council.

After a 16-year term as national vice-president of the seventh district of the AFGE, Kaplan, in 1986, was chosen as the organization's sixth national secretary-treasurer.

For over two decades, Allen H. Kaplan has been active in the organization of government employees on both the local and national levels. He has a somewhat different view of employer-employee relationships, believing in cooperative action involving the union, management, and government. That view is in stark contrast to a scenario where employers and employees are always in a confrontational situation, with the government attempting to serve as a reconciler.

Keating-Owen Act (1916)

During the Progressive Era, 1900–1920, many reformers on both the state and national level campaigned for the correction of abuses in child labor conditions. A progressive muckraker, John Spargo, pricked the conscience of the country with a scathing indictment of child labor in *The Bitter Cry of the Children.* By 1912, 38 states had enacted child labor laws that limited the age at which children could be employed and the number of hours they could work, and provided for the health, welfare, and safety of children in the country's factories, mills, and mines.

Successes on the state level eventually pervaded the halls of Congress, where in 1916, as part of President Woodrow Wilson's New Freedom program, the Keating-Owen Act was enacted. The federal law attempted to regulate child labor by keeping out of interstate commerce products manufactured by firms utilizing child labor. This victory of progressives, who had succeeded in getting the first federal child labor law passed, was a hollow one, however, for in 1918 a conservative Supreme Court struck the law down in the *Hammer v. Dagenhart* case.

Congress responded by passing the Child Labor Tax law in 1919, but it too was invalidated by the Court in (*Bailey v. Drexel Furniture Company*). It was not until the New Deal years of Franklin Delano Roosevelt that an effective child labor law passed both Congress and judicial tests. In 1938, as part of the reform legislation of Roosevelt's second New Deal, a heavily Democratic Congress passed the Fair Labor Standards Act, which limited both the ages and hours of child workers. This time an activist Supreme Court upheld the Fair Labor Standards Act in the 1941 *United States v. Darby Lumber Company* decision. Child labor has thus been federally regulated since 1938, but some employers circumvent the law by employing children for part-time work and in seasonal occupations.

See also *Bailey v. Drexel Furniture Company; Fair Labor Standards Act; Hammer v. Dagenhart.*

Kennedy, Robert F. (1925–1968)

The brother of former U.S. President John Fitzgerald Kennedy, Robert F. Kennedy, in 1957, was selected chief counsel to the Senate Select Committee on Improper Activities in the Labor or Management Field. As the committee's chief attorney, Kennedy relentlessly attacked corruption, extortion, and racketeering in the Teamsters Union, headed by Dave Beck. Committee hearings, which were nationally televised, attracted the attention of the nation as they brought to light all sorts of malfeasance and misfeasance in several labor unions. With Kennedy at the helm of the investigation, Teamster chief Beck was forced out of office. He was replaced by Jimmy Hoffa.

In 1961, after John F. Kennedy had defeated Richard M. Nixon for the presidency, Robert F. Kennedy assumed the post of attorney general in the Kennedy cabinet. Kennedy continued his attack on the Teamsters under Hoffa's dictatorial and arbitrary leadership. Hoffa used his power and position to counter every government move against him despite being adjudged guilty of jury-tampering in 1964. During this era, Robert Kennedy referred to the Teamsters under Hoffa as the "Hoodlum Empire."

Despite Kennedy's never-ending assault on the Teamsters and Hoffa, the union executive stayed out of jail until 1967, when he began a federal prison sentence. After serving four years, Hoffa, a staunch Republican, was released from jail by President Nixon.

The Kennedys were supportive of labor and received the backing of organized labor in the campaign of 1960. Before his untimely death in 1968 at the hands of assassin Sirhan Sirhan, Robert F. Kennedy became an avid supporter of Cesar Chavez and the United Farm Workers in their crusade against the grape growers. In fact he backed both the strike and boycott against California's grape industry.

Throughout his brief career as a lawyer and as U.S. attorney general, Robert F. Kennedy was both a friend of organized labor and at the same time a vigorous opponent and prosecutor of corruption, chicanery, and gangsterism in the labor movement.

Kirkland, Joseph Lane (1922–)

The current president of the American Federation of Labor (AFL), Lane Kirkland, is a native of Camden, South Carolina. Elected to lead the AFL in 1979 on the retirement of George Meany, Kirkland's educational background included attendance at Newberry College in South Carolina, graduation from the U.S. Merchant Marine Academy (1942), and a B.S. degree from the Georgetown University School of Foreign Service (1948).

During World War II Kirkland was a U.S. Merchant Marine pilot, and he affiliated with the National Organization of Masters, Mates, and Pilots of America.

After the war he became a nautical scientist in the U.S. Navy Department's Hydrographic Office.

Kirkland's career as a labor leader with the American Federation of Labor apparently began in 1948 when he joined the association's research staff. From that post, over the next three decades he was assistant director of the AFL's social security department, executive assistant to President Meany (1961), and secretary-treasurer of the AFL (1969) before being named AFL president in 1979. Before becoming head of the AFL-CIO, Kirkland was president of the Institute of Collective Bargaining and Group Relations and director of the American Foundation on Automation and Employment. He also has been involved in various civic and fraternal organizations.

As president of the AFL-CIO, Kirkland has offered a contrasting style of leadership from that of his predecessor, George Meany. For example, Meany opposed AFL-CIO involvement and participation in marches and demonstrations. With Kirkland's leadership, however, the AFL-CIO joined in such movements as what has become Solidarity Day, a massive parade by organized labor in Washington, D.C., in late summer. Kirkland also attempted to reshape the AFL-CIO so it would particularly attract white-collar professionals as well as women and ethnic groups. He also appealed to the United Automobile Workers to rejoin the AFL-CIO, which it did in 1981.

Kirkland is in the tradition of most modern American labor leaders with his support of Democrats and the Democratic Party. He vigorously opposed the Reagan administration,Reaganomics, and what he perceived to be the Republican's anti-labor policies.

In the last decade or so Lane Kirkland has been able to attract more women workers into the AFL-CIO. He also established a precedent when Joyce Miller, leader of the Coalition of Labor Unions, was named the first woman member of the AFL-CIO executive council.

As one of the country's foremost labor leaders, college-educated Lane Kirkland projects the image of a contemporary professional executive. Refined, cultured, and an affluent speaker, Kirkland is a far cry from the bombastic Samuel Gompers and the crusty George Meany, who went before him as AFL bosses. He offers stable, strong leadership to the AFL-CIO at a time when organized labor is struggling. The urbane Kirkland is a new breed of American labor leader who is at home with the rank and file and at the same time comfortable with executives, political leaders, and professionals.

Knights of Labor

The Noble and Holy Order of the Knights of Labor (Knights of Labor) was established on 9 December 1869 by nine tailors in a meeting hall in Philadelphia. For the next 25 years, the Noble Order was the principal labor organization in the United States. From 1869 to 1876, the Knights of Labor was guided by Uriah Stephens, who was one of its founders. Upon the retirement of Stephens, Terence V. Powderly assumed the top position in the Knights of Labor. As the union declined rapidly in the early 1890s, James R. Sovereign replaced Powderly as Knights of Labor chief. Sovereign presided over the final demise of the Knights of Labor.

The Noble and Holy Order appealed to the vast number of immigrants who flooded the United States from southeastern Europe. Its basic premise was to organize all workers into a single national union. Therefore its membership included both skilled and unskilled workers, male and female employees, and workers of diverse ethnic backgrounds. At peak strength in the 1880s, the Knights of Labor had a membership of about 750,000. Among its members were Texas cowboys, who toiled long hours for extremely low wages.

While the Knights of Labor, in its inception, opposed strikes in favor of arbitration, it was through strikes that it gained several notable victories and increased prestige. In the 1880s it won a strike against Union Pacific Railroad, forcing the restoration of wage cuts. Later the Knights of Labor took on Jay Gould, one of the country's top railroad barons. Union members effectively shut down Gould's Southwestern railway system, causing him to end discrimination against Knights of Labor members. Because of those impressive victories the Knights of Labor expanded its authority and increased its membership. In the meantime Powderly, who basically believed in an antistrike policy, was heralded the nation's labor czar.

As the Knights of Labor reached their zenith in the mid-1880s, workers chorused:

> Toiling millions now are waking—see
> them marching on;
> All the tyrants now are shaking, ere
> their power's gone.
> Storm the fort, ye Knights of Labor,
> Battle for your cause;
> Equal rights for every neighbor—
> Down with Tyrant laws!

The Knights of Labor members were euphoric, but Jay Gould was not through. A second railroad strike in the Southwest ended disastrously for the union, as Powderly tried unsuccessfully to arbitrate a dispute with Gould. The decline of the Noble Order had begun. In 1886 Knights of Labor members were involved in Chicago's famous Haymarket Square strike and riots even though the Noble Order did not officially sanction their participation. With the breaking of that strike and the convictions of eight Haymarket rioters, the Knights of Labor suffered yet another serious reversal. It was blamed for the disturbance, although the union did not directly support the strike.

The weakened union was never the same following the Haymarket episode. Its membership dwindled to only 200,000 in a two-year span. Futilely it tried to rebuild by embracing various political movements such as land and currency reforms, but to no avail. Grand Master Workman Powderly even threw his support behind Henry George and his single-tax platform in New York City's mayoral campaign. As a last desperate act to hold the union together, Powderly urged the Noble Order to call off strikes, boycotts, and lockouts in favor of using legislative power to break the stranglehold of the robber barons on politics. The days of the Knights of Labor were indeed numbered.

Powderly was replaced by Sovereign, who was at the helm when the old union died. Despite its dreadful climax, the Noble and Holy Order of the Knights of Labor had made one significant and lasting contribution to the labor movement—it established a sense of unity and solidarity among American workers, and in so doing gave pause to the American industrial complex that labor was indeed a force to be reckoned with in the future.

See also Haymarket Square Riots; Powderly, Terence V.

Knudsen, William S. (1879–1948)

Vice-president of General Motors Corporation (GMC) during the Great Sitdown Strike at Flint, Michigan, in 1936–1937, William S. Knudsen initially assumed the position that if GMC workers had any complaints, they should go to local plant managers. Knudsen's stance was anti-union when the strike commenced on 30 December 1936. As the workers shut down the plant and invoked the sit-down technique, he condemned the strike as an all-out assault on company property rights. Knudsen and GMC management adopted an unwavering attitude of noncompromise with the United Automobile Workers (UAW), which supported the strike.

As the strike dragged on into February 1937 with increasing violence, Governor

Frank Murphy of Michigan called for negotiation to settle the dispute. He pressured Knudsen to meet with him and union officials in an attempt to resolve the stalemate. For over a week Murphy, Knudsen, and CIO czar John L. Lewis engaged in talks seeking an end to the bitter strike and strife. Finally, with the strikers still occupying the Flint plants, agreement was reached, ending the six-week-long sit-down strike. While the UAW did not register an outright victory, GMC did agree that it would not engage in collective bargaining with any other union.

As one of GMC's top executives, William S. Knudsen took a position similar to that of most management in 1936–1937 despite the enactment by Congress of the National Labor Relations Act—he was strongly anti-union, completely unresponsive to the appeal of the working class. In no way did he desire to negotiate with a labor union, and it was not until he was pressured by Governor Murphy and President Roosevelt that he finally agreed to sit down at the bargaining table. William S. Knudsen was a prime example of the recalcitrant American businessman of the 1930s who would not accept the union. During World War II, however, he exhibited a cooperative attitude with labor by serving as codirector, along with the CIO's Sidney Hillman, of the Office of Production Management.

La Follette Civil Liberties Committee

The La Follette Civil Liberties Committee, a subcommittee of the U.S. Senate Committee on Education and Labor, was formed in 1936 to investigate management's refusal to allow labor to organize and to engage in collective bargaining. The committee was chaired by Republican Senator Robert M. La Follette, Jr., of Wisconsin. Assisting La Follette were Senator Elbert Thomas, Utah Democrat; attorney John Abt; and Robert Wohlforth, the committee's executive secretary.

For four years, from 1936 to 1940, the subcommittee probed abuses by corporations against the working class in violation of the National Labor Relations Act, the Norris-LaGuardia Act, and other federal statutes.

The revelations of the La Follette inquiry were both startling and shocking. Its investigations included the Harlan County, Kentucky, coal mines; the steel industry; the automobile industry; the farming industry; and the rubber industry. It probed United States Steel, Republic Steel, Ford Motor Company, and B.F. Goodrich, to name a few corporations that allegedly denied workers the right to collectively bargain with their employers so they might join a labor union. The committee heard many witnesses during its four-year tenure. Workers freely charged employer interference with their attempts to attend union meetings, distribute union literature, and join an independent labor union. Organizers testified that thugs hired by employers repeatedly harassed them as they tried to contact the workers. Witness after witness related that they could not join a union because they were denied First Amendment freedoms—freedom of speech, press, and assembly by employers and their compatriots. One employer told the committee that he had never heard of the Norris-LaGuardia Act, which outlawed yellow-dog contracts, and that he still asked his employees to sign one. One lawman unabashedly referred to himself as a thug and said he went "thuggin'." When asked by La Follette what that meant, he responded, "Huntin' union organizers."

At the conclusion of its four-year investigation, the La Follette Committee released a report that indicted U.S. corporations and corporate executives with violating the Wagner Act and the Norris-LaGuardia Act. The report suggested that a blue book of American corporations had deprived American workers the right to join a labor union by using three methods:

1. Industrial Munitions. The committee learned, through invoices produced by corporations, that many companies had stockpiled weapons in arsenals for use against the working class. The weapons were purchased from Federal Laboratories and Lake Erie Chemical Company. Among the weapons purchased were gas grenades (both tear gas and sickening gas), riot guns, machine guns, high-powered rifles, submachine guns, military and police revolvers, and ammunition. From documents subpoenaed by the committee, it was revealed that the largest purchases of munitions occurred either before a strike or during a strike. Between 1933 and 1937, 80 of the largest buyers of munitions accounted for nearly half a million dollars of gas equipment, with 15 steel corporations buying about 50 per cent of that amount.

2. Industrial Spies. The committee discovered that national detective agencies

and employers' associations furnished strikebreakers (scabs) and spies to employers. It became the norm for companies to hire professional strikebreakers who, after the strike was broken, moved on to other locales to engage in the same activity. The names or code numbers of strikebreakers were found on the payrolls of a number of corporations. Of course spies were hired to spy on the workers; the spies also were professionals.

3. Industrial Policemen. Many corporations used industrial policemen, deputy sheriffs, and professional detectives, all of whom the workers called thugs, in attempts to prevent workers from joining labor unions. In Harlan County, Kentucky, the sheriffs deputized over 300 men, most of whom were on the payrolls of coal corporations. A number of the deputies had criminal backgrounds, having served time for crimes ranging from detaining a female against her will to murder. United States Steel Corporation operated a camp outside Washington, D.C., where its policemen, during a two-week-long summer program, were trained in the use of all sorts of weapons and riot control. The committee viewed newsreels that showed Republic Steel's policemen firing into a crowd of retreating strikers in south Chicago in what was called the Memorial Day Massacre of 30 May 1937.

The La Follette investigation and report spotlighted for the entire country the methods used by big business to deter unionism. As a result the federal government was prodded into action in the late 1930s. It took the combined efforts of the U.S. Labor Department, the Justice Department, the Federal Bureau of Investigation, and the Civil Rights Division of the attorney general's office to bring about compliance with federal law, namely the Wagner Act and the Norris-LaGuardia Act, and it took the full enforcement powers of the executive branch to achieve for the American worker what those laws provided—the right to join the labor union of their choice without interference and recrimination by employers.

Because of the La Follette probe, by 1940 a new civil right was added to those of free speech, press, and assembly: the right to join a labor union.

La Follette, Robert Marion, Sr. (1855–1925)

A graduate of the University of Wisconsin, Robert Marion La Follette, Sr., became a lawyer and entered Wisconsin politics in the late nineteenth century. From the outset of his political career, La Follette opposed both bosses and the local power structure. Campaigning against Republican machines, he was first elected district attorney and then to the U.S. Congress, where he served from 1885 to 1891. The campaign against Republican bossism led La Follette to seek the Wisconsin governorship in the 1890s. He lost his first two bids, but in 1900 he was elected as Wisconsin's chief executive. In the 1900 campaign La Follette took his case to the people of Wisconsin, verbally attacking Wisconsin party leaders as he spoke from a wagon flatbed in shirt sleeves.

In 1901 La Follette occupied the statehouse, where he became a progressive Republican governor. He put into operation his Wisconsin Idea, which became a nationwide model of state government. In addition to opposing business by going directly to the people, La Follette surrounded himself with experts, mainly from the University of Wisconsin campus, who became his key advisors. As governor, La Follette got the legislature to enact a direct primary law, to establish a statewide railroad commission to regulate Wisconsin's railroads, and to bring the railroads, corporations, and insurance companies under state control. A worker's compensation law was also passed while he was governor. After serving three terms as Wisconsin's governor, in 1906 La Follette was elected to the U.S. Senate, where he also served three terms.

In the Senate, La Follette continued his opposition to bosses, big business, and special interest groups. He opposed the highly protectionist Payne-Aldrich Tariff, supported the regulation of railroad rates, and introduced the La Follette Seamen's Act to reform conditions among the country's seamen. In short, as senator he became "Mr. Progressive."

In the 1912 presidential contest, La Follette sought the Progressive Party nomination, which eventually went to Chief Bull Mooser, Theodore Roosevelt. During World War I he was antiwar but supported the war effort. Following the war, he voted against the Treaty of Versailles and U.S. entry into the League of Nations.

In the 1920s La Follette was a liberal, and it has been argued that he was also a radical. He became the titular head of the Progressive Party in 1924, accepting its nomination for president. In the presidential election La Follette strongly opposed Calvin Coolidge and garnered about five million votes.

Near the end of an eventful life in politics, La Follette authored his autobiography, entitled *Alone in the Senate*. Truly, during his career he was a voice crying in the wilderness against entrenched power in business and politics. Many times he was nearly alone in the Senate as a foe of machines, bosses, and corporate privilege. His policies were pro-people and pro-labor. In addition to his sponsorship of the La Follette Seamen's Act, La Follete was opposed to governing by injunction.

For 25 years, as governor of Wisconsin and as U.S. senator, Robert Marion La Follette, Sr. was a man of the people. Often referred to as Fighting Bob, La Follette fought for farmers and workers and against corporate interests. In turn, labor unionists and the railroad brotherhoods supported him.

Under La Follette's leadership, Wisconsin became the "most progressive and best-governed state in the union." Most of the reforms La Follette championed eventually became legislation.

La Follette, Robert Marion, Jr. (1895–1953)

The son of the famous "Fighting Bob" La Follette, Robert Marion La Follette, Jr., who might well be called "Fighting Bob, Jr.," followed in his father's footsteps as a progressive Republican from Wisconsin. His most memorable activity in the U.S. Senate was chairing the La Follette Civil Liberties Committee from 1936 to 1940.

After attending the University of Wisconsin, he served as secretary to his father, who by that time was a U.S. Senator. When the senior La Follette died in 1925, Robert, Jr., was elected to take his place in the Senate. From 1925 to his defeat in 1946, the younger La Follette served Wisconsin in the Senate and, like his father, was a strong insurgent Republican.

La Follette served on a number of important Senate committees and received several presidential appointments to special committees and commissions. His famous La Follette Civil Liberties Committee inquired into the nationwide abuses of labor by management, the most sensational facet of the investigation coming when the committee spotlighted Harlan County, Kentucky. Following a preliminary peek into violations against Harlan's coal miners by coal operators in February 1937, the committee opened full-length hearings on 22 March 1937. For about three months, as Senators La Follette and Elbert Thomas quizzed witness after witness, the nation learned that Harlan County's coal operators, in league with the county administration, used over 300 armed deputy sheriffs, most of whom were paid by the coal operators, to harass, intimidate, threaten, assault, and murder the coal miners and United Mine Workers of America (UMW) organizers who went to Harlan County to establish the union. The committee learned that from about 1933 to 1937 coal miners were denied the right to join a labor union because they did not have freedom of speech, press, and assembly. On 7 July 1935, 14 armed deputy sheriffs dispersed a UMW rally by attacking 66-year-old William "Rockhouse" Munholland, by waving their guns and shouting threats at a crowd that had gathered to hear the Wagner Act discussed, and by blowing their automobile horns incessantly to drown out union speakers. On two occasions in 1933, UMW organizer Lawrence "Peggy" Dwyer's apartment in Pineville, Kentucky, 34 miles from Harlan, was dynamited. Dwyer miraculously escaped serious injury.

Harlan had two thug gangs—one led by chief thug Ben F. Unthank, the other supervised by Mean Merle H. Middleton. These two gangs, along with over 300 deputy sheriffs, committed acts of terrorism against Harlan miners and UMW organizers for about six years. A chief target was Marshall A. Musick, who was arrested, beaten, and shot at by thugs. When Musick was advised to leave the area for personal safety, night riders drove by and shot into his house, killing his son, 16-year-old Bennett Musick, a coal miner and UMW member. Earlier, road killers had shot into the home of another Harlan organizer, William Clontz, barely missing his sleeping son as bullets sprayed the headboard of the bed.

The murder of Bennett Musick on 9 February 1937 was the provocative crime that occasioned the La Follette inquiry into Harlan County's labor turmoil. Following the La Follette investigation, the FBI conducted its own probe, which resulted in the federal indictment of 69 Harlan County coal corporations, coal company executives, and deputy sheriffs on 27 September 1937. The next spring the defendants were tried in federal court

in London, Kentucky. In a case known as the Mary Helen Conspiracy trial, which lasted almost the entire summer of 1938, the eyes of the entire nation were focused on Harlan County. The trial ended in a mistrial, but it brought to a head Harlan's rejection of the union. Soon after the trial the operators came to terms with the UMW, and Harlan County's labor troubles came to an end.

It was the La Follette hearings and the publicity given by the committee to a reign of terror against the coal miners by Harlan operators and gun thugs that finally paved the way for coal miners to join the union without fear of recrimination. As chair of the La Follette Civil Liberties Committee, Senator Robert Marion La Follette, Jr., performed an invaluable service to labor by bringing about the right of workers to join a labor union throughout the nation.

La Follette Seamen's Act (1915)

Sponsored by Senator Robert M. La Follette, Sr., the 1915 La Follette Seamen's Act corrected many of the horrible working conditions for American seamen on merchant ships. Among its key provisions were abolition of imprisonment for desertion in a safe harbor; limiting the penalty for desertion to forfeiture of a seamen's personal effects; and the right to demand one-half their wages earned and still unpaid in a port where a cargo was loaded and/or discharged. The law also prescribed living conditions and food allowances for merchant marines. It established a nine-hour day in port as well as safety regulations on ships. Under the law, owners of ships were liable for corporal punishment administered to sailors.

One of the most important stipulations of the La Follette Seamen's Act was the abolition of the crimp system. The crimp was a combination shipping master-boarding house operator who took in sailors who were between jobs. When the sailors ran up a large bill and the amount was large enough, he was provided with a voyage. Upon assuming the job, the seaman signed over to the crimp several months pay. As soon as the ship cleared port, the shipping company was paid. This system placed many seamen in serious debt to the crimp and in effect instituted a system of peonage. Seamen were caught in a never-ending scheme comparable to workers in company towns who were issued scrip redeemable at company stores and who received credit at the same emporium. It was extremely difficult to get out of debt under these arrangements. Senator La Follette, always interested in the welfare of seamen and workers, saw the crimp system as an injustice to sailors. The practice was eliminated in his bill, thus improving the plight of seamen considerably.

The La Follette Seamen's Act stood as a monument to Fighting Bob's efforts to improve the conditions and life-styles of merchant marine employees early in the twentieth century.

Labor Spies

In 1937 two books were published that described elaborate labor espionage systems used by employers. Clinch Calkins authored *Spy Overhead: The Story of Industrial Espionage*, and Leo Huberman circulated *The Labor Spy Rackets*. Both books detailed the extent to which management resorted to labor spies to thwart attempts by employees to join labor organizations. Both authors published their works two years following the passage by Congress of the National Labor Relations Act, which gave workers the right to join labor unions of their choice.

Labor spies were acquired in several ways. In some instances employers used sheriff's deputies to infiltrate union meetings to spy on the workers. The deputies also shadowed workers, and sometimes used a technique called "rough shadowing," following a worker so closely that the "spy" would step on the worker's heels as he walked.

On other occasions a worker was induced to spy on his fellow employees. In those situations the worker would often work alongside his companion and would associate with him after work, observing all he did, to whom he conversed, where he went—in short, all his habits. If the worker involved himself in union business, the spy would report to the person who hired him, who would in turn notify the employer. The employee would then be terminated. The practice of entrapping an employee to spy on his coworkers was known as "hooking." The "hooker" was the individual who enticed the worker to become a spy. If the worker did not know that he was spying on fellow workers and that his boss had access to the information, he (the spy) was classified as a "hooked man." A spy inside a mine, mill, or plant was referred to as an "inside man." If a spy was not employed in a factory, but was engaged in circulating anti-union and anti-strike information to workers and their spouses, he was called a "missionary." Undercover spies who were not employees were hailed as "outside men." When a spy formed a relationship with a union man to acquire information, the practice was referred to as "roping."

National organizations furnished "ops" (operatives) to employers. The term *op* was used to identify a spy employed by an agency. One major agency that supplied ops to management was the Pinkerton Detective Agency. In the 1870s James McParlan, Pinkerton detective, was hired to spy on Molly Maguires (coal miners in Pennsylvania.) McParlan did his work so well that ten Mollies were executed for rebelling against their employer and horrible working conditions in the mines. The Pinkertons were used by many corporations to spy on employees and union members in the 1930s.

Another organization that supplied labor spies to businesses was Corporations Auxiliary. Like the Pinkerton agency,

Corporations Auxiliary deployed operatives to employers for the express purpose of keeping workers from joining labor unions. Still another firm that was in the business of sending spies to employers was the Railway Audit and Inspection Company. The bottom line is that a blue book of U.S. corporations used labor spies during the 1930s in attempts to prevent American workers from exercising their rights under the Wagner Act, including the right to engage in collective bargaining with their employers and the right to join a labor union of their choice. Through the use of labor espionage, businesses were often able to keep employees from affiliating with independent labor unions.

Labor's Bill of Rights (1919)

In the aftermath of a strike in the Seattle shipyards, the Boston police strike, and national strikes by coal miners and steelworkers following World War I, and despite gains made by over 100 labor unions affiliated with the American Federation of Labor (AFL), the AFL in the 1920s faced the onslaught of the depression as well as the lack of governmental support from the conservative Republican presidential administrations of Warren G. Harding, Calvin Coolidge, and Herbert C. Hoover. In fact, labor in the 1920s experienced the revitalization of injunctions.

In the face of labor's lean years, the AFL could have, as some counseled, become a political organization or joined in the formation of a labor party, comparable to the People's Party of the 1890s. With conditions as they were, it was a temptation for the union to become a vital part of the political process. However, under the leadership of its tenacious president, Samuel Gompers, and later under the astute guidance of William Green, the AFL rejected involvement in political activity and in the formation of a third party to address the issues and goals of the toiling masses.

The AFL decided to remain nonpolitical, true to its long-standing tradition. In 1919 it framed and endorsed a document called Labor's Bill of Rights, which contained three major objectives: (1) recognition of the AFL by the U.S. business establishment; (2) the increase of wages to afford the working class a suitable and comfortable life-style; and (3) a definite limitation of the issuance of injunctions in labor disputes and strikes. The proclamation of Labor's Bill of Rights was the extent to which the AFL wished to go at that time. It must be pointed out that in more recent years the AFL has become more political, especially in its support of Democratic administrations and its contributions to Democratic candidates on both the state and national levels.

Labor's Non-Partisan League

When President Franklin Delano Roosevelt ran for a second term in 1936, John L. Lewis, president of the Congress of Industrial Organizations (CIO) and the United Mine Workers of America (UMW), along with several other CIO stalwarts, helped organize labor's Non-Partisan League to support Roosevelt's reelection bid. Attempts were made by the CIO to enlist American Federation of Labor (AFL) support for the league, and George L. Berry, representing the Printing Pressmen's Union, an AFL affiliate, was the league's first president. The AFL, however, adopted a hands-off policy toward the league, and President William Green chided the CIO for its political involvement.

The CIO, meanwhile, strongly backed the Roosevelt campaign. It contributed thousands of dollars; Lewis's UMW alone made a single donation of $500,000. The CIO threw its support behind Roosevelt because of gains made by labor during his first term. The Non-Partisan League may be credited in no small measure for Roosevelt's landslide victory over Kansas Republican Alfred M. Landon in 1936.

On the state level, the Non-Partisan League focussed on the states of Pennsylvania, New York, New Jersey, and Michigan. It backed Mayor Fiorello LaGuardia's successful reelection bid in New York City in 1937. It also supported pro-labor candidates in Detroit and in the 1938 congressional elections.

Because of the success of candidates backed by the Non-Partisan League, there was discussion in the 1930s with regard to forming a third party, a labor party. Since the New Deal was pro-labor, however, the third party movement never really gained momentum. Conservatives criticized the Non-Partisan League for its radicalism and what they perceived to be its leftist orientation. There were even charges from anti–New Dealers that the league had a communistic tinge. Despite the criticism, the fact is that the organization became politically active in the 1930s and its activism promoted the success of Democratic candidates nationally, on the state level, and locally. As CIO head Lewis put it, "Labor has gained more under President Roosevelt than under any president in memory. Obviously it is the duty of labor to support Roosevelt 100 per cent in the next [1936] election."

Lake Erie Chemical Company

The Lake Erie Chemical Company was a Cleveland-based concern that manufactured and distributed chemical weapons, including tear gas equipment, shoulder gas guns, and tear gas grenades, to U.S. corporations during the 1930s.

In testimony before the La Follette Civil Liberties Committee, A. S. Ailes, vice-president and sales manager of the Lake Erie Chemical Company, admitted the following: (1) his company manufactured the gas equipment; (2) his company kept in close touch with businesses with regard to labor relations, labor unrest, strikes, etc.; and (3) when strikes became imminent, having been kept abreast of the situation by the corporation involved,

Lake Erie Chemical Company was prepared to move into a company arsenal large quantities of chemical weapons, including tear gas equipment.

Senators La Follette and Elbert Thomas used correspondence between Mr. Ailes and company officials to document the relationship between Lake Erie Chemical Company and U.S. corporations that purchased the weapons to combat unions. Senator Thomas also brought out, in his interrogation of Mr. Ailes, that the chemical weapons purchased from Lake Erie Chemical Company were often placed in the hands of irresponsible guards and strikebreakers for use against workers. The vice-president of the munitions concern justified the sale of chemical weapons to corporations on the grounds that they needed protection against strikers.

The bigger the strike, the bigger the sale of weapons to businesses. Lake Erie Chemical Company, like Federal Laboratories, was one of the concerns that, during the labor warfare of the 1930s, dispensed large amounts of gas equipment, weapons, and munitions to a blue book of U.S. corporations for storage in arsenals to prevent American workers from organizing and from joining labor unions.

Landrum-Griffin Act (1959)

Officially known as the Labor Management Reporting and Disclosure Act and popularly referred to as Hoffa's law, this measure was cosponsored by Democratic Congressman Phil Landrum of Jasper, (Pickens County) Georgia, and Republican Senator Robert Griffin of Michigan. It was passed two years after the McClellan Committee's investigation of corruption and racketeering in labor unions, specifically the Teamsters organization.

The Landrum-Griffin Act went beyond the Taft-Hartley Act (1947) to curb the unbridled power of labor unions. Under the new law (1) union funds were protected from misuse by union officials, who were subject to fines and imprisonment; (2) forceful interference with rights of union members became a federal violation; (3) persons convicted of crimes and Communist Party members were restrained from holding office in a union for five years after leaving prison or the party; (4) the ban on secondary boycotts was tightened to keep a union from pressuring one employer to make him stop doing business with a rival employer; (5) extortion picketing was outlawed; (6) unions in the construction industry and garment industry were protected from nonunion subcontractors; and (7) states had jurisdiction in labor disputes considered too insignificant for National Labor Relations Board action. It also laid down specific guidelines for the holding of union elections to make them more responsible and responsive to the will of the union rank and file, a proviso designed to eliminate the manipulation of union elections by union hierarchy.

The Landrum-Griffin Act was a decent attempt by the federal government to oversee union internal operations and to curb the power, corruption, and racketeering in labor unions. It marked, for the first time perhaps, direct federal intervention in the affairs of labor organizations. The new law was a signal for labor unions to manage their business in a more responsible manner for the benefit of the entire membership.

Lauf v. Shinner and Company (U.S., 1938)

In *Lauf v. Shinner and Company*, the Supreme Court upheld the constitutionality of the Norris-LaGuardia Act passed by Congress in 1932. The thrust of the Norris-LaGuardia Act was twofold: to outlaw the use of yellow-dog or anti-union contracts by employers, and to limit the use of injunctions in labor disputes. In stating the Court's decision, Justice Owen Roberts held that Congress had the power to define the jurisdiction of lower federal courts.

In essence *Lauf v. Shinner and Co.* overturned the Court's previous decision in *Duplex Printing Press Co. v. Deering* (1921), which emasculated the intent of the Clayton Anti-Trust Act (1914) to restrict injunctions. The Clayton Act was considered an anti-injunction law until the *Duplex* decision, which made the Norris-LaGuardia Act necessary.

The Supreme Court followed its decision in the *Lauf* case with two other opinions—*New Negro Alliance Co. v. Sanitary Grocery Co.* (1938) and *United States v. Hutcheson* (1941), both of which sustained the anti-injunction provision of the Norris-LaGuardia Act.

See also *Adair v. United States; Coppage v. Kansas;* Injunctions; Norris-LaGuardia Act; Yellow-Dog Contracts.

Laurrell, Ferdinand

Ferdinand Laurrell, along with Adolph Strasser and Samuel Gompers, was one of the aggressive organizers who helped to revitalize the struggling Cigar Makers International Union in the 1870s. Laurrell, who was of Swedish immigrant background and was exposed to most European theories of radicalism, including those of Karl Marx and Friedrich Engels, introduced Gompers to Marxist theory. Telling the American Federation of Labor chief to look into the philosophies expounded by Marx and Engels, Laurrell at the same time warned Gompers about embracing their theories. He also advised Gompers against affiliating with the Socialist Labor party. He said, "Study your union card, Sam, and if the idea does not square with that, it ain't true."

The triumvirate of Strasser, Gompers, and Laurrell reorganized and breathed new life into the Cigar Markers' Union, forerunner to the American Federation of Labor. Both unions were quite class conscious but stopped short of swallowing Marxian socialism. "Class conscious?" Gompers queried. "As a matter of fact there is no other organization in the entire world that is so class conscious as are the trade unions."

Lawrence Textile Strike (1912)

The Lawrence Textile Strike took place from 12 January to 12 March 1912 in Lawrence, Massachusetts, and involved approximately 30,000 workers in that city's textile mills. The two-month strike was occasioned by a wage cut imposed on mostly immigrant workers, whose average pay was less than $9 per week. Along with the wage reduction, the workers also worked long hours in the mills.

While most of the workers were unorganized, a handful were affiliated with the American Federation of Labor's United Textile Workers and a thousand or so were members of the Industrial Workers of the World (IWW). When the walkout began, the IWW dispatched Joseph J. Ettor and Arturo Giovannitti to Lawrence to oversee the strike. For the next eight weeks the two IWW leaders planned mass meetings, set up picket lines, and, most importantly, provided relief for the strikers and their families in the form of soup kitchens.

Despite IWW attempts to keep the strike orderly and lawful, when reports circulated that dynamite charges were planted throughout the city, the IWW was blamed. Then it was revealed that a local undertaker and the head of the American Woolen Company (where most of the strikers were employed) were involved in planting the dynamite, apparently in an attempt to bring disrepute on the union and strikers.

Ignoring the issues that caused the strike, the American Woolen Mills attempted to resume operations. This led

Strikers confront Massachusetts militia

to an incident that mirrored many similar scenarios in the history of the American labor movement: workers opposed the reopening of the plant, policemen were summoned, a fight broke out, an Italian immigrant female worker was slain, martial law was invoked, and the militia was called out to restore order. In the aftermath of the violence, Ettor and Giovannitti were apprehended in connection with the death of the Italian woman. With the two IWW leaders incarcerated, Big Bill Haywood, IWW president, arrived in Lawrence to take charge of the strike.

With the strike in a stalemate, IWW relief efforts continued. A new problem arose when it became apparent that feeding the workers' children was an almost insurmountable task. To ease the situation, plans were made to relocate children in nearby towns. Some were removed, but as others were about to entrain, policemen, without provocation, according to one witness, began to flail away at the children and their parents, beating many.

Almost immediately outcries of anger poured in from all over the United States. As a result, the Lawrence authorities and mill owners abandoned their policies, the mills reopened, workers returned to their jobs, and the strike was ended.

The Lawrence Textile Strike was concluded with the strikers getting all their demands. In the wake of the strike's settlement, Ettor and Giovannitti were acquitted. The strike was regarded as successful, giving the IWW a major victory among textile workers of the Northeast.

Lewis, John L. (1880–1969)

Born on 12 February 1880 in Lucas, Iowa, John L. Lewis was the son of a Welsh coal miner who was a strong union man. At age 14 Lewis became a coal miner himself, and seven years later he trekked across the country working in various coal mines to acquaint himself with mines and miners throughout the United States. A mine explosion at Hannah, Wyoming, which snuffed out the lives of 236 men and boys, made a deep and lasting impression on Lewis, who helped remove the bodies. "The descent into the mine that had become a charnel house was a descent in hell," he said. "What really ripped my emotions to shreds was the sight of numb, mute faces of the wives now suddenly widows of the men they loved. It was at Hannah that I was baptized in my own tears."

Lewis was a self-educated man. He read widely from novels, historical works, the Bible, and Shakespeare. He also possessed the gift of oratory and had a domineering, intimidating personality. A dynamic speaker, Lewis early in his career became involved in the United Mine Workers of America (UMW). On one occasion he served as a UMW lobbyist in the Illinois state legislature. When a mine blast at Cherry, Illinois, killed 160 coal miners, Lewis charged into the legislature, where he insisted that legislators enact mine safety and worker's compensation laws. To get those bills passed he resorted to typical Lewis behavior: He "raged and banged his fists on the speaker's rostrum" and threatened "to physically demolish each state legislator."

Lewis's stature as a labor leader soon attracted American Federation of Labor (AFL) President Samuel Gompers, who named him AFL field representative, beginning Lewis's rapid rise to the top as the nation's labor czar. Within the AFL he created a UMW machine. In 1916 he was chosen UMW statistician and in 1917 managing editor of the *United Mine Workers Journal*. These positions were learning experiences for Lewis, who became quite knowledgeable regarding the UMW and the coal industry. In 1918 he was made UMW vice-president, the next year acting president, and in 1920 UMW international president.

From 1920 to his resignation as UMW head in 1960, Lewis reigned over the

John L. Lewis

UMW as the country's most powerful and dynamic labor leader. During the first decade of his presidency he immersed himself in industrial unionism. Later he led the UMW out of the AFL. During the 1930s the UMW became an integral part of the Congress of Industrial Organizations, also headed by Lewis.

Lewis took on all challengers to his position as labor czar. Within the UMW he summarily destroyed all those who threatened his power base. In fact he became very much a dictator. He also lashed out at U.S. presidents who disagreed with his policies. In 1919 President Woodrow Wilson endorsed an injunction that broke a coal strike. Enraged, Lewis blasted, "President Wilson's attitude is the climax of a long series of attempted usurpations of executive power." Following the reelection of FDR in 1936, Lewis and Roosevelt engaged in a serious verbal tiff because FDR, whom organized labor had strongly supported for a second term, failed to back the Steel Workers' Organizing Committee (SWOC) in its strike against Little Steel. A troubled and irate Lewis lambasted the president: "It ill behooves one who has supped at labor's table and who has been sheltered in labor's house to curse with equal fervor and fine impartiality both labor and its adversaries when they become locked in a deadly embrace."

During the New Deal years, Lewis consolidated his power as labor czar. With the passage of National Industrial Recovery Act and the Wagner Act, he ordered massive organizing campaigns in the bituminous coal fields of West Virginia, Kentucky, and the remainder of the southern Appalachians. In two months UMW membership mushroomed from 100,000 to 400,000. By 1933 most of West Virginia and Kentucky were under the UMW banner. The lone exception in Kentucky was fiercely anti-union Harlan County, which did not acquiesce until 1939.

Lewis's success in the coalfields led him to call upon the AFL to attend more closely to the needs of the industrial unions. When it failed to do so, the UMW left the AFL and was a key player in the formation of the Congress of Industrial Organizations (CIO) in 1935. Lewis presided as CIO chief as industrial union affiliates cracked strongholds of anti-unionism to organize rubber workers, auto workers, and steelworkers. Lewis was entrenched as the most powerful labor leader of his time. Many considered him more powerful than FDR.

In 1940, after labor rejected his endorsement of GOP presidential candidate Wendell L. Willkie, Lewis quit as CIO president, withdrawing the UMW from the CIO in 1942. For the next two decades, however, he continued to lead the coal miners. A singular achievement of Lewis in the mid-1940s was to set up a UMW welfare and pension fund from royalties on coal tonnage. From that fund he built ten hospitals throughout the Appalachian coalfields. The fund also provided pensions for retired coal miners as well as medical care for miners and their families.

Upon his resignation as UMW president in 1960, Lewis remained president emeritus, head of the union's board of trustees, and chief executive officer of the union's welfare and retirement fund.

At the age of 89, the physically drained and exhausted czar of American labor died on 11 June 1969. Numerous eulogies were offered upon his passing. One coal operator, while admitting that he hated Lewis "with a passion," added "Damn, I wish he were on our side."

Coal miners and their families adored John L. Lewis. The wife of a disabled miner wrote:

Who can we replace when he,
Our president John L. Lewis
* is gone.*
Who has been so faithful

Who has been so kind
Who has been so thoughtful
To the needy, lame and blind.

A Pennsylvania coal miner composed this poem:

I came to this world
Without my consent
I will leave it against my will.
I worked in a mine
That came to an end
Now John L. Lewis is my
*   only friend.*

In Harlan County, Kentucky, UMW miners baptized nonunion workers with these words: "I baptize you in the name of the Father, the Son, and John L. Lewis."
See also Congress of Industrial Organizations; United Mine Workers of America.

Little Steel
The term *Little Steel* refers to four American steel corporations—Republic Steel, Youngstown Sheet and Tube, Inland Steel, and Bethlehem Steel—which were strongly anti-union during the union organizing drives of the 1930s. Tom M. Girdler, the anti-labor president of Republic, marshaled the other Little Steel companies in resisting efforts of the Steel Workers' Organizing Committee (SWOC) to unionize 75,000 steelworkers.

When a strike was called in May 1937, the Little Steel combine resisted in a manner typical of that period by using tear gas against organizers, using troops to protect scabs, attacking picket lines, and arresting strike leaders.

The strike was not without violence. The major outbreak occurred at the South Chicago plant of Republic Steel on 30 May. In what is known in labor history as the Memorial Day Massacre, ten workers were slain and over 100 wounded when Chicago policemen fired on un-armed workers enjoying a holiday picnic. Although the workers did not initiate the assault, they were blamed for it, and in the end the Congress of Industrial Organizations (CIO) lost a major strike. It simply could not overcome the power of the Little Steel conglomerate and its use of gas, weapons, and policemen. Not until the La Follette Civil Liberties Committee had finished its inquiry and filed its report did Little Steel capitulate to union organizers.
See also Girdler, Tom Mercer; Memorial Day Massacre.

Little Steel Formula
During World War II the four Little Steel companies clamored for a $1 per day wage hike. The National War Labor Board took the plea under consideration and decided to link a wage increase to the cost-of-living index. Reviewing information released by the Bureau of Labor Statistics, which showed the cost-of-living index had risen 15 points between January 1941 and May 1942, the War Labor Board granted the Little Steel employer a wage increase of 44 cents a day instead of the $1 per day requested.

By using the cost-of-living index to decide wage hikes during World War II, the War Labor Board established what was called the Little Steel formula. Throughout the war years this formula was the guideline used for wage increases for workers. A major shortcoming with the formula was that it had been adopted on the premise that prices had leveled off. The rise of prices remained unchecked, however, and the War Labor Board was faced with the difficult task of still trying to apply the Little Steel formula.

Lochner v. New York (U.S., 1905)
During the Progressive Era of the early twentieth century, laws were passed, especially on the state level, establishing the maximum number of hours women

and men could work in plants. Oregon implemented a law restricting women laundry workers to ten hours per day. New York passed a statute restricting male workers in bakeries to ten hours per day. The New York law was challenged in the courts, and in 1905 a conservative Supreme Court declared that state's ten-hour law unconstitutional. In a 5 to 4 decision, Justice R. W. Peckham, writing for the conservative majority, stated: "There is no reasonable ground for interfering with the liberty of persons on the right of free contract, by determining the hours of labor, in the occupation of a baker." The Court's majority decried the loss of freedom of contract that the New York ten-hour law attempted to provide. In so doing it placed property rights ahead of human rights, making it possible for employers to continue contracts requiring employees to work over ten hours per day and 60 hours per week.

The *Lochner* decision established a precedent that was not overturned by the Court for about two decades. Finally in the 1930s, the Roosevelt Court began to take a more liberal stance toward laws restricting the hours of both female and male employees.

Lockout

An effective weapon in the hands of employers, a lockout was used in the late nineteenth century when workers walked out on strike. As the strike began, the employer locked company gates so that striking workers could not return to their jobs. In 1892 at Homestead, Pennsylvania, Carnegie Steel imposed a lockout against its employees.

Following the lockout, the company used company policemen to guard the gates and to protect company property. At times the company attempted to bring in strikebreakers or scabs to break the strike. Because strikers opposed scabs breaking the strike and taking their jobs, the scabs had to be protected by company guards or policemen, Pinkerton de-

tectives, state militia, or federal troops. A lockout was often accompanied by a violent battle between strikers and scabs, along with company guards.

With the presence of company guards or an outside security force on hand, a company would end the lockout, bring in and protect replacement workers to take the jobs of the striking employees, and end the strike. Once the strike was broken, the employees who walked out lost their jobs. In this manner the union lost, and management scored another victory over organized labor.

It was not until the twentieth century, with the passage of the National Industrial Recovery Act, the Wagner Act, and similar laws, that the lockout ceased to be an effective instrument in the hands of employers against labor.

See also Homestead Lockout.

Locomotive Engineers, Brotherhood of

See Brotherhood of Locomotive Engineers.

Locomotive Firemen and Enginemen, Brotherhood of

See Brotherhood of Locomotive Firemen and Enginemen.

Loewe v. Lawlor (U.S., 1916)

Popularly known as the Danbury Hatters case, the *Loewe v. Lawlor* litigation revolved around the question as to whether or not a union, in calling for a national boycott in support of a strike by workers for union recognition, was engaged in a conspiracy to restrain interstate commerce.

When a local union attempted to organize the workers of the Danbury, Connecticut, hatmaking firm of D. E. Loewe and Company, the company's anti-union policies led to a strike by employees. In support of the striking workers, the United Hatters Union in 1902 called for a nationwide boycott of goods manufactured by D. E. Loewe. The company responded by filing a suit against the United Hatters, charging the union with a conspiracy to restrain interstate commerce in violation of the 1890 Sherman Anti-Trust Act. The company also asked for triple damages against the union members who called the strike. After years of legal maneuvering, the case came before the U.S. Supreme Court, and the company was awarded damages in excess of $250,000. The United Hatters and the American Federation of Labor (AFL) cooperated to pay the fines.

In its opinion, the Supreme Court, Chief Justice Melville Fuller speaking for the majority, declared that the union had conspired to restrain interstate commerce in violation of the Sherman Act. Noting that the United Hatters Union consisted of 9,000 members, included "a large number of subordinate unions," and was combined with 1.4 million AFL members, Fuller ruled that the union was engaged in a national conspiracy to force hat manufacturers to grant it recognition. Such action, Fuller wrote, was in violation of the law and could not be condoned by the court. The fact that Loewe Company hats were sold in at least 20 states and the boycott applied to all those states could not be allowed under the law, according to Chief Justice Fuller.

The Supreme Court's decision in *Loewe v. Lawlor* dealt a serious blow to the labor movement, one that produced shock waves for at least three decades. Together with the government injunction supporting Buck's Stove and Range Company, *Loewe* served notice that the Court's personnel would have to change before organized labor could make much progress.

It was not until the administration of Franklin D. Roosevelt, during which Congress passed the National Labor Relations Act and the Supreme Court came to regard organized labor in a more favorable light, that workers gained the right to join the labor union of their choice. Because of the *Loewe v. Lawlor*

decision, labor unions had to fight the stigma of conspiracy for more than 30 years.

See also Buck's Stove and Range Company.

Longshoremen

Longshoremen are workers who are employed on waterfronts or dockside, loading and unloading cargoes from vessels engaged in transoceanic and intracoastal commerce. Longshoremen are also known as laborers, stevedores, or loaders.

Longshoremen in the United States have been noted for their aggressiveness and militancy. As early as 1836 they were described as militant workers, yet they remained unorganized until 1864, when the first dockworkers union was formed. American dockworkers have been unionized from that date to the present. In more recent times, longshoremen unions have been involved in corruption and racketeering. Some of their more prominent leaders have been linked to communism.

Today longshoremen are found in seaports on both the Atlantic and Pacific coasts as well as along the Gulf Coast and in the Great Lakes region. They are an invaluable asset to the U.S. shipping industry.

Lowell Textile Mills

Lowell, Massachusetts, was one of the country's first textile towns. The mill dominated the town; in fact, it owned the town. The labor force for the Lowell textile mills in the 1840s was supplied at first by New England farm girls. There they were strictly supervised and housed in apartments much like dormitories. In the rooming houses the factory girls were exposed to music, books, and magazines. English novelist Charles Dickens, who toured Lowell in 1842, noted pianos in the houses where the girls stayed, the girls availing themselves of a circulating library, and that the *Lowell Offering*, a magazine, carried stories by the factory workers. By the expressions on their faces the factory girls seemed satisfied with their work. For mill workers they were nicely attired, wearing bonnets, cloaks, shawls, and silk stockings.

The factories where the girls toiled contained window flower boxes and rooms that were well ventilated and well lighted. They worked long hours, lived in crowded rooms, and were under the strict control of their bosses, who imposed a paternalistic system. They had to attend church, be in their quarters by 10:00 P.M., and no profanity or immorality was allowed.

As young girls, many of them away from home for the first time, most of them welcomed their new-found freedom. They formed relationships with their female workers, and as they earned money, they saved it for impending matrimony and familial situations. They were not career factory girls, since most hoped to move from the mill to other stations in life.

As time passed and with the coming of competing mills, the Lowell factories tightened up on their employees substantially. Wages were cut, hours increased, and the girls were told to increase their capacity. Most toiled a 75-hour work week for $1.50. In essence they became pawns in the hands of their employers. Compared to European standards, American girls lived in crowded, hot, unsanitary rooms, worked longer hours, had only half an hour for lunch, and were forced to stand for so long that they developed maladies such as varicose veins and swelling of feet and legs.

Some even turned to strikes, but those were generally unsuccessful. As conditions worsened, many farm girls left the mills, and others were not even attracted to the factories. Factory owners in the years before the Civil War turned to immigrant labor, and German and Irish girls replaced their American counterparts. Since these expatriots were often extremely needy, they accepted employment on the owners' terms without regard to hours and wages. Cheap labor became the rule of thumb in Lowell and other New England mill towns.

As a result, mill owners operated what became known as sweatshops, with conditions that Southerners quickly compared to Negro slavery. Although slavery ended in the South in 1865, Northern sweatshops and a form of peonage in factories continued well into the twentieth century.

Ludlow Massacre (1913)

In 1913 at Ludlow, Colorado, coal miners employed by John D. Rockefeller's Colorado Fuel and Iron Company struck for the right to join the United Mine Workers of America (UMW). The company, operating on the open shop principle, rejected the union and savagely opposed the miners with industrial policemen and the state militia.

Since Colorado Fuel and Iron owned the town in which the strikers lived, it displaced the miners, who took up residence in a tent provided by the union. For months a bloody conflict raged between company security and the strikers. On 20 April 1914 Colorado state militia attacked the strikers at Ludlow. First, state troops machine-gunned the tent colony and then torched the tents, in which terrified women and children knelt, many in holes dug in the ground to escape both the machine-gun fire and the flames. Afterward eleven small children and two women were found, victims of the flames and smoke inhalation.

In an attack that, according to papers in the files of the Colorado Fuel and Iron Company, was unprovoked, innocent children and women perished. While the Ludlow Massacre shocked the entire nation, the company refused to accept the United Mine Workers of America.

The House Committee on Mines and Mining conducted a hearing into the outrage. John D. Rockefeller, Jr., offered testimony in which he affirmed that his company would take whatever steps were

Only wreckage and debris remain following the attack by state troops on striking miners and their families in Ludlow, Colorado.

necessary to keep a nonunion mine. Stating that his camp would continue operation on an open shop basis, he blamed outside organizers for coming into Ludlow to arouse the coal miners. Rockefeller maintained that he would never give in to the demands of the union.

Mother Jones angrily exclaimed: "Little children being roasted alive makes a front-page story. Dying by inches of starvation and exposure does not."

The Ludlow Massacre was another in a long line of anti-union attacks by U.S. corporations in the early decades of the twentieth century. Company abuses of employees continued well into the 1930s and early 1940s before federal law forced corporations to negotiate union contracts with American workers.

See also Colorado Fuel and Iron Company.

McClellan Committee (1957)

Officially known as the Select Committee on Improper Activities in the Labor or Management Field, the U.S. Senate subcommittee chaired by Democratic Senator John McClellan of Arkansas was impaneled on 30 January 1957 to investigate alleged wrongdoings by labor union officials and management. Chief counsel to the committee was Robert F. Kennedy.

The McClellan Committee conducted hearings between 1957 and 1959, and many of them were nationally televised. For about three years the committee listened to 1,526 witnesses, whose testimony filled about 50,000 transcribed pages. Witnesses testified to the misuse of union funds by top union officials, including Teamster President Dave Beck, who reportedly embezzled $320,000. When Beck was called by the committee to testify, he invoked the Fifth Amendment, refusing to answer on grounds of self-incrimination, a pattern that became standard for union leaders who appeared before the committee.

The committee also listened to testimony that charged union officials with dictatorlike tactics in the operation of unions. Witnesses also linked unions to racketeering, gangsterism, and the mafia. Corruption in unions was rampant, according to the hearings, and in many cases union hierarchy manipulated elections as a means of remaining entrenched in power.

While it is true that widespread corruption involved only a few unions—the Teamsters, Hotel and Restaurant Employees, Bakery and Confectionery Workers, Laundry Workers, Operating Engineers, Allied Industrial Workers, and the United Textile Workers—the testimony heard by the committee seemingly cast a dark shadow on the whole of the American labor movement. According to witnesses, the Teamsters was the most corrupt union, the one most infiltrated by racketeers and gangsters.

While the McClellan Committee indicted neither labor nor management, its record revealed a multitude of illegal and unethical union activities over a long period of time. The committee's hearings impacted the American labor scene in several ways. Gone as Teamster president was Dave Beck, who was replaced by Jimmy Hoffa, so nothing really changed in Teamster leadership.

In 1959 Congress passed the Labor-Management Reporting and Disclosure Act, popularly known as the Landrum-Griffin Act, which was designed to make union officials more accountable in the operation of their organizations and in the use of union funds. While the law was only a partial solution to the problems in unions, it did serve notice that labor was going to be kept under close surveillance by the U.S. government. In the final analysis, however, mismanagement of union funds, dictatorship tactics, stolen elections, racketeering, and gangsterism remained the norm in some labor unions.

McDonald, David John (1902–1979)

David John McDonald was born in Pittsburgh, Pennsylvania. The son of a steelworker, he went to work at age 15 for Jones-Laughlin Steel Corporation. Following his graduation from high school, he was employed as a machinist's helper in a National Tube Company plant. Since he was in the workplace daily, McDonald quickly picked up on grievances of his fellow laborers and as a result became sympathetic toward the labor movement.

McDonald's role as a labor leader began in 1923 when, at age 20, he was appointed secretary to United Mine Workers of America (UMW) Vice-president Philip Murray. He remained with the UMW for over a decade, and when the Congress of Industrial Organizations (CIO) was formed in 1936, Murray named McDonald secretary-treasurer of the Steel Workers Organizing Committee.

For almost three decades, David McDonald was the foremost labor leader of the steelworkers. In 1936, when the Steelworkers of America (SWA) was born, he was named secretary-treasurer. A decade later, upon the death of Murray, he became acting president and the next year president. At that same time he was appointed vice-president of the AFL-CIO executive council.

McDonald served the steelworkers well. As president, he was successful in negotiating improved wages and fringe benefits. In 1956 he gained a supplemental unemployment benefit program, and following the prolonged steel strike of 1959, he won a better pension plan for the steelworkers. He also established a human relations commission to expedite continuous top-level union-management talks to resolve grievances. Because of McDonald's incisive leadership, there were no major steel strikes in the 1960s.

Despite the gains he achieved for the SWA, there were dissidents who were always trying to dislodge McDonald as union president. In the mid-1950s, dues protestors unsuccessfully tried to defeat him. Later he was criticized for being too promanagement and not responsive to the rank-and-file membership. McDonald overcame these attacks within the union by getting the constitution amended so he could serve two additional four-year terms. Finally, in 1965, SWA secretary-treasurer I. W. Abel defeated him for the union presidency. For over a decade

McDonald had been the forceful leader of the Steelworkers of America. During his tenure as president he won many benefits for the steelworkers, improving their life-style.

Machinists and Blacksmith's, National Union of (NUMB)

Fourteen machinists and blacksmiths in Philadelphia began to meet together in 1858 to discuss common problems relating to their trades. That number soon grew to 300 as machinists and blacksmiths in four additional cities followed the example of their Pennsylvania brethren. A year later 21 delegates established the National Union of Machinists and Blacksmiths (NUMB). By 1860 NUMB had 2,828 members in 57 locals. Along came the Civil War, which disrupted the union. Southerners withdrew as Northerners went off to war. After the war the union revived briefly, but then declined as depression struck.

Among its major achievements, the NUMB produced stalwart American leaders Terence V. Powderly and Ira Steward. Since Steward was a leading proponent of the eight-hour day, the NUMB endorsed that maximum-hour standard. The NUMB also called for the creation of a national labor union. When the National Labor Union (NLU) was founded in 1866, NUMB first joined, then four years later broke away as the NLU became involved in politics.

In 1873 the NUMB established the New Industrial Congress, which was similar to the American Federation of Labor. The union experienced rapid growth in the early 1870s as membership ballooned from 1,500 to 18,000 before internal strife and the panic of 1873 caused a collapse. A skeletal group absorbed by the Knights of Labor remained active until the close of the century. Eventually in the modern era the International Association of Machinists (IAM) replaced the NUMB.

McParlan, D. James (1844–1919)

A native of the province of Ulster in Ireland, James McParlan, before coming to the United States in 1867, was employed in an English chemical factory and a Belfast linen warehouse. His first job in the United States was in a New York City grocery, and he later worked in a Medina, New York, dry goods emporium. He received his baptism of fire as a detective when he was hired by a Chicago agency as a "preventive policeman." In 1871 he took a job with the Allan Pinkerton Detective Agency, with which he stayed until his death in 1919.

In the anthracite coalfields of eastern Pennsylvania in the 1870s, Irish coal miners worked in mines owned by Philadelphia and Reading Railroad, whose president, Franklin B. Gowen, was vehemently opposed to labor unions. The miners worked long hours for low wages in hazardous coal mines. Many of them belonged to the Workingmen's Benevolent Association (WBA), a sort of union in the area, and to the Miners' and Mine Laborers' Benevolent Association. While the union had earlier concluded an agreement with the area's anthracite operators, the mine owners in December 1874 broke the pact by cutting wages. In January 1875 the "long strike" erupted in Pennsylvania's eastern anthracite fields around Pottsville, Scranton, and Wilkes-Barre. As the disturbance unfolded, the miners resorted to sabotage of company property, attacks on mine personnel, and derailment of coal trains, along with other acts of terrorism.

In an attempt to stop the terroristic activity and to ferret out those responsible, Gowen brought in McParlan—alias James McKenna, allegedly a fugitive from justice—to infiltrate a secret order of coal miners known as the Molly Maguires or "Mollies," who were blamed for acts of terrorism. Earlier Gowen had successfully broken the WBA, but the Molly McGuires and another organization of Irishmen, the Ancient Order of Hiberians, continued the agitation.

McParlan was in the eastern Pennsylvania coalfields from 27 October 1873 until 7 March 1876. During that time, he gathered information about the Mollies and filed reports to Gowen.

In late 1875 Pennsylvania authorities arrested many of the Molly Maguires in connection with the coalfield disturbances. In the mass trials that followed, McParlan testified for the state against his former comrades. Twenty-four Molly Maguires were found guilty; ten were hanged, and the remainder received jail terms ranging from two to seven years. McParlan's testimony proved damaging in the conviction of the Molly Maguires.

Later, as a Pinkerton operative in Colorado, McParlan used his ingenuity to force a confession from Harry Orchard in connection with the murder of Idaho Governor Frank Steunenberg, a radical foe of the Western Federation of Miners (WFM). Orchard's confession implicated WFM President William "Big Bill" Haywood, who was indicted and tried on the murder charge. Haywood's brilliant defense attorney, the famous Clarence Darrow, used Orchard's confession to free Haywood. Orchard was found guilty, and received a verdict of death by hanging, which was later changed to a life prison term.

By the time of the Haywood and Orchard trials, James McParlan had changed his name to McParland. While he had succeeded in breaking the resistance of the Molly Maguires in eastern Pennsylvania with convictions, executions, and prison sentences, in Idaho he failed to convict Haywood and WFM officials, opening himself and Pinkerton officials to ridicule and embarrassment.

Major League Baseball Player's Association (MLBPA)

In its early years, major league baseball resembled, according to one source, the feudalism of the Middle Ages. There was the manor (the club franchise) and the lord (the club owner), the vassals (coaches, managers, and front office staff), and the serfs (the players). Players had little or no freedom and could be sold or traded much like serfs or slaves.

It was not until 1946, when the Mexican League began its raid on the major leagues in the United States, that attention was paid to a players' association. As players went south of the border, baseball commissioner A. B. "Happy" Chandler issued a five-year edict against players jumping. Meanwhile, the American Baseball Guild was formed with Robert Murphy, the legal examiner of the National Labor Relations Board, as director. The Guild, in its infancy, focused on a player's pension plan, minimum wages, and compensation during spring training.

Of the six major league clubs, the team that most strongly supported the American Baseball Guild was the Pittsburgh Pirates. The Pirates sought union recognition and collective bargaining, but Pirate management refused. A threatened strike collapsed when management rejected player demands for a union representation election. The American Baseball Guild was dead. For a time major league clubs formed company unions with employee representation chosen by the owners. A pension plan, a minimum wage of $5,000, and a $25 per day spring training allowance were conceded by the owners.

From the company unions evolved the Major League Baseball Players Association (MLBPA). As it grew into an independent, hard-bargaining entity, it hired attorney J. Norman Lewis as its chief agent. In 1966 Marvin J. Miller was selected MLBPA director. While the owners opposed Miller, the players offered their overwhelming endorsement.

Under Miller's direction the MLBPA became a unified, democratically organized outfit. An owner's effort to undermine the pension plan was vetoed, and in 1968 the first contract was signed by the owners and the MLBPA. That agreement was renewed in 1970.

Several landmarks occasioned MLBPA activity in the 1970s. In 1971 it successfully appealed the case of Alex Johnson, who had been suspended for failing to play with sufficient vigor. The following year the Supreme Court dismissed the challenge of St. Louis Cardinals' outfielder Curtis Flood to baseball's reserve clause. That same year baseball's first general strike, which lasted 11 days and forced cancellation of 86 games, ended with owners agreeing to increase pension fund contributions by $1 million. In 1973 an arbitration system was created, giving baseball players the right to arbitrate a salary dispute with a professional arbitrator.

Today the MLBPA, with Donald M. Fehr as executive director, boasts 800 members. It remains the bargaining agent for major league baseball players. While there have been recent points of conflict between owners and players, on the whole negotiation and arbitration have resolved the conflicts with minimal disruption of the baseball seasons.

Malone, Dudley Field (1882–1950)

An American Civil Liberties Union (ACLU) attorney, Dudley Field Malone of Cleveland, Ohio, traveled in May 1932 to southeastern Kentucky as part of an ACLU entourage to make a constitutional and civil rights test in the troubled coalfields of Bell and Harlan counties. Making the journey with Malone were New York lawyer Arthur Garfield Hays, spokesman for the group; Professor Broadus Mitchell of Johns Hopkins University; Reverend C. C. Webber of New York's Union Theological Seminary; Washington lawyer Jesse C. Duke; and Dr. Ernest Sutherland Bates, a renowned author, editor, and former college professor from New York City.

Malone and his colleagues wished to make the constitutional and civil rights test because of stories from the coalfields that suggested that nonunion coal miners did not enjoy free speech, free press, and freedom of assembly. The ACLU groups notified Bell County, Kentucky, officials of their plans. As they proceeded into the environs, they were met at the Bell-Knox county line by a motorcade headed by Pineville, Kentucky, Mayor J. M. Brooks and Bell County attorney Walter B. Smith, who blocked the highway and refused them entry into the county.

Malone and his cohorts returned to London, Kentucky, site of the federal district court for southeastern Kentucky, to seek an injunction against Bell County officials from Judge A. M. J. Cochran. When Judge Cochran refused to grant the injunction, which would have allowed the ACLU travelers to carry out their plans, the visitors departed, proclaiming that it was clear that civil liberties were nonexistent in the two Kentucky coal counties.

Before his trip to Kentucky, Malone and fellow ACLU compatriot Arthur Garfield Hays were part of the defense staff in Dayton, Tennessee's, famous Monkey Trial in 1925.

Martin, Warren Homer (1902–1968)

Homer Martin was a Baptist minister in Leeds, Missouri who, after upsetting his parishioners by making comments favorable to labor, departed the ministry and wandered into Michigan. There he hired on at the General Motors Corporation's Chevrolet plant. At once Martin became a labor leader as president of an American Federation of Labor (AFL) local organized in the plant where he toiled. The company fired him, resulting in his move to Detroit, where in 1934 he helped organize the United Automobile Workers (UAW). A year later, when the UAW was chartered by the AFL, Martin was named vice-president. In 1936 he became president of the UAW.

Homer Martin soon led the UAW into the Congress of Industrial Organizations (CIO). For three years he successfully guided the UAW, yet he was always in the middle of bitter and divisive conflicts because of his impulsive and temperamental personality. Those conflicts led to Martin's downfall by 1939. Before he resigned the presidency of the UAW, he led a small core of UAW unions back into the AFL.

Turning from his role as labor leader, Martin became a farmer. Still maintaining an interest in labor affairs, he led a movement to reduce UAW influence in Michigan's Democratic Party. Finally he left the Midwest for California, where he became a labor counselor for the Tulane and King's County Employer Council. Martin died in California on 22 January 1968.

The legacy of Homer Martin was that he led the UAW during the difficult days of unionization in Michigan's automobile industry. Under his controversial presidency, the auto workers were organized into a strong union that successfully bargained with Ford, General Motors, and Chrysler Corporation. For almost seven years he was the champion of the automobile workers. When he left, the union was in the strong and capable hands of his successor, Walter Reuther.

Matewan Massacre

See Bloody Mingo.

Maximum Hours Laws

In the early years of the American labor movement, employers worked employees without regard to maximum hours laws. In the nineteenth century, for example, the workday for many people ranged from 12 to 14 hours, and the work week comprised 60 to 80 hours—nearly always six days and sometimes seven, with workers getting an hour off on Sunday to attend church if they wished. In some cases responsible male workers were allowed time for courting purposes.

Reformists desired to limit work hours beginning in the late nineteenth century. Ira Steward was regarded as the chief apostle of the eight-hour movement, and the Omaha Platform of the People's Party (1892) advocated the eight-hour day. During the Progressive Era (1900–1920), certain progressives pushed for maximum hours laws, and in many states ten-hour laws were enacted. A conservative Supreme Court overturned a ten-hour law for male workers in *Lochner v. New York* (1905) and let stand a similar law for female workers in the *Muller v. Oregon* (1908) decision. On the federal level the Adamson Act (1916) established an eight-hour day for railroad workers.

It was not until the administration of President Franklin Delano Roosevelt (1932–1945) that maximum hours were put in place on a nationwide basis. First, Congress passed the National Industrial Recovery Act (NIRA), which contained maximum hours laws for both the workday and work week. Again a conservative Supreme Court declared NIRA unconstitutional in the 1935 *Schechter v. United States* case. So it was that during what is often regarded as FDR's second New Deal (1935–1938) Congress passed the Fair Labor Standards Act (FLSA), a great victory for maximum hours advocates. Though challenged by employers, the FLSA was upheld by the Supreme Court in *United States v. Darby Lumber Company* (1941).

In effect the FLSA implanted the traditional nine-to-five or eight-hour workday and the 40-hour work week. If an employee worked beyond those hours, extra compensation was paid by the employer. Today, except for certain types of employment, mainly part-time, seasonal, and perhaps emergency work, most American workers enjoy an eight-hour day and a 40-hour week.

Meany, George (1894–1980)

Upon completion of public school in New York City, George Meany went to work as a plumber's apprentice in 1910. Five years later he qualified as a journeyman plumber. At age 21 he joined the United Association of Plumbers and Steam Fitters of the United States and Canada (UA), and for the rest of his life Meany was involved in the American labor movement.

Meany was chosen business agent of the UA's New York Local 463 in 1922. He served as delegate to the New York City Central Trades & Labor Assembly, and in 1932 was elected vice-president of the New York State Federation of Labor. Seven years later he was chosen secretary-treasurer of the American Federation of Labor (AFL). During World War II Meany was labor delegate to the National Defense Mediation Board and the National War Labor Board. Following the war he became the first director of Labor's League for Political Education.

Following the death of AFL President William Green in 1952, the AFL executive council named Meany acting president, then president. During his lengthy tenure as AFL chief, Meany focused on unity in the labor movement, elimination of corruption in labor, and the ending of communism in U.S. trade unions. Working with Congress of Industrial Organizations (CIO) head Walter Reuther, the two giants of American labor consummated the AFL-CIO merger arrangement with Meany as president of the powerful labor union. As AFL-CIO president, Meany went after labor union corruption and racketeering. He was quite successful in his crusade against chicanery in labor, expelling three unions from the AFL-CIO, including the powerful Teamsters. Always a foe of communism, George Meany relentlessly attacked its infiltration into American labor unions.

During the 1960s, the bombastic Meany successfully squelched all opposition to his leadership of the AFL-CIO. As labor czar he cast aside all opposition, including that of CIO chieftain Walter Reuther.

A powerful labor leader, Meany was courted by many politicians. Normally he threw his support behind Democrats on both the national and local levels. In

1972, however, Meany broke an AFL-CIO tradition that dated back to the 1955 merger by refusing to endorse Democratic presidential nominee George McGovern of South Dakota.

Meany retired as AFL-CIO president in 1979. His successor was Lane Kirkland, the organization's present president. During his almost three-decade tenure as AFL-CIO president, Meany left an indelible stamp upon the labor movement with the AFL-CIO merger and his crusade against corruption and communism. He opposed public demonstrations, however, and following his death in 1980, his successor, Lane Kirkland, inaugurated 19 September 1981 as labor's Solidarity Day.

See also American Federation of Labor; Congress of Industrial Organizations.

Mechanics' Lien Laws

Mechanics' lien laws were supported by workingmen's parties in Northeastern industrial states in the first half of the nineteenth century. Basically the laws were designed to ensure a worker's wages in case the employer went bankrupt, so a worker could still collect what he was owed. In New York State workingmen's groups endorsed mechanics' lien laws, which were in turn embraced by that state's longtime political machine, Tammany Hall. With the combined support of workingmen's associations and politicians, the New York legislature enacted such a law. Once New York had passed a mechanics' lien law, other industrialized states in the Northeastern phalanx adopted similar legislation. By the time of the Civil War, most of the industrialized states had adopted mechanics' lien laws.

Medicare (1965)

In 1965, as part of President Lyndon B. Johnson's Great Society program, the U.S. Congress added an amendment to the Social Security Act of 1935, which was passed during the New Deal era of President Franklin D. Roosevelt. The amendment provided a federally funded program of hospital and health insurance—Medicare, implemented by the Social Security Administration. Medicare, which is currently operable, provides hospital benefits for retired workers beyond the age of 65. To receive Medicare benefits, a worker must have been covered while employed by Social Security and must be retired at age 65. Once reaching his sixty-fifth birthday, the worker, of both the white- and blue-collar class, is eligible to apply for Medicare hospital insurance. The health insurance part of Medicare is strictly voluntary.

Medicare benefits are the same throughout the United States, but its scope is limited. While hospital insurance is provided, Medicare recipients cannot claim benefits for prescription drugs, eyeglasses, and dental care.

Since many workers are covered by Social Security during their days of employment, they can receive Medicare benefits at age 65. A fallacy of the system is that with the meteoric rise in health care and hospital costs, Medicare is not sufficient to meet the needs of many workers.

While Medicare provides national hospital and health insurance for retired American workers, the United States still has not gone the way of its neighbor to the north, the Dominion of Canada, which maintains a socialized medicine system for its people.

Memorial Day Massacre (1937)

The Steel Workers Organizing Committee (SWOC) in 1937 attempted to implant the Steelworkers of America (SWA) into the four Little Steel factories of Republic, Bethlehem, Youngstown Sheet and Tube, and Inland. Tom M. Girdler, an outspoken critic of SWOC, led strong, concentrated opposition to the union campaign using industrial munitions, policemen, and espionage.

To gain union recognition at the Little Steel companies, the workers called a strike that continued for several months. The companies marshalled all their resources to crush the strike and the strikers. Inevitable violence flared. The pivotal episode erupted on Memorial Day, 30 May 1937, at the South Chicago plant of Republic Steel. Holidaying workers and their families, enjoying a picnic, turned to demonstrating before the gates of Republic Steel. Chicago city policemen attempted to disperse the crowd. As newsreels viewed by the La Follette Civil Liberties Committee depicted, they opened fire and shot down ten strikers as the group ran for cover when the shooting broke out. Over 100 workers were seriously wounded in the affray.

The Memorial Day Massacre momentarily ended efforts by the SWOC to organize Little Steel. It was not until after the La Follette inquiry into the episode and subsequent federal intervention into the conflict that Little Steel capitulated to the SWOC and SWA.

The Memorial Day Massacre was another bloody stain in labor-management relations of the 1930s as laborers strove for the right to join unions of their choice.

See also Girdler, Tom Mercer; Little Steel.

Middleton, Theodore Roosevelt

Chief law enforcement officer of coal-producing Harlan County, Kentucky, from 1933 to 1937, Sheriff Theodore Roosevelt Middleton used his office to stop the United Mine Workers of America (UMW) from organizing the county's 12,000 coal miners.

Before his election as sheriff, Middleton had operated a poolroom in the county, run a grocery, worked in coal mines owned by his mother, worked as a real estate agent in Tacoma, Washington, and operated a Harlan restaurant. Prior to his election as sheriff, he had served as Harlan's police chief. While police chief he acquired ten shares of stock in a Harlan County coal mine and operated a

county dairy farm. During prohibition he spent six months in prison for violation of the prohibition laws. Middleton also served four years in the U.S. Army as an enlisted man during World War I, then took the oath of an officer on 19 June 1917. Following the war he applied for a commission as a regular officer. The army turned him down for "lack of personal veracity."

In 1933 Middleton ran for sheriff of Harlan County on a "new deal" platform. Apparently he received the support of coal miners because he promised he would not appoint former deputies who harassed both them and union organizers. Shortly after his election, however, he named as deputies many of those who had badgered coal miners and union men. In addition, his sheriff's performance bonds were signed by leading Harlan coal operators. The "new deal" promised by Sheriff Middleton did not materialize.

From 1934 to 1937, then, the sheriff's office, controlled by the coal operators, became a stalwart instrument to repel the UMW in Harlan County. During those years, Middleton had 379 deputy sheriffs, most of whom were paid by Harlan County coal operators. Many of the deputies had criminal records and habitually had oppressed union organizers and union-affiliated coal miners.

Appearing as a witness before the La Follette Civil Liberties Committee in the spring of 1937, Middleton gave sensational testimony revealing strong business ties with other county officials, political leaders, and coal operators. When the committee pried too closely into Middleton's personal financial background, on the advice of counsel, he took the Fifth Amendment. Evidence uncovered by the committee showed that in a four-year period, Middleton's personal fortune had ballooned to over $100,000, although his statutory salary as sheriff was a maximum of $5,000 per year.

Middleton's revelations to the La Follette Committee revealed the lease of coal lands to Harlan coal corporations, interest in a coal company commissary, royalties on coal mined on land leased by him, and the sale of milk from his dairy farm to coal company commissaries. While he was sheriff, Middleton was also president of a Harlan County coal company, which strongly opposed the UMW.

Middleton's testimony before the La Follette Committee was nationally publicized, and Harlan County was soon headlined as "Bloody Harlan" throughout the nation. For four years, Middleton-appointed deputies shot, beat, and took UMW organizers for rides; they also blocked public highways, used tear gas, bombed union cars, and ambushed organizers, all to keep the union out of the county. The sheriff, a coal operator himself, did little to stem the anti-union tide.

By Kentucky law, Middleton was unable to succeed himself in 1937. He was a defendant in federal court in 1938 for using his office to terrorize union men and organizers. He was not convicted because the jury was unable to agree on a verdict. The La Follette inquiry did lead to his indictment and trial, and despite a mistrial being declared, in late 1938 the UMW signed a contract with most of Harlan County's coal operators.

In 1942 union foe Theodore Roosevelt Middleton succumbed to a heart attack.

Migrant Workers

In agricultural areas throughout the United States, an important and inexpensive source of labor, especially at harvest time, has traditionally been furnished by migrant workers. Migrant workers come from various ethnic backgrounds. Mexican background is very prominent, but in certain Southern areas Cubans, Puerto Ricans, and other groups of Latin ancestry furnish migratory labor.

These workers are called migrant or migratory because, beginning on the East Coast of the Deep South, they move north to harvest crops during the varied harvest seasons. In Florida, for example, they harvest citrus and vegetables, then move north to pick peaches during the summer months. In essence migrant workers move to where the crops are ready to be harvested.

Migrant workers are engaged primarily in seasonal work. The landowner for whom they toil usually provides a migrant labor camp in which the workers live during harvest time. The camp consists of small huts with tiny rooms in which the workers eat and sleep. The huts usually are crowded, poorly lighted, poorly ventilated, dirty, and unsanitary. The workers often live in squalor and are paid menial wages.

Migrant workers are usually under the supervision of a crew chief who migrates along with them. The crew chief is their boss and therefore is responsible for seeing that the work is done. The crew chief reports directly to the landowner or crop owner, receives money from the landowner, and in turn pays the workers. The

Larry Itliong organized Filipino farm workers in California during the 1960s.

crew chief also is responsible for the purchase of any necessities or nonnecessities the workers want. For example, workers tell the crew chief they want cigarettes and beer; the crew chief buys the products from the money owed the workers. An unscrupulous crew chief can buy what the workers request and overcharge them, meaning they do not always receive all the wages they earned. Basically, migrant workers are at the mercy of both the landowner and the crew chief.

In recent years both the federal government and state governments have been involved in attempting to improve conditions under which migrant laborers work. At the same time, social services workers of the Catholic church have been engaged in trying to force landowners to upgrade facilities for the workers. Still, while some farmers provide migrant workers with cleaner, better-ventilated, more spacious quarters and furnish a variety of nourishing foods, the fact is that most migrant workers still exist in squalid housing and are underfed and undernourished.

Miller, Joyce Dannen (1928–)

Joyce Dannen Miller was born in Chicago, Illinois. At age 24 she joined the Amalgamated Clothing Workers of America (ACWA). For about one year Miller was the Pittsburgh area director of ACWA, and from 1962 to 1966 she served as educational director for the Chicago Board of ACWA. In 1966 she was named assistant director of social services for ACWA, a position she held until 1972, when she became executive assistant to ACWA's general officers and director of social services.

Following the 1976 merger of ACWA and the Textile Workers Union, which created the Amalgamated Clothing and Textile Workers Union (ACTWU), Miller was tapped as international vice-president of the Coalition of Labor Union Women (CLWU). Four years later she achieved a singular honor when she was named an AFL-CIO vice-president and seated on that union's executive council. She became the first woman chosen to occupy a seat on the AFL-CIO's top governing body.

Miller has also held a number of other responsible positions on various labor boards and councils: East Coast Coalition of Labor Women, National Committee on Working Women, AFL-CIO Committee on Civil Rights, National Trade Union Council for Human Rights, and the Trade Union Women's Study Program at Cornell University's Institute of Labor and Industrial Relations, to mention a few.

A trailblazer, pioneer, and pacesetter, Joyce Miller has worn many hats as an important women's labor leader in the textile industry and as a member of the AFL-CIO executive council. Always she has worked to improve the status of women in the workplace.

One of the ACTWU's greatest victories occurred when, after 17 years of bitter struggle, the union successfully organized the tough anti-union J. P. Stevens Company in the Carolinas. Joyce Miller was in the forefront of that startling union triumph.

Minimum Wage

Until the early years of the twentieth century, especially during the Progressive period from 1900 to 1920, little attention was paid to minimum wages for American workers. Since most workers did not have a union contract, they worked at whatever wage the employer paid. Consequently many workers toiled for menial wages, with male workers receiving better pay than female workers. For example, some women textile workers in the Piedmont South received 90 cents per day for a ten- to twelve-hour day. On the other hand, male factory workers earned anywhere from $1.25 to $2.50 per day.

With the inception of the Progressive period, progressives in both the Democratic and Republican parties began to address the issue of minimum wages on the state level. Minimum wage legislation was enacted in seven states. Employers challenged the laws in the courts, and the Supreme Court was split over whether such legislation was constitutional.

In 1918 Congress decreed a minimum wage law for both women and children workers in the District of Columbia. Employers challenged the statute on the grounds that it abrogated freedom of contract guaranteed by the due process clause of the Fifth Amendment. In *Adkins v. Children's Hospital* (1923), the Court invalidated the District of Columbia's minimum wage law for women and children. In the opinion of Justice George Sutherland, it was "a naked, arbitrary exercise of power."

So it was that the federal government did not legislate in the area of minimum wages until the passage of the National Industrial Recovery Act (NIRA) in 1933. Under the New Deal measure, codes of fair competition negotiated under NIRA contained minimum wage laws. The Supreme Court overturned NIRA in 1935 in the *Schechter* case. Not until the passage of the Fair Labor Standards Act (FLSA) of 1938, which the Court upheld in 1941, did Congress enact a national minimum wage law. Initially the FLSA called for minimum wages of between 25 and 40 cents per hour. Under the FLSA, minimum wages have increased periodically to the present $4.25 per hour. Some employers evade the law through the use of part-time help and seasonal work.

Mitchell, Harry Leland (1906–)

A native of Halls, Tennessee, Harry Leland "Mitch" Mitchell, bespectacled and white-haired today, was a social activist-labor organizer during the 1930s and 1940s. His major contribution to the American labor movement was the organization of the Southern Tenant Farmer Union (STFU) in 1934. As executive secretary of the STFU, Mitch led farmers' strikes in Arkansas and Tennessee at harvest time in 1935. Those strikes catapulted the STFU into national headlines. So successful were the strikes that membership in the STFU skyrocketed to 30,000 tenant farmers and sharecroppers by 1937.

Always a crusader for the tenant farmer, Mitchell testified before both public and private agencies on agricultural problems in attempts to obtain aid for tenants and sharecroppers from federal agencies and national organizations. As leader of the STFU, Mitchell emphasized its role as a pressure group to gain publicity and legislation on behalf of tenant farmers. Alas, in 1937 Mitchell's STFU reluctantly merged with the communist-dominated United Cannery, Agricultural, Packing and Allied Workers of America (UCAPAWA), with which it was associated for about two years. In 1939, following a Missouri sharecroppers strike, Mitchell withdrew from UCAPAWA.

In 1944 Mitchell was tapped as president of the STFU, which he led into the American Federation of Labor (AFL). As an AFL affiliate, the STFU was renamed the National Farm Labor Union (NFLU). For a decade Mitchell was NFLU president, as well as president of its successor, the National Agricultural Workers Union (NAWU). In 1960 NAWU merged with the Amalgamated Meat Cutters and Butcher Workers of North America.

Harry Leland Mitchell has devoted a lifetime to improving the status of tenant farmers and sharecroppers. An agricultural specialist, he organized dairy farm and plant workers; rice mill, sugar plantation, and seasonal workers; and menhaden fishermen on the Gulf of Mexico. He was also a consultant to the U.S. Department of Labor and the International Labor Organization. A socialist until 1932, Mitchell cast his lot with the Democratic Party in 1936.

In recent years Mitchell has traveled and lectured about his days as an STFU organizer and official. He has also collected, compiled, and circulated official papers and documents pertaining to the STFU. A liberal, Mitchell has been vitally interested in the plight of all farmers, especially injustices to black tenant farmers and black sharecroppers. He helped publicize with graphic accounts, for example, the lynching of black farm workers in the South, particularly the Claude Neal case in Florida in 1934.

Mitchell, John (1870–1919)

The son of an Illinois coal miner, John Mitchell entered the mines at the age of 12. As a teenager, he took off on a trip to the mines of Colorado and Wyoming, returning to Illinois a year or so later. In 1887 he joined the Knights of Labor and participated in a yearlong strike that led to a wage decrease.

Sensing the need for a separate union for coal miners, Mitchell joined a newly formed local of the United Mine Workers of America (UMW) in 1890. A year later, after marrying a miner's daughter, Mitchell's course as a UMW labor leader was charted. In 1894 he joined 125,000 miners on strike and was fired at strike's end. After an acquaintance persuaded him to become secretary-treasurer of an Illinois UMW subdistrict, Mitchell rose rapidly in the ranks as a union official. In 1897 he became a member of the Illinois state executive board, and following his involvement in a successful nationwide strike, he was named delegate to the UMW national convention. After a brief tenure as union vice-president in 1898, John Mitchell was elected president of the UMW.

The nationwide coal strike of 1902 projected Mitchell into the national limelight. That walkout included over 150,000 English and non-English mine workers in Pennsylvania's anthracite region. Following a five-month walkout, the union gained a wage increase, a reduction in work hours, and an agreement to arbitrate future grievances. At age 32 Mitchell was the successful leader of

union immigrant labor from southeastern Europe.

Mitchell led the UMW for a decade. Then a depression in the bituminous fields and subsequent strike failures caused his downfall in 1907. While he retained the loyalty of anthracite workers, bituminous miners turned away from his leadership. His presidency ended in 1908, after which he lectured on trade unionism and led the trade agreement department of the National Civic Federation.

Of slight and wiry build, Mitchell possessed a sober, thoughtful appearance. Conservative in manner and dress, his favorite attire consisted of a long, ministerial black coat. During the 1902 anthracite strike talks, Mitchell was bitterly attacked by coal operators who had refused to confer until mandated by President Theodore Roosevelt, causing the president to remark of Mitchell: "There was only one man in the room who behaved like a gentleman, and that man was not I."

Mohawk Valley Formula

The La Follette Civil Liberties Committee, in its investigation of anti-labor violations, uncovered what became known as the Mohawk Valley formula. The Remington Rand Company apparently was the first corporation to implement the scheme; then it was adopted and expanded by the National Association of Manufacturers. The purpose of the formula was to wipe out trade unionism.

The Mohawk Valley formula consisted of the following principles: (1) all union organizers were radicals, syndicalists, and revolutionists who desired to overthrow the capitalistic system; (2) building public opinion behind employers who favored law and the status quo; (3) using industrial policemen, sheriff's deputies, city policemen, and/or the state militia to harass strikers by denying them freedom of assembly, speech, and press; (4) bringing in employees who were not on strike (in other words, using scabs); and

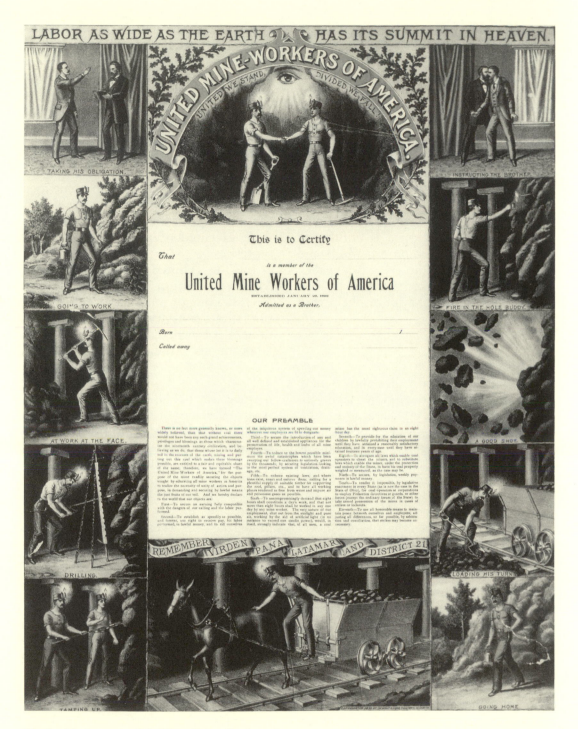

Membership document of the United Mine Workers of America

(5) organizing watch dog groups to get the factory operable as quickly as possible.

The Mohawk Valley formula, according to the La Follette Committee, was effective in delaying the rise of labor unionism by stigmatizing labor leaders as syndicalists. Another significant factor in the formula was that management was not beyond relocating a business if local citizens did nothing to stop the organization of workers.

The bottom line in the 1930s was that management stopped at nothing in efforts to keep out union organizers and union members. The Mohawk Valley formula is a perfect example of that strong anti-union behavior on the part of most employers.

Molly Maguires

In nineteenth-century Ireland, tenant farmers were victimized by landlords who harassed them by charging exorbitant rents for land. A courageous Irish woman, Molly Maguire, organized the tenants and successfully led them in a demonstration against their bosses, the landlords. Under Molly Maguire, Ireland's tenant farmers really did "dump the bosses off their backs." Molly never came to the United States, but many of her fellow countrymen migrated and settled in eastern Pennsylvania, where they became coal miners.

As coal miners, Irishmen were victimized by coal operators who paid them low wages and also cut their wages. They worked long hours in unsafe mines. Remembering Molly back in Ireland and her crusade against tyrannical landlords, the coal miners established a small, secret organization officially called the Ancient Order of Hibernians and unofficially the Molly Maguires ("Mollies").

In the 1870s the Mollies conducted a campaign of terrorism against the coal operators. They bushwhacked superiors and foremen, derailed coal trains, destroyed coal tipples and other company property, and, in essence, shut down the mines by turning back all scabs who attempted to enter.

Since the organization was small and secretive, the coal operators hired James McParlan, a Pinkerton agent, to come in, infiltrate the Mollies, and find the troublemakers. Over a two-and-a-half year period, McParlan gathered evidence that led to the rounding up of 24 Mollies. They were charged with an assortment of crimes, tried in courts controlled by the coal operators, and convicted. Ten were executed, the others received jail sentences.

In the United States the Molly Maguires were not as successful as in Ireland. It was not until the twentieth century that Pennsylvania coal miners, and miners everywhere, were able to join the labor unions of their choice.

Moore, Ely (1798–1860)

A strong leader of labor during the Jacksonian era, Ely Moore was born near Belvidere, New Jersey. He practiced medicine for a time before becoming a journeyman printer. Almost at once he got involved in the early labor movement, distinguishing himself as both an effective organizer and capable administrator in union affairs.

Moore's first position in labor was president of craft unions in New York City. From that office he rose to head the General Trades' Union and then the National Trades Union. Moore may be considered the first labor leader of national importance in the United States. An eloquent speaker, he became a political activist and in 1834, with the backing of New York's Tammany Hall, was elected to represent his district in the House of Representatives. Reelected in 1836, Moore, who carried a cane with an ivory head and who was in ill health at the time, spent his last ounce of strength defending labor against a verbal attack by a South Carolina congressman who spoke in terms of a revolution by labor. In fact,

Moore leaned on the cane as he spoke, although his voice resounded throughout the House. Finally he fell and was caught by a colleague. That performance was his last hurrah in behalf of the labor movement of the 1830s. His influence was so great that the courts refused to outlaw unions during the Jacksonian period.

While it is true that the modern American labor movement was conceived in the post–Civil War era, Ely Moore presided over the conception and adolescence of antebellum labor.

Most, Johann (1846–1906)

Johann Most was born in Augsburg, Germany, and at age 17 he took up the bookbinder's trade. For five years he was an itinerant laborer throughout central Europe. Migrating to Switzerland, Most joined the International Workingmen's Association in Zurich where he became a devout socialist. A brilliant writer, he edited socialist newspapers in several European cities. He also spent approximately five years in prison in Austria and Germany because of his radical views. Finally, after being expelled from both countries, Most crossed the English Channel to London, where he edited a weekly socialist publication. By 1880 he had become an avowed anarchist and was back in prison for hailing the assassination of Tsar Alexander II of Russia.

After his release from jail, Most migrated to the United States in 1882. Settling in New York City, he reestablished the socialist publication, *Die Freiheit*. A powerful orator, Most soon dominated the anarchist movement in the United States. In 1883 he was the major figure at the Pittsburgh Anarchist Convention, which formed the Revolutionary Socialist Party. In the United States, Most was imprisoned at least twice—the first right before Chicago's Haymarket Riots (1886), and the second after the assassination of President William McKinley in 1901. In the 1880s Most was an associate of anarchist Alexander Berkman.

By 1901 Most had gone full circle to criticize direct individual action by anarchists against the status quo. He broke with Berkman and offended younger, more militant anarchists by denouncing the attempted assassination of Carnegie Steel's Henry Clay Frick. Johann Most died in Cincinnati in 1906.

Muckrakers

Muckrakers were journalists and writers at the beginning of the twentieth century who mostly wrote exposés citing corruption in politics and business. Several writers uncovered the exploitation of American workers by bosses.

President Theodore Roosevelt, borrowing the term from John Bunyan's *Pilgrim's Progress*, which depicted a man with a muckrake spending his entire life raking muck in search of money, twisted the name to suit his own purpose: "There is filth on the floor, and it must be scraped up with a muckrake; and there are times and places where this service is the most needed of all services that can

Author Upton Sinclair wrote revealing, critical novels about the Chicago stockyards, diet fads, and conditions in the Colorado mining industry.

be performed. But the man who never does anything else, who never speaks or writes save of his feats with the muck-rake, speedily becomes, not a help to society, not an incitement to good, but one of the most potent forces of evil."

Some muckrakers exaggerated and others fabricated, while several wrote about conditions as they were. Among those who graphically and explicitly described the exploitation of the working class were Jack London, John Spargo, and Theodore Dreiser. London, in *The Iron Heel*, portrayed the oppression of the toiling masses by the tycoons of the Gilded Age. Spargo described horrible conditions in the nation's sweatshops, where young children were driven until they dropped from exhaustion at their machines. In *The Bitter Cry of the Children*, Spargo aroused the conscience of the nation to correct abuses in child labor. Dreiser, in a poignant novel called *Sister Carrie*, wrote vividly about the exploitation and harassment of working girls in New York City.

Although Spargo and London were identified with the Socialist Party and were severe critics of the capitalist system, their writings awakened the consciences of presidents, congressmen, senators, and, of course, the public. As a result, reforms in child labor conditions and for women workers came during the Progressive Era (1900–1920). A conservative Supreme Court struck down the first federal child labor law in 1918, but in time effective regulation of child workers as well as adult workers came. In the end the efforts of the muckrakers, though criticized, bore fruit.

Muller v. Oregon (U.S., 1908)

The Supreme Court in 1908 upheld an Oregon law limiting working hours for women to a ten-hour day. In its decision, the Court ruled that the Oregon ten-hour law for female laundry employees did not impair the liberty of contract guaranteed by the Fourteenth Amendment.

In the case, Louis Dembitz Brandeis of Louisville, Kentucky, who represented the state, introduced his famous "Brandeis brief." In his brief, Brandeis, who was later appointed to the Supreme Court in 1916 by President Woodrow Wilson, used statistics as well as sociological, economic, and historical data to contend that long hours at work had a detrimental impact upon women and their physical makeup. Brandeis also argued that it was within the police power of the state of Oregon to regulate the hours of its women workers. It was his view that employers who forced women to work long hours at hard labor damaged a woman's body. "That woman's physical structure and the performance of maternal functions place her at a disadvantage in the struggle for subsistence is obvious. This is especially true when the burdens of motherhood are upon her. Even when they are not, by abundant testimony of the medical fraternity continuance for a long time on her feet at work, repeating this from day to day, tends to injurious effects upon the body, and as healthy mothers are essential to vigorous offspring, the physical well-being of a woman becomes an object of public interest and care in order to preserve the strength and vigor of the race."

While modern feminists may disagree, the "Brandeis brief" in *Muller v. Oregon* swayed the Court to uphold Oregon's ten-hour law for women workers. As such it was a clear victory for the social activists of the Progressive Era and their muckraking counterparts.

See also Brandeis, Louis Dembitz; *Bunting v. Oregon.*

Murray, Philip (1886–1952)

Born in Scotland, Philip Murray was the son of a coal miner who was president of a local Scottish miner's union. At age ten he started working in coal mines in his homeland. When he was 16 years old, Murray came to the United States and settled in the bituminous coalfield of western Pennsylvania, where he worked in the mines. At age 18, before he gained U.S. citizenship, he was elected president of his United Mine Workers of America (UMW) local union following a dispute with coal operators that cost him his job.

For the next three decades Murray became one of the country's premier labor leaders. In 1916 he was chosen to head the District 5 organization of the UMW. After serving on the UMW executive board from 1912, Murray, in 1919, was made vice-president. During World War I he served on the National Bituminous Coal Production Committee.

During the New Deal years, Murray was a central figure in the rise of the modern American labor movement. In 1933 he was named to the Labor and Industrial Advisory Board of the National Recovery Administration. Two years later he helped in the formulation and enactment of the Guffey-Snyder Bituminous Coal Stabilization Act, which was passed by Congress after the Supreme Court voided the National Industrial Recovery Act.

Alongside John L. Lewis, Murray assisted in the establishment of the Congress of Industrial Organizations (CIO). He also was chairman of the Steel Workers Organizing Committee (SWOC) from 1936 to 1942, when it became the United Steel Workers of America (USWA). Elected to head the CIO in 1940 following the resignation of Lewis, Murray was also chosen international USWA president in 1942. That same year he was expelled from the UMW following a feud with John L. Lewis.

As a staunch supporter of most of Franklin D. Roosevelt's New Deal programs, Murray was appointed to the National Defense Mediation Board and to several other boards during World War II. After the war he led major and successful steel strikes in 1946, 1949, and 1952. A conservative CIO member, Murray was an ardent foe of communism in labor in the post–World War II era.

Murray was a severe critic of the Taft-Hartley Act passed by Congress in 1947 during the administration of Harry S Truman. He was indicted once for violating Taft-Hartley provisions with regard to expenditures in political campaigns. Although the indictment was dismissed by the Supreme Court, he remained a stalwart supporter and contributor to Democratic candidates who were favorable to organized labor.

From the time he first set foot in the United States, Philip Murray, a workingman himself, espoused the cause of labor unions. He was directly involved in the affairs of three major organizations, the UMW, the CIO, and the USWA. Certainly he was one of the country's strongest proponents of labor unionism for five decades. During all those years he never lost touch with he rank and file. On 1 March 1931, as the international vice-president of the UMW, he addressed nearly 2,000 Kentucky coal miners in the Gaines Theatre in tiny Pineville, Kentucky. Despite the depression that gnawed at their very existence, Murray exhorted the coal miners to support a UMW organizational campaign in the coalfields of Bell and Harlan counties of Kentucky.

The Nation

The Nation is a liberal periodical that in the 1930s focused on the plight and problems of American workers. During the labor turmoil of the New Deal years, *The Nation* published numerous articles and editorialized on behalf of the toiling masses. For example, in the midst of the turbulence in Harlan County, Kentucky, from 1931 to 1939, *The Nation* sided with coal miners against their bosses.

While mainstream newspapers and periodicals defended employers, *The Nation* devoted its columns to a crusade for the rights of the American working class. Examples of the articles published in *The Nation* include "Harlan County: Act of God?"; "The Right To Get Shot," by American Civil Liberties counsel Arthur Garfield Hays; and "Starvation and the Reds in Kentucky."

National Bituminous Coal Act

See Guffey-Snyder Act.

National Civic Federation

The National Civic Federation was an organization established in 1898 in an attempt to resolve the intense labor-management conflict of the late nineteenth century. Its membership was impressive: business leader Mark Hanna; American Federation of Labor President Samuel Gompers; former President Grover Cleveland; and Harvard President Charles W. Eliot. Representing management, in addition to Mark Hanna, were John D. Rockefeller, Jr., Charles M. Schwab, and August Belmont; labor was represented by Gompers and United Mine Workers of America chief John Mitchell.

The main thrust of the federation was to replace the confrontation of the late nineteenth century with cooperation in the twentieth century. To accomplish this purpose, unions were recognized, labor was no longer equated with anarchism, and arbitration was acceptable to both labor and management. Initially there was a cooperative attitude between unions and bosses. For example, railroad barons accepted the railroad brotherhoods, newspaper publishers came to terms with the publishers union, and machinists were recognized by foundries. Union membership jumped impressively. Employers who refused to negotiate with unions were regarded as un-American.

For a time the new atmosphere between labor and capital promoted peace and good will. By 1903 the idea inherent in the National Civic Federation had died, however. United States Steel had refused to negotiate with the steelworkers and had broken a lengthy strike. President Theodore Roosevelt had used his executive powers to bring about a settlement in the anthracite strike of 1902, a solution favorable to labor. Unions had experienced phenomenal growth from 868,500 enrollees in 1900 to more than 2 million in 1904, but the National Civic Federation began to back off from its earlier stance for employer-employee cooperation. Employers and the public became apprehensive of the new power of labor unions.

For an instant, it appeared that there would be labor-capital cooperation and negotiation and arbitration instead of strife. Then it was over as employers began to use yellow-dog contracts and other anti-union techniques to thwart the rise of organized labor. Replacing an interim of cordiality was a spirit of combativeness as capitalists invoked blacklists, labor spies, scabs, and thugs to resist labor unions. So it was that despite the good intentions of the National Civic Federation, improved labor-management relations did not transpire, for the most part, until the federal government intervened again in the 1930s.

National Committee for the Defense of Political Prisoners (NCDPP)

Organized by New York novelist Theodore Dreiser, a chief purpose of the National Committee for the Defense of Political Prisoners (NCDPP) was to encourage an investigation of an alleged reign of terror among coal miners in the Bell-Harlan coalfields of Kentucky in 1931. Beginning in mid-October, Dreiser invited a number of distinguished Americans to join his committee, including U.S. Senator George W. Norris of Nebraska, Robert M. La Follette, Jr., of Wisconsin, James R. Couzens of Michigan, and Henrik Shipstead of Minnesota. Other prominent people who were extended invitations by Dreiser were Daniel Willard, president of the Baltimore and Ohio railroad; Professor Felix Frankfurter of Harvard Law School; Roy Howard, Chairman of the Board, Scripps-Howard Newspapers; Charles P. Taft II, son of ex-President Taft; William Allen White, a famous editor from Emporia, Kansas; and several other editors, ministers, and college presidents. All declined Dreiser's invitation except for editor Bruce Crawford of *Crawford's Weekly*, Norton, Virginia.

Toward the end of October 1931 Dreiser had called on Senator William E. Borah of Idaho to conduct a senatorial investigation of conditions in the coalfields. Borah denied Dreiser's request, prompting the author to form his own committee. Thus the NCDPP was born.

The NCDPP included famous American novelist John Dos Passos, Mr. & Mrs. Charles Rumford Walker, Josephine Herbst, Lester Cohen, Samuel Ornitz, and Bruce Crawford, all writers and journalists; George Maurer, a representative of the International Labor Defense; and Harry Gannes, a New York representative of the National Miners' Union.

Dreiser and his committee spent less than a week in the strife-torn Kentucky coalfields. During their brief stay they interviewed mostly local miners and their wives, who testified to impoverished living conditions and to harassment at the hands of local sheriffs and their armed deputies. Dreiser, who admitted that he did not believe in charity and gave nothing to it, later published *Harlan Miners Speak*, a compilation of the committee's findings in the coalfields. Several other writers, including Dos Passos, published articles about their impressions of the coalfield visit.

The trip by Dreiser and his committee opened the door for other outsiders to go and investigate conditions in Kentucky. Finally, in May 1932 a United States Senate subcommittee of the Committee on Manufactures, chaired by Senator Bronson Cutting of New Mexico, conducted a preliminary hearing into the Kentucky situation. The subcommittee, for about a week, listened to testimony from coal miners, their spouses, several outsiders who visited the coal region, and a Kentucky National Guard official who was in the area during the turbulent summer of 1931. The subcommittee concluded that a thorough inquiry into the coalfield troubles was not warranted. It was not until 1936–1937 that the La Follette Civil Liberties Committee made the first full-scale investigation into the conditions at Bell-Harlan coalfields.

National Football League Player's Association (NFLPA)

Formed in 1956, the National Football League Players Association (NFLPA) at the outset was a collective bargaining agent. Players in the rival American Football League followed by establishing their own association. When the two leagues merged in 1969, the NFLPA absorbed its American League counterpart.

National football league owners recognized the NFLPA in 1970 by signing a four-year contract that provided for $20 million in player benefits. When the pact expired in 1974, contracts talks collapsed because NFLPA negotiators insisted upon the right of players to move from one team to another upon expiration of contracts. The controversy evolved when San Francisco's David Parks signed with the New Orleans Saints after playing out his option. When the Saints and the '49ers could not agree on fair compensation, NFL commissioner Pete Rozelle ordered the Saints to relinquish their first round draft choice for two years. The so-called Rozelle Rule regarding the freedom issue became a significant item in player-owner negotiations.

The 1974 National Football League (NFL) season involved the longest strike in professional sports history. It continued throughout the exhibition schedule as the NFLPA, on 27 August 1974, a week before the regular season opened, rejected the owners' final offer by a 25 to 1 vote. NFL players played the 1974 schedule without a contract.

The stalemate continued into the 1975 NFL season. Randy Vataha, a wide receiver and player's representative of the New England Patriots, announced that his team voted to boycott the last pre-season game until contract talks resumed. The New York Jets, the Washington Redskins, the Detroit Lions, and the New York Giants joined the strike as players from 11 NFL teams refused to play. Federal mediator W. J. Usery, Jr., assured the players that the owners would bargain in good faith. Meanwhile, NFL owners, exploiting disunity among the players, refused to give in to their demands. Talks continued between the owners and NFLPA Executive Director Ed Garvey as differences surfaced between the older and younger players. The older players emphasized the pension plan, the younger emphasized the freedom issue. Older players were also more interested in insurance. Diversity also loomed between black and white players. Black players supported the freedom issue while whites were lukewarm on that point.

While the conflict continued, white players crossed picket lines that had been set up. Finally on 30 December 1975 a federal district court in Minneapolis ruled the Rozelle Rule violated antitrust laws. With that decision the principal issue separating owners and players was resolved.

From the late 1970s to the present, discord has continued between the NFLPA and NFL owners. While recent strikes have not resulted in the loss of games, NFL owners have resorted to using replacement players, or scabs, to get the games in. The NFLPA has answered by setting up picket lines. As replacement players crossed picket lines, tense scenes developed when threats were made and violence occurred. The games went on, however, and once the strike was settled, very few replacement players remained on team rosters.

Today the chief bargaining agent for NFL players is the NFLPA. It is made up of one player representative from each NFL team. The players' representatives select an executive director to bargain with the NFL Management Council.

National Hockey League Players Association (NHLPA)

In December 1966, Springfield Indians hockey players struck in protest of a number of grievances. The strike denoted a burgeoning restlessness on the part of players in both the National Hockey League (NHL) and the American Hockey League (AHL). The strikers hired Toronto attorney R. Alan Eagleson to represent them. An effective negotiator, Eagleson earlier had counseled individual NHL personnel.

On 28 December 1966 the Boston Bruins convened with Eagleson to discuss the possibility of setting up a players association. Eagleson met with players from both the American Hockey League and World Hockey League (WHL), who enthusiastically endorsed the proposal. In June 1967 player representatives from six clubs attended the annual meeting of NHL owners in Montreal. At a player-council conclave, the owners were informed that the NHLPA had been established. Owners gave the association immediate recognition and agreed to payments for exhibition games and meal allowances.

During the first year of NHLPA operation, several players did not report to training camps. The players believed that owners had agreed that all personnel had to report before training camp opened. The owners disagreed. After several meetings between the owners and the NHLPA, a compromise was reached.

Meanwhile the management of the Toronto Maple Leafs seemed determined to break the NHLPA. That ended when all but three club members affiliated with the association.

Early collective bargaining sessions between NHL owners and the NHLPA involved a pension plan that was adjusted to suit the association, increased compensation for exhibition games, and the right of the NHLPA to meet with each NHL team at its training camp.

NHLPA's finances were placed on a stable basis when officials agreed with License Corporation of America to put the NHLPA logo on commercial products, providing enough income to make the association self-sustaining.

For the most part, the NHLPA has not suffered the stormy and troubled history of the National Football League Player's Association (NFLPA). Collective bargaining has resolved grievances between owners and players satisfactorily for both parties.

National Industrial Recovery Act (NIRA)

Passed as part of President Franklin D. Roosevelt's Hundred Days program in 1933, the National Industrial Recovery Act (NIRA) was designed to stimulate the recovery of both business and labor from the depression. The law provided for the negotiation of codes of fair competition between the employer and employee stating conditions of employment. The most important part of the bill, Section 7a, guaranteed employees the right of collective bargaining with their employers. The codes also provided for maximum hours and minimum wages. Workers could not be compelled to join a company union; instead they had the right to join the union of their choice.

The purpose of the measure, called by President Roosevelt "the most important and far-reaching legislation ever enacted by the American Congress," was, in the president's words, "To put people back to work." As time passed, the law and the codes became entangled in a bureaucratic morass, rendering the measure largely ineffective. In 1935 a conservative Supreme Court declared NIRA, except for Section 7a, unconstitutional in *Schechter Poultry Corporation v. United States*. Section 7a, however, was incorporated into the National Labor Relations Act just before the Supreme Court's decision in *Schechter Poultry Corporation*, thus preserving the right of collective bargaining.

See also National Recovery Administration; *Schechter Poultry Corporation v. United States*.

National Labor Board

The National Labor Board was created in 1933 to handle disputes between management and labor arising under the National Industrial Recovery Act (NIRA). Many codes of fair competition were negotiated under NIRA, and many of them were violated by employers. The National Labor Board, which was divided into regional labor boards across the country, investigated complaints and grievances that the employer had not honored a particular code.

In many areas regional labor boards were flooded by workers' grievances. Once complaints were filed, the National Labor Board went into an area, conducted hearings to test the validity of the violations, and issued a decision involving a cease and desist order, that is, the employer had to cease code violation and refrain from the violation in the future.

The real problem with the cease and desist order was that the board had no enforcement powers, leaving that up to courts that all too often failed to enforce board orders. As a result, the National Labor Board was entangled in a bureaucratic jungle of nonenforcement of NIRA codes, rendering both the law and the boards ineffective.

National Labor Relations Act (1935)

Often referred to as the Wagner Act, sponsored in the U.S. Senate by Democratic Senator Robert F. Wagner of New York, the National Labor Relations Act of 1935 was labor's Declaration of Independence, its Emancipation Proclamation. The law, of course, was challenged in the courts. In a landmark case, *National Labor Relations Board v. Jones-Laughlin Steel Company* (1937), the Supreme Court upheld the Wagner Act by a 5 to 4 vote.

The Wagner Act contained three key sections. Section 7 guaranteed American workers the right of collective bargaining with their employers and the right to join the labor union of their choice without employer interference. Section 8 prohibited a number of unfair labor practices. For example, employers could not refuse to engage in collective bargaining with employees, could not discriminate against employees who filed grievances under the law, could not discriminate against workers who affiliated with a labor union, could not interfere in employees' unions, and could not bother employees who exercised their rights under the law. Section 9 established a National Labor Relations Board (NLRB), which had three primary functions. First, it held elections so employees could vote for or against the union. If they voted for the union, they could designate their union of choice for collective bargaining purposes. Second, it heard grievances filed by employees

against employers. To expedite the hearings process, regional labor relations boards were set up. Third, upon conclusion of a hearing, the NLRB could issue a cease and desist order enforceable by the courts.

Following the *National Labor Relations Board v. Jones-Laughlin* decision, and with the full power of the federal government behind unions, by the end of the 1930s the country's toiling masses were free to join a labor union without fear of employer recrimination for the first time in history. Big labor became a reality because of the Wagner Act.

National Labor Relations Board v. Jones-Laughlin Steel Corporation (U.S., 1937)

A landmark Supreme Court decision in which the court by a 5 to 4 vote upheld the constitutionality of the National Labor Relations Act, also known as the Wagner Act, which was passed by Congress on 5 July 1935 as part of Franklin Delano Roosevelt's second New Deal.

Specifically the law contained three major sections. Section 7a, which the court had left intact in 1935 when it declared the National Industrial Recovery Act unconstitutional in *Schechter Corp. v. United States*, conceded workers the right to collective bargaining with their employers. Section 8 contained a long list of unfair labor practices that restrained the employer from discriminating against an employee for joining a labor union, from firing an employee because he "has filed charges or given testimony under this Act," from refusing to engage in collective bargaining with employees' representatives, and from promoting a company union. Section 9 of the law established a National Labor Relations Board, empowering it with three functions: (1) to hold elections so employees can decide for or against union representation and select the union of their choice; (2) to conduct hearings based on grievances and violations of the law filed against employers by employees; and (3) to issue cease and desist orders against employers.

In the Court's decision, Chief Justice Charles Evans Hughes wrote the majority opinion. He stated that employees have a "fundamental right" of self-organization and of collective bargaining with employers through representatives they choose. The Court pointed out that an employee was helpless in dealing with an employer and that a labor union was a suitable vehicle to alleviate that helplessness. Chief Justice Hughes recognized the inequality that existed between the employee and employer, and recognized a labor organization as a proper institution to remedy the inequity. In short, the Court's decision in the *Jones-Laughlin* case outlawed company unions, yellow-dog contracts, blacklists, and the use of labor spies. The case put into place the union shop and the closed shop as well as allowing for peaceful picketing. Employees now could organize, and employers could not prevent the rise of employee unions. The decision of 29 March 1937 opportunely emancipated the American working population.

The Court's decision in the *Jones-Laughlin* case also came at an appropriate time for the Roosevelt administration. Following his landslide reelection over Alf Landon in 1936, Roosevelt, disturbed over a conservative Court's anti–New Deal decisions invalidating the National Industrial Recovery Act and the Agricultural Adjustment Act, launched his court-packing onslaught. With the Court's *Jones-Laughlin* opinion, the court-packing attempt by FDR was effectively stymied. Roosevelt, in effect, rejoiced over the sustaining of the Wagner Act. It might be said that the *Jones-Laughlin* decision, along with several companion cases, saved the Court in the spring of 1937.

National Labor Union (NLU)

Seventy-seven delegates from 13 states and the District of Columbia met in Bal-timore's Front Street Theater on 20 August 1866 to establish the first national labor organization in the United States. The initial assembly was dominated by representatives from local trade unions and city trades assemblies.

At the outset the National Labor Union (NLU) had a political-reformist orientation. Its major goal was an eight-hour law. Soon the NLU branched out to encompass land reform, prison labor reform, cooperatives, African American workers, and antimonopoly reform.

The union floundered until 1868, when William H. Sylvis was elected president. Sylvis provided strong leadership and direction, but with his sudden death in 1869 the NLU declined. The union became more political, isolating it from labor's mainstream, which focused on economic activity. Conflict also arose over the inclusion of women and black workers.

By 1870 the NLU had separated into two distinct sections: industrial and political. Two years later the political wing formed the Labor Reform Party.

The legacy of the National Labor Union is that it gave workers a sense of class-consciousness. With the demise of the NLU, the Knights of Labor arose to give direction to workers' goals. During its brief tenure, the NLU was successful in attaining an eight-hour day for federal employees and the repeal of the contract labor law. It also smoothed the way for the Knights of Labor and the American Federation of Labor.

See also Sylvis, William H.

National Labor Union, Colored (CNLU)

The National Labor Union, Colored (CNLU) grew from efforts by African American workers to gain membership in the National Labor Union. Led by Isaac Meyers of Baltimore, African American delegates attended an NLU convention in the late 1860s. When the NLU refused to integrate, black workers convened the first CNLU conclave. Most of the delegates to the first assembly were lawyers and preachers, most black workers being too poor to attend.

The CNLU called for open hiring and free public education while strongly supporting the temperance movement. It was a loose confederation of autonomous state and local unions composed of skilled, unskilled, male, female, and agricultural workers. With Meyers as its chief organizing agent, the CNLU expressed a desire to cooperate with the NLU, but held itself away from partisan political activity.

In 1871 Meyers was replaced by the dynamic Frederick Douglass, who embraced political activism for the CNLU. Douglass established a political agenda for the CNLU in close cooperation with other black workers' interests, and the CNLU soon ceased to exist as an independent entity.

National Maritime Union (NMU)

American seamen were organized during the 1930s. One of the first unions of maritime workers was the International Seamen's Union of America (ISU). In December 1935 the ISU negotiated an agreement with the American Steamship Association that extended an existing contract. The pact seemingly favored West Coast seamen over East Coast workers, causing a rift within the ISU.

Early in 1936 East Coast workers called "quickie" strikes against individual ships. The crew of the *SS Pennsylvania* abandoned ship in San Francisco, demanding pay equal to that of their West Coast brethren. ISU officials, calling the action an outlaw strike, brought in scabs to replace the strikers. Other similar protests failed, but in March 1936 the crew of the *SS California*, on a return voyage to New York from San Pedro, remained on board while refusing to work. Although the company called the seamen mutineers, the strikers refused to budge. Secretary of Labor Frances Perkins in-

tervened to break the impasse by pledging to help the company in bargaining with the crew and to help the workers from being coerced. When the vessel arrived in New York, however, 64 strikers were fired and blacklisted. A wildcat strike erupted in New York, causing over 200 ships to be detained in port. The ISU finally broke the strike. Meanwhile, internal conflict raged within the ISU as West Coast seamen struck and the rank and file of the ISU demanded that Gulf and Atlantic seamen join them. ISU leadership refused to support the strike. An 86-day strike by rump leaders disrupted shipping temporarily before it was broken by the union.

Out of the chaos within the ISU, the National Maritime Union (NMU) was born at a New York City mass rally in May 1937. Within three months the NMU had enrolled 37,000 seamen and affiliated with the Congress of Industrial Organizations (CIO). The new union petitioned the National Labor Relations Board for elections among East Coast seamen. Alarmed by the sudden rise and success of the NMU, the American Federation of Labor revoked the ISU charter in favor of the Seafarers International Union (SIU). While the SIU was successful in the West, it could not challenge the NMU in the East. The NMU enjoyed outstanding success on the East Coast but was engaged in constant conflict with the SIU on the West Coast. Thus a dual unionism resulted among American seamen, with the SIU claiming 80,250 members in the 1970s and the NMU encompassing 50,000 members.

National Miners Union (NMU)

In the 1920s the Communist Party in the United States discontinued its boring-from-within strategy in the American trade union movement. Instead the party adopted a new technique—the formation of independent unions. One such organization, the National Miners' Union (NMU), was created on 16 September

1928 in Pittsburgh, Pennsylvania, and was an affiliate of the communist Trade Union Unity League (TUUL).

The NMU, in tune with communist ideology, called for class warfare and a class struggle in the mining industry. It also urged a minimum wage of $35 per month, a six-hour day, a five-day week, a union check-weighman, and overtime pay.

Appealing mainly to black coal miners, the NMU launched active organizing campaigns in Pennsylvania, West Virginia, Ohio, and Illinois. In late 1931, following the crushing of a United Mine Workers of America strike in Bloody Harlan County, Kentucky, the NMU entered the area to organize coal miners. Its strategy involved enlisting miners, sending the leaders to Pittsburgh for indoctrination sessions, and bringing them back to Kentucky to organize more miners. The NMU also set up soup kitchens to feed hungry Kentucky miners and their families during the depression. A Kentucky coal miner who became prominent in NMU activities and nationally known as an organizer, composer, and singer of protest songs was Jim Garland of Bell County.

The NMU called a strike of Harlan County coal miners for 1 January 1932, but only 83 of the county's miners responded. The days of the NMU in Harlan County were numbered. The union also called strikes among miners in western Pennsylvania and eastern Ohio. Those strikes, which were accompanied by violence, were also crushed. By the end of 1931 and early 1932 the efforts of the NMU to organize coal miners collapsed. The era of the National Miners' Union was a short, violent one in the annals of U.S. labor history.

National Recovery Administration (NRA)

Established in 1933 by the National Industrial Recovery Act (NIRA) and headed by General Hugh S. Johnson, the National Recovery Administration (NRA) was an executive agency created to implement the codes of fair competition negotiated under the authority of NIRA. The purpose of the NRA was to limit unfair competition and calamitous overproduction and to provide better wages by limiting work hours. Initially the NRA was acclaimed nationwide as an instrument of recovery for both business and labor. Hundreds of codes were soon in effect, and the symbol of the NRA—the blue eagle—sprang up everywhere, even on the bare backs of women workers who wore sun dresses in an NRA parade in New York City.

While many codes of fair competition were negotiated, many were violated by employers. The National Labor Board, created to see that the codes were carried out, was soon inundated by complaints from workers. The board was powerless to enforce the codes. The NIRA also guaranteed workers the right of collective bargaining so they could form labor unions. Employers, in an effort to circumvent the law, formed company unions that the NRA recognized as legitimate associations for workers. Soon the NRA was jokingly dubbed the "National Run-around."

The NRA, caught in a maelstrom of ineptitude, was invalidated by the Supreme Court in 1935. For the most part, it was unsuccessful in stimulating the recovery of business and labor from the depression. In essence business and labor did not get moving again until the beginning of World War II.

National Right-To-Work Committee

A committee made up of American businessmen, the National Right-To-Work Committee during the 1970s vigorously opposed reform in the nation's labor laws. The American Federation of Labor and Congress of Industrial Organizations (AFL-CIO), while the Ninety-Fifth Congress was in session, attempted changes in the Wagner Act specifically to hasten the handling of "unfair labor practice cases and representation elections." Labor also advocated "increased penalties for employer violations of the law," the withholding of "federal contracts from willful violators," and giving "organizers an equal opportunity to address employees in representation elections." While these changes were considered minute and not a boon to organized labor, businessmen, both conservative and liberal, presented a united front against the reforms.

The defeat of labor law reform was a bitter one for organized labor, especially since it threw its support behind Democratic congressional and senatorial candidates and Democratic presidential candidate Jimmy Carter in the election of 1976. Certainly labor expected the passage of labor law reforms. What was considered a friendly Congress and a friendly White House refused, however, to legislate the changes labor wanted. Obviously the businessmen's coalition exerted greater influence on the Ninety-Fifth Congress than organized labor. As AFL-CIO President George Meany put it, the anti-labor stance of business was a "heavily financed, well orchestrated coalition between big business and right-wing extremists." Its aim—to defeat labor law reform. In that it succeeded well.

National Textile Workers Union (NTWU)

With strong ties to the communistic Trade Union Unity League (TUUL), the National Textile Workers Union (NTWU) competed with the United Textile Workers of America (UTWA) for unskilled immigrant labor in the Northeast's and Deep South's textile mills. Unable to maintain membership growth, the NTWU was finally absorbed by the UTWA in 1930.

Founded in New Bedford, Massachusetts, the NTWU, the first TUUL affiliate, called for higher wages, shorter hours, equal pay for equal work, and the aboli-

tion of child labor. Major organizing campaigns were conducted by the NTWU in the South. Its greatest success came in the Gastonia, North Carolina, Loray mill of the Manville-Jenckes Corporation. When the company repudiated union demands for a 40-hour week and an increased wage scale, a strike was called in April 1929. Of the 2,200 workers at the Gastonia operation, 1,700 walked out. The strike became violent as mill officials and local authorities moved against it. The brutality of the mill owners, however, aroused sympathy for the strikers.

The deck was stacked against the workers and the union, though. In a no-win scenario, several NTWU leaders were tried and convicted on charges of conspiracy to commit murder. The convictions undermined the brief success of the NTWU, causing the union to ultimately collapse in Dixie. Thereafter its chief haven was in New England.

With the NTWU's defeat in North Carolina, the Red International imposed a boring-from-within strategy in efforts to take over existing unions. The NTWU soon dissolved as its leaders urged workers to seek membership in the conservative American Federation of Labor.

See also Beal, Fred E.

National Trades' Union

Composed of General Trades' Unions members from New York, Philadelphia, and Boston, the National Trades' Union brought together workingmen to seek reform during the Jacksonian era. While the National Trades' Union was largely an economic organization, it did endorse reforms supported by Jacksonian Democrats. For example, it was opposed to the national bank because of its monopolistic practices.

One of the principal goals of the National Trades' Union was the ten-hour day. It also united workingmen in their struggle for improved working conditions. In many respects the National

Trades' Union of the 1830s was a fore-runner of the National Labor Union of the post–Civil War era.

Among the important leaders of the National Trades' Union was John Ferral of Philadelphia, whose crowning achievement came in his leadership of a ten-hour strike in that city. Another union official of prominence was Philadelphia's William English, a shoemaker. On more than one occasion his flaming oratory aroused workingmen to action. New England workingmen were best represented by Charles Douglas, who eminently addressed the problems of textile mill workers. Colorfully attired Seth Luther spoke eloquently and critically on behalf of women and children who relentlessly toiled for foremen who paid scant attention to their health, welfare, and safety.

Ferral, English, Douglas, and Luther were in a sense local leaders of the National Trades' Union who helped unite workers in a common cause and who gave voice to the concerns of labor in the Jacksonian era. Their steady leadership provided the base from which Ely Moore rose to become the first national president of the National Trades' Union in the 1830s.

National War Labor Board

Two war labor boards have been set up since the turn of the century. The first was created in April 1918 for the duration of World War I. The second was established by President Franklin Delano Roosevelt ten days after Japan bombed Pearl Harbor. The purposes of the two boards were similar.

The World War I board was made up of five presidentially appointed members. Its primary goal was to arbitrate all labor-management controversies that could not be settled through other channels. Generally labor and management agreed to a no-strike policy for the duration of the war. In return the Wilson administration agreed to support labor's

right to collective bargaining, honor all prewar agreements with respect either to open or union shops, enforce an eight-hour day wherever feasible, pay women equally for equal work, and recognize the desire of all workers for sufficient wages.

With the War Labor Board, many workers during the conflict enjoyed an eight-hour day. There were also few work stoppages, and when those occurred, the board strongly intervened. Wages for workers accelerated and trade unionism flourished. Following the November 1918 armistice, and with the end of the steadying influence of the War Labor Board, labor-management strife was renewed.

The War Labor Board of the World War II era was composed of 12 members equally representing labor, management, and the public sector. Its purpose was essentially the same as that of the World War I board. A no-strike agreement was pledged by both sides; in return union security was promised for union members, although there would be no closed- or union-shop scenario. While collective bargaining was also maintained, government oversight of wages and prices along with wartime inflation led some unions, most notably John L. Lewis's United Mine Workers of America (UMW), to call for wage hikes to keep pace with rising prices. From that union demand, the War Labor Board established the Little Steel formula, which implemented wage increases in accord with the rise of prices. That formula was used for the war's duration to arbitrate disputes arising over wages.

While strikes decreased during the war, there were two serious stoppages—a national coal strike and a railway strike. In the coal strike, the government seized mines twice before a settlement was reached that met most of the UMW's demands. In the railway strike, the president also ordered the seizure of railroads until an eleventh-hour accord, going well beyond the Little Steel formula, returned the railroads to their owners.

Despite these two serious strikes, the War Labor Board of World War II worked diligently to prevent disputes that might disrupt the war effort. Its successes far outweighed its failures, proving that labor, management, and the public sector could manage industrial relations and the economy during critical war years. In fact, both war labor boards operated successfully to keep industrial strife from seriously damaging the war efforts.

Negro American Labor Council (NALC)

Capably led by Brotherhood of Sleeping Car Porters executive Asa Philip Randolph, the Negro American Labor Council (NALC) in the 1960s worked to end discrimination in labor, particularly in the American Federation of Labor and Congress of Industrial Organizations (AFL-CIO) ranks. The NALC pressured the AFL-CIO to increase employment opportunities for African American workers and to encourage their entry into trades controlled by AFL-CIO affiliates. Recognizing that considerable progress had been made in both areas, the NALC criticized the AFL-CIO for not moving rapidly to curtail discrimination.

In response to Randolph's impassioned plea, the AFL-CIO, while endorsing federal civil right legislation in the 1960s, criticized the black labor leader for creating a wedge between labor and the African American community. AFL-CIO leaders also lambasted Randolph for discriminating against white workers in the Brotherhood of Sleeping Car Porters. The crisis eased in 1961 following a meeting between AFL-CIO chief George Meany, Randolph, and 18 delegates from NALC.

From 1962 to 1965, an uneasy truce existed between the NALC and the AFL-CIO. The NALC joined the Southern Christian Leadership Conference, the Congress of Racial Equality, the Student Non-Violent Coordinating Committee, and the National Association for the Advancement of Colored People for the civil rights march on Washington in 1963. The demonstration, designed to pressure President John F. Kennedy to increase employment opportunities for African Americans, end segregation in unemployment, and support a civil rights bill, was condemned by Meany, who opposed direct political action. CIO head Walter Reuther supported the march, in which one-fourth of the demonstrators were union members.

In 1964 and 1965 the NALC also endorsed civil rights marches in Selma and Montgomery, Alabama, and in Chicago, Illinois. Randolph finally softened his criticism of the AFL-CIO as civil rights measures were enacted and as African American workers made progress. In 1966 he resigned as NALC president.

For over half a decade Asa Philip Randolph and the NALC agitated for freedom and increased economic opportunities for African American workers. He and his council succeeded in attaining both goals.

The New Republic

Similar to *The Nation*, *The New Republic*, edited by renowned American journalist Malcolm Cowley, was a vehicle for liberal, leftist correspondents in the 1930s. Its columns contained article after article befriending the working class. Its editorials championed the cause of employees against employers. Cowley, who watched the Soviet experience in the years following the Russian Revolution, apparently grew increasingly enamored with the Soviet system and finally became a card-carrying Communist Party member just before World War II.

John Dos Passos also wrote regularly for *The New Republic*. Among the articles that appeared in the publication were "I Get Shot" and "Working under the Gun," by Dos Passos; "Kentucky Coal

Town," by Cowley; and "Toothpicks," Theodore Dreiser's account of his trials and tribulations in the Kentucky coal country in 1931 and 1932.

The New Republic today remains an extremely liberal journal with a strong leftist persuasion.

New York Central Railroad v. White (U.S., 1917)

In New York the state legislature enacted a worker's compensation law in 1914. New York was one of about 30 states to pass such a measure during the Progressive Era. A worker's compensation statute placed liability for an employee's injury at the workplace on the employer. In other words, the employer, if negligibility was ascertained, was responsible for a worker's hospital and medical costs as well as time lost from work because of an injury suffered on the job. Never before had an employer been accountable for a worker's mishap.

The New York law was challenged in the courts in *New York Central Railroad v. White*. In 1917 the U.S. Supreme Court unanimously upheld the New York worker's compensation law, which, in addition to providing compensation for accidental injury and/or death of a worker, included a no-fault clause. The court's decision was a clear victory for New York workers.

See also Worker's Compensation Laws.

New York Workingmen's Party

The New York Workingmen's party was one of several similar organizations conceived during the Jacksonian era. It was born on 23 April 1829 when New York workingmen of various trades came together in support of the ten-hour day. Nearly 6,000 people attended the party's first convention, which drafted a document setting forth the party's platform. The platform thoroughly criticized the status quo and called for the working class to elect candidates responsive to the goals of the workers.

In its formative stages the party was led by machinist Thomas Skidmore. Skidmore, in addition to supporting the ten-hour day, favored a national economy that guaranteed workers a comfortable life-style. In essence, Skidmore believed in the sort of communism that nineteenth-century Shakers embraced—no private ownership of property.

Other important party leaders were George Henry Evans, a printer, and two people of socialist persuasion—Robert Dale Owen of New Harmony, Indiana, communal fame and the famous Frances (Fanny) Wright of the Nashoba, Tennessee, colonization experiment. Evans followed in the footsteps of Skidmore. He published the *Working Man's Advocate*, which stated that "all children are entitled to equal education; all adults to equal property; and all mankind, to equal privileges."

While both Skidmore and Evans supported a brand of socialism, communitarianism, and perhaps communism, Owen and Wright went further—Owen with his advocacy of nationalized education and Wright with her opposition to the existing social order based on social inequity. In essence both Owen and Wright desired to replace the capitalistic system with a socialistic government.

Conservatives were disturbed by the agenda of the Workingmen's Party. In the election of 1829 they fielded a slate of candidates to oppose the radicals. Their fears were short-lived, however, as the Workingmen's Party slate elected only one candidate to the assembly.

As time passed, internal discord and rivalry among the party's leaders caused rifts that led to its eventual collapse. While it offered only a temporary panacea to the ills of the working class, the party was a harbinger of things to come in the post–Civil War years, with the formation of the Greenback-Labor Party, the People's Party, the Farmer-

Labor Party, and Labor's Non-Partisan League.

Norris-LaGuardia Act (1932)

Passed in 1932 during the final days of the Hoover administration, the Norris-LaGuardia Act, cosponsored by Republican Senator George W. Norris (the "fighting liberal" from Nebraska) and Democratic Congressman Fiorello LaGuardia of New York, the Norris-LaGuardia Act was the beginning of the emancipation of the working class.

The Norris-LaGuardia Act contained two major provisions: it significantly limited the use of injunctions in labor disputes, and it outlawed the use of yellow-dog contracts. Basically, injunctions could be issued and enforced only in cases of irreparable damage to company property for which there was no recourse in the courts.

In the late 1930s and early 1940s the Supreme Court delivered three opinions upholding the Norris-LaGuardia Act.

The Court in the 1938 case of *Lauf v. Shinner and Co.* simply declared the law constitutional. The same year the Court came to a similar conclusion in *New Negro Alliance Co. v. Sanitary Grocery Co.* Three years later, in *United States v. Hutcheson*, the Supreme Court decided that the Norris-LaGuardia Act largely exempted labor unions from prosecution as conspiracies to restrain trade in violation of the 1890 Sherman Anti-Trust Act. The Norris-LaGuardia Act closed the breach left by the Clayton Anti-Trust Act of 1914.

Employers ignored and evaded the Norris-LaGuardia Act until forced into compliance by the federal government. Pearl Bassham, a Kentucky coal operator, told the La Follette Civil Liberties Committee in 1937 that he had never heard of the law. The Roosevelt Court upheld the Norris-LaGuardia Act, and the Roosevelt administration enforced the act to bring relief to thousands of American workers and labor unions.

See also Injunctions; Yellow-Dog Contracts.

Olney, Richard (1835–1917)

Richard Olney was U.S. attorney general from 1893 to 1895 in the Grover Cleveland administration. As attorney general, he was procorporate and pro-injunction. During the Pullman Strike of 1894, Olney, friend of the railroads, ordered 3,400 men into Chicago, where they were deputized and paid by railroad executives to ensure the operation of the trains. When violence erupted between the deputies and the strikers, the railroad owners notified Cleveland that the situation had gotten out of hand, prompting him to dispatch federal troops to break the strike.

Olney also practiced government by injunction during the Pullman Strike. As the dispute continued and violence flourished, Olney requested federal Judge Peter J. Grosscup to issue a blanket injunction against the strikers and the American Railway Union. In fact the entire power of the federal government was hurled against the railway workers. Olney's government by injunction ended the Pullman Strike when its leader, Eugene V. Debs, was shuttled off to jail for violation of the court order. The railroads triumphed and labor was trounced. Olney's use of the injunction was in tune with the anti-labor mindset of the system in the late nineteenth century.

O'Neal, Frederick (1905–1992)

A Mississippian by birth, Frederick O'Neal was active in the entertainment arena, especially television and motion pictures, as both an actor and director. He was also a visiting professor at the campuses of Clark College and Southern Illinois University. In the 1960s and 1970s, O'Neal headed the Actor's Equity Association, and later guided the Associated Actors and Artists of America (AAAA).

In the field of labor relations, in addition to his presidency of AAAA, O'Neal chaired the AFL-CIO Civil Rights Committee. He was vice-president of the Catholic Actors' Guild and served on the advisory council of Industrial and Labor Relations of Cornell University.

Educated in New York City, O'Neal was active in African-American theater circles in both the United States and England. He received many honors and awards, including honorary doctorates from Lincoln University, Tougaloo College in Mississippi, and New York's St. John's University. In 1979 the National Association for the Advancement of Colored People tapped O'Neal as its man of the year. O'Neal, a union member for half a century, was an ardent supporter of unions and the labor movement. At the same time he decried the ignorance about labor and the labor movement manifested by the general public. To O'Neal the strength of the United States could be found in the strength of its labor unions.

The AAAA, popularly called the "4 A's," is an umbrella agency in the entertainment field. Belonging to AAAA are nine independent national unions, among them the Actor's Equity Association, the American Federation of Television and Radio Artists, and the Screen Actors Guild. The AAAA has a council made up of officials from the nine unions. In sharp contrast to other labor unions, the AAAA's officials receive no salaries.

Open Shop

The open shop refers to a workplace where hiring is not based on union membership. Workers do not have to belong to a union; they have freedom of choice with regard to union affiliation.

Early in the twentieth century the National Association of Manufacturers endorsed the open shop. Likewise most American employers operated their businesses as an open shop. Following World War I, the American Plan, which embraced the open shop, was accepted and encouraged by the National Association of Manufacturers (NAM) and big business in general. During the days of the open shop, union membership was almost nonexistent.

It was not until the New Deal era that the federal government stepped in to assure workers the option of union membership. The passage of the National Labor Relations Act in 1935 made union membership a condition of employment. Employers had to bargain with a union, and if a majority of workers voted for the union, a workplace made the transition from an open to a closed shop. In the 1930s the closed shop replaced the open shop as union membership skyrocketed.

During the Truman administration, Congress enacted the 1947 Taft-Hartley Act, which was passed over "Give 'em Hell" Harry's veto. Section 14b of that law applied a right-to-work principle, giving workers the option of choosing or rejecting union membership. Section 14b, in effect, ended the closed shop, replacing it with a union shop where today's workers can but are not required to join a union. Organized labor opposed and still opposes Section 14b, but in a number of states, particularly Southern states, Section 14b is both accepted and used.

From open shop to closed shop to union shop, the American worker again has freedom of choice when it comes to the union.

See also Closed Shop.

Operation Dixie

With the end of World War II, the Congress of Industrial Organizations (CIO) launched an intensive campaign to organize blue-collar workers in the South. Southern unionization efforts by CIO affiliates were largely successful in coal mining regions. In other industries, notably textile, automobile, and tobacco plants, organizational attempts were mostly unsuccessful. For the most part Southern workers showed little inclination to join unions. Outside the South, while about 54 percent of the blue-collar class belonged to a union, in Dixie that number was only about 30 percent. Beyond the South approximately 44 percent of black workers were unionists, but in the South only 12 percent of black employees were unionized.

To boost its union membership among Southern industrial workers and to end discrimination in the workplace, the CIO initiated an 11-million-dollar drive shortly after World War II ended. Organizers infiltrated the South to sign up workers, especially in the textile mills. Following a concentrated effort of more than five years, the CIO had few new members to show for its efforts. Postwar prosperity and inflation hampered CIO strategy.

A few scattered unions—the United Mine Workers of America, Textile Workers Union of America, Teamsters, and Longshoremen—could boast of thousands of union members in the South by the early 1950s. Unionism among the region's textile workers actually declined during the same period.

Operation Dixie, then, was largely a failure in the South. By 1952, for example, the CIO could count only 500,000 union members compared to the American Federation of Labor's 2 million. Of approximately 9.3 million Southern blue-collar employees, only about 2.7 million or one-fourth were card-carrying, dues-paying unionists. Of that number only about 700,000 black workers had enrolled in a union.

The death knell for the CIO's Operation Dixie was the 1947 Taft-Hartley Act with its anti-union Section 14b. A number of states became right-to-work states, laying Operation Dixie to perpetual rest.

Today the South remains largely anti-union territory. In some instances, announced union elections are mysteriously postponed for an indefinite period. In others, plants close and vacate a town rather than accede to a union. Some employers have adopted the practice of sending work abroad to take advantage of cheap, nonunion labor. These owner tactics make the South of the 1990s a union desert.

See also Congress of Industrial Organizations; Taft-Hartley Act.

Order of Railway Conductors and Brakemen (ORC)

In Amboy, Illinois, in 1868 conductors on the Illinois Central Railroad met to form the Conductors Union. That same year conductors on the Chicago, Burlington, and Quincy Railroad convened in Galesburg, Illinois, to establish Division Two of the Conductors Union. The two bodies merged into the Order of Railway Conductors and Brakemen (ORC). Other conductors formed a union called the Brotherhood of Railway Conductors (BRC).

The ORC at first was a temperate and benevolent society, emphasizing fraternalistic and ritualistic activities. It opposed strikes and threatened to expel strikers. Although it was antistrike, the ORC encountered hostility from the railroad barons. Other railway brotherhoods regarded ORC members as strikebreakers. In 1885 the ORC changed gears as it began to assist members in resolving disputes with railroad managers. While the new ORC policy did not meet with the approval of all conductors, the union grew. The BRC merged into the ORC in 1890, expanding the organization's membership to 48,000 conductors by World War I. The ORC successfully lobbied for the passage of the Adamson Act during the Wilson administration.

Since World War II, conductors, brakemen, trainmen, switchmen, firemen, and enginemen have bonded to create the United Transportation Union (UTU).

O'Reilly, Lenora

Lenora O'Reilly was an employee in the New York City garment industry in the first decade of the twentieth century. She was also a union member and organizer in the aftermath of the tragic 1911 Triangle Shirtwaist fire in which 146 garment workers were killed. Lenora O'Reilly described in graphic terms the horrendous conditions in factories in the city's garment district. Her explicit revelations were made before a New York factory investigative commission, led by Alfred E. Smith and Robert F. Wagner, Sr.

In her testimony, O'Reilly spoke of long hours, menial wages, and astonishing squalor. Wages, for example, ranged from $5 to $10 a week for different jobs. In summer factories were unbearably hot; in winter they were bone-chilling cold. Cardboard was used in place of broken window panes. Filthy toilets, water used for both washing and drinking, dirty unswept floors, dark stairwells, and a lack of fire escapes were common in all the factories.

O'Reilly's explicit testimony before the New York investigative panel led to efforts by both Smith and Wagner to correct subhuman conditions in the state's factory system. As a result, legislation to make factories more safe and clean for women and children made the state of New York a pacesetter in labor reform in the second decade of the twentieth century.

O'Reilly summoned working women to the union standard as a viable means of correcting horrible conditions in the garment district. Because of her efforts among the garment workers, Lenora O'Reilly was a significant women's labor leader of her era.

See also Triangle Shirtwaist Fire.

Parsons, Albert Ross (1848–1887)

A native of Montgomery, Alabama, Albert Parsons, after serving in the Confederate army during the Civil War, went to Texas for a brief time. In 1871 he moved to Chicago to work as a printer. In the windy city, Parsons joined the International Typographical Union (ITU), helped organize the Knights of Labor, and enrolled in the Socialist Party. After running unsuccessfully for public office in Cook County, Parsons was involved in the 1877 nationwide railroad strike as a socialist orator-agitator. He also was chosen secretary of Chicago's Eight-Hour League.

In 1881 Parsons joined the Anarchist Black International. As editor of the *Alarm*, he was one of the leaders of the 1886 strike against McCormick's Harvester operation in support of an eight-hour day. While he was out of the city when the *Alarm* called for the mass demonstration at Haymarket Square on 4 May 1886 to protest the deaths of four strikers the previous day, Parsons was arrested in connection with the murder of seven policemen. He was indicted, tried, and convicted along with several other anarchists. Referred to as "the most famous of the anarcho-communists," Parsons was hanged after his sentence was affirmed by the Illinois supreme court.

Pass, Albert Edward (1921–)

A hard-core United Mine Workers of America (UMW) official and a staunch supporter of UMW President William Anthony "Tony" Boyle, Albert Pass in 1969 was a member of the union's International Executive Board and secretary-treasurer of UMW District 19, which included the twin Kentucky coal counties of Bell and Harlan. Although William Turnblazer, Jr., was District 19 president, Pass governed the region in dictatorlike fashion.

At the 1964 UMW convention in Miami Beach, Pass, thoroughly devoted to Boyle, wore a white hard hat as he and his colleagues ruled the assembly in an iron-fisted manner. At that gathering, Pass saw that microphones were cut off when UMW dissidents attempted to speak from the convention floor. At other times a signal was given to the band to strike up and drown out anti-Boyle unionists. In short, the real power in District 19 rested with Albert Pass.

In 1969 Tony Boyle ran for another term as UMW president. Because of his lack of concern for mine safety and his arbitrary leadership, UMW board member Joseph "Jock" Yablonski, from Pennsylvania's District 5, decided to oppose Boyle. Albert Pass flew to Washington, he and Boyle huddled in UMW headquarters, and the decision was made to assassinate Yablonski. The mastermind behind the plot—Albert Pass.

Pass returned to District 19 headquarters in Middlesboro, Kentucky, and conferred with William Jackson Prater, District 19 field representative. Prater contacted Silous Huddleston, a retired miner and UMW pensioner, to put the assassination plot into motion. Huddleston had a daughter, Annette, who lived in Cleveland, Ohio, and was married to an erstwhile house painter, Paul Gilly. Huddleston talked Annette into enlisting Paul, who in turn solicited two other Cleveland men, both of whom had criminal backgrounds, to kill Yablonski. Gilly, Claude Vealey, and James Charles Phillips became the hunters, Yablonski the hunted. Phillips later took himself out of the picture and was replaced by Aubran "Buddy" Martin.

A fund amounting to nearly $20,000 was raised in District 19 to pay the killers. Twenty-three miners, mostly retired pensioners, were paid to organize in District 19. Since they did no organizing because there was none to do, the pensioners returned the money to Pass, who was to use it to pay Gilly, Vealey, and Martin after they had murdered Yablonski. Edith Roark, a Middlesboro resident and UMW employee, wrote the checks on orders from Pass without realizing how the money was to be spent.

On New Year's Eve, 1969, the three killers slipped into Yablonski's darkened home in Clarksville, Pennsylvania, and shot to death in cold blood Jock Yablonski, his wife Margaret, and their daughter Charlotte.

Three years later, in the summer of 1973, the ever-smiling Albert Pass was tried, convicted, and sentenced to three consecutive life terms as the director of the murder scheme. He was led out of the courtroom in Erie, Pennsylvania, to begin serving the sentences. As he departed in the company of Pennsylvania lawmen, the smile had vanished from the countenance of Albert Pass.

Paterson Silk Strike (1913)

After the Lawrence, Massachusetts, textile strike, the second most important strike on the East Coast involving the Industrial Workers of the World (IWW) was the Paterson, New Jersey, Silk Strike of 1913. IWW leaders who directly participated in the dispute included Big Bill Haywood and Joseph J. Ettor. The strike, which lasted for five bitter months, was marked by an unusual amount of violence. Strikers were arrested and beaten. Picket lines were summarily breached by authorities, who herded scores of workers into local jails.

John Reed, a Harvard graduate who at age 24 was a radical and revolutionary (he was later buried in the Kremlin), described the strike in *Ten Days That Shook the World*. He was so impressed by strikers who sang as they were marched off to jail that he helped publicize the strike across the country by putting on a performance at New York's Madison Square Garden.

In the end, money ran out, and as it did the IWW was forced to concede. While the IWW won an impressive victory at Lawrence, the union suffered a staggering defeat at Paterson. To be sure, the IWW continued for a few more years, but it never fully recovered from the Paterson Silk Strike.

See also Industrial Workers of the World.

People v. Fisher (New York, 1835)

In New York State a group of journeymen shoemakers were sued for conspiracy to raise wages, which in effect, according to their employers, restrained commerce.

The New York Supreme Court ruled in favor of the company. The decision was both anti-labor and anti-union. It was a harbinger of things to come, since the U.S. Supreme Court in the late nineteenth and twentieth centuries decided that strikes and labor unions were conspiracies that restrained interstate commerce in violation of the 1890 Sherman Anti-Trust Act.

People's Party

The People's Party was also called the Populist Party. Its members were known as "Popocrats," "Hicks," "Hayseeds," and "Wild-eyed Radicals." Founded in 1892 in Omaha, Nebraska, the party evolved out of the free-silver movement and the farm alliances of the 1880s. Basically, it was a political movement that catered to the farmers and their goals, yet it appealed to the working class as well.

In its first national convention the party drafted the Omaha Platform. While many of the platform's planks addressed farm issues, there were several that appealed to workers. For example,

Leaders of the Industrial Workers of the World, including Elizabeth Gurley Flynn, center, Carl Tesco, and William Hayward, came to Paterson, New Jersey, to support striking silk workers.

the platform called for an eight-hour day, immigration quotas, the abolition of anti-labor injunctions, and the end of the use of Pinkertons in labor disputes.

The People's Party platform gained several notable supporters from the ranks of organized labor. The Knights of Labor identified with the goals of the party. Both Henry George, who proposed the single tax, and Edward Bellamy, socialist author of *Looking Backward*, favored the Populist program. Labor leader Eugene V. Debs also endorsed the party's proposals. The American Federation of Labor, led by Samuel Gompers, withheld its assent.

Although the People's Party attracted many workers and several important labor leaders, it failed to impact the political process in the 1890s. Most of the pro-labor planks in the Omaha Platform were not enacted into law at that time. In the twentieth century, however, under both Republican and Democratic administrations, much of the platform, especially those items that labor embraced,

became the law of the land. By the 1930s Populism had gone full circle with the New Deal.

The real impact of the People's Party, according to historian Richard Hofstadter, was that it was the first political organization in the United States to call attention to the fact that the federal government had a responsibility to promote the general welfare of all the people.

Perkins, Frances (1882–1965)

Frances Perkins, a native of Massachusetts, was born in Boston, grew up in Worcester, and graduated from Mount Holyoke College. After her graduation, she forsook her home state for the Midwest and Chicago, where she joined Jane Addams as a social worker and reformer. Following a brief sojourn in Philadelphia, where she embraced the study of economics, Perkins, at age 28, relocated in New York State, where she became active in consumer affairs as an official and a lobbyist. It was in New York that she formed an acquaintance with powerful Tammany Hall politicians and with Al Smith and Robert Wagner. In the social work arena, Perkins became a crusader. From 1910 to the early 1930s she was involved in a variety of state agencies that oversaw industry and the New York factory system. She was named state industrial commissioner by Governor Franklin D. Roosevelt.

In 1933, when Roosevelt was elected president of the United States, he blazed a new trail by naming Frances Perkins secretary of labor, the first female cabinet member in U.S. history. Perkins headed the Labor Department during Roosevelt's three terms as president.

During her 12-year tenure, Frances Perkins became known as Madam Secretary. As secretary of labor she was less interested in unions and the unionization of workers than in trying to improve conditions of labor and the quality of life for American workers. She was also vitally concerned about some sort of provision for workers upon retirement. Nonetheless, Perkins was involved in labor's civil war, and her department acted as mediator and conciliator in the strife between labor and management in the 1930s and 1940s. Perkins also realized the fulfillment of one of her goals for workers with the passage of the Social Security Act of 1935. Since two of her principal desires were minimum wages and maximum hours for laborers, the Fair Labor Standards Act of 1938 was of abiding satisfaction to her.

Frances Perkins was an outstanding secretary of labor. She pioneered many gains for workers, setting a standard for her successors in the Department of Labor. An appropriate tribute to Perkins came early in Roosevelt's first term when she became a member of what was known as the president's Inner Cabinet, along with New Dealers Harold Ickes, Henry Wallace, Harry Hopkins, Henry Morgenthau, and Hugh Johnson.

Phillips, Wendell (1811–1884)

Wendell Phillips, a lawyer and Boston aristocrat, was an ardent antislavery zealot before the Civil War. He criticized the Constitution because he believed it supported slavery. Phillips was also antichurch because to him it upheld the peculiar institution.

With the end of the Civil War, Phillips assumed the presidency of the American Anti-Slavery Society. He used his position to campaign for women's rights and civil rights for freed men.

As slavery ended, Phillips began an attack on the ills of the country's industrial empire. An outstanding speaker, he criticized wage slavery and collaborated with union workers in support of a ten-hour day and then an eight-hour day. Phillips spoke out in favor of equal pay for equal work for women as well as for laws to control and end monopolies.

The true measure of the wellborn Phillips is that he was opposed to slavery. He first was against African slavery, then crusaded against wage slavery. In short, Wendell Phillips favored freedom for all persons irrespective of color, class, or economic status.

Picketing

Picketing refers to a practice adopted by American workers in a strike. Once a strike is called and workers leave their jobs, strikers set up a picket line. When the picket line is in place, striking employees congregate in front of a shop, factory, or business with banners or placards, marching up and down and citing the establishment as unfair to organized labor and the union. Picketing also occurs at the gate or entrance to a place of employment.

With the picket line intact workers are discouraged from crossing it to enter a workplace. If an employee tries to violate the picket line, more often than not that worker is forcibly restrained and prevented from doing so.

In years past, infringement upon the picket line usually led to a violent altercations in which blows were exchanged and shots fired. On many occasions workers on the picket line were armed. In mining areas roving bands of pickets often descended on the drift mouth of the mine to discourage workers. At first the courts denied that picketing was a form of free expression protected by the First Amendment. Later, especially during the World War II era, the courts did an about-face and began upholding picketing as lawful.

Today picketing is acceptable as long as workers who desire to work are not coerced and as long as irreparable injury to employers and their property is not involved.

See also American Steel Foundries v. Tri-City Central Trade Council.

Pinkerton Detectives

Pinkerton detectives were supplied to U.S. corporations by the Allan Pinkerton Detective Agency, established in Chicago before the Civil War. During that conflict the Pinkerton agency furnished detectives who were used for intelligence gathering by the U.S. Army. After the war their experience as spies was translated into spying on American workers for business tycoons.

From the 1870s to at least the World War II era, Pinkerton detectives were extensively employed by big business. Of course they were used as guards or security, but that service was quickly transformed into spying and thuggery. Pinkerton agent James McParlan was a spy in the eastern Pennsylvania coal region during the Molly Maguire episode. Three hundred Pinkerton detectives were employed against strikers at Andrew Carnegie's Homestead, Pennsylvania, operation in 1892.

The La Follette Civil Liberties Committee, during its probe of business violations against organized labor in the 1930s, learned that a blue book of corporations was using Pinkerton detectives as labor spies, thugs, guards, and strikebreakers. The committee's findings led to federal intervention on behalf of labor and labor unions. Subsequent to federal involvement, the use of Pinkerton detectives in labor disputes diminished. Presently Pinkertons are used to provide security in the private sector.

Populist Party
See People's Party.

Portal-to-Portal Pay

The United Mine Workers of America (UMW), through their president, John L. Lewis, insisted upon what was known as portal-to-portal pay—that is, payment for the time miners spent making their way from the mine's drift mouth, or opening, to their place of work underground. While some coal miners had to go only a few hundred yards to work, others had to journey several miles. The union believed that the men should be compensated for actual work as well as for the time, be it minutes or hours, spent going to and from their assigned workplace. When Lewis negotiated contracts for the coal miners during World War II, he demanded both an increase in wages and portal-to-portal pay. When the UMW president called for a work stoppage during wartime, which prompted FDR to seize the mines, Lewis was successful in getting portal-to-portal pay included in the contract with the coal operators.

Portal-to-portal pay later involved compensation for time miners spent travelling from their homes to the mine, if they lived outside the company town. In several instances some coal miners drove 25 to 50 miles to and from the mine. The union wanted compensation for that travelling time.

Porter, Robert G.

A dedicated unionist most of his life, Robert G. Porter was a schoolteacher in East St. Louis, Illinois, where he helped establish the East St. Louis Teachers Union. As treasurer of the local union, Porter was instrumental in setting up one of the nation's first union elections for teachers.

Following his involvement in the affairs of the East St. Louis local, Porter was elected secretary-treasurer of the American Federation of Teachers (AFT), a position he has held since 1963. He is also an active member of the AFL-CIO's Committee on Political Education (COPE) and has attended several AFL-CIO conventions as a delegate from the AFT. Porter, who makes no apologies for a teacher's union and for strikes by teachers, is deeply concerned about the protection of academic freedom through the AFT's defense committee, of which he is a member.

Today Porter's AFT has around 665,000 members, consisting of both public schoolteachers and college and university professors. The AFT has also strenuously opposed school segregation and strongly favored equal pay for women teachers. Presently the AFT is the strongest teacher's union in the United States.

Powderly, Terence V. (1849–1924)

A native of Carbondale, Pennsylvania, Terence Powderly attended school until he reached age 13, when he dropped out to work on the railroad. At age 17 he became a machinist's apprentice for about a decade. His first contact with a labor organization came when he joined the machinists' and blacksmiths' union in 1871. For three years he worked as a labor organizer in western Pennsylvania.

Powderly's career with the Noble and Holy Order of the Knights of Labor (Knights of Labor) began in 1876 when he was initiated into that union. His course charted, he was affiliated with the Knights of Labor for the next 17 years. Meanwhile, as a candidate on the Greenback-Labor Party ticket, he served three two-year terms as mayor of Scranton, Pennsylvania. When his presidency of the Knights of Labor ended, he was admitted to the Pennsylvania bar. In the latter stages of his life, he joined the Republican Party, supporting William McKinley for president in 1896. From 1897 to 1902 he was U.S. commissioner general of immigration. Following that, he became somewhat of a fixture in the U.S. Department of Labor.

As grand master workman of the Knights of Labor, Powderly favored industrial unionism and opposed craft and trade unionism. Under his tutelage the Knights of Labor signed up approximately 750,000 workers nationwide. The Knights of Labor had no racial or sexual barriers and admitted all kinds of laborers, including Texas cowboys. Although opposed to militancy, preferring instead mediation and conciliation, the Knights of Labor, under Powderly's direction, won several major strikes, including one strike against Jay Gould's Western railroad empire.

Powderly was not the prototype labor leader. Instead he was well dressed, well mannered, prim, proper, and courteous. He was not a social mixer, did not drink, and did not go where the boys and girls were. On one occasion, he remarked: "I will talk at no picnics. When I speak on the labor question I want the individual attention of my hearers and I want that attention for at least two hours, and in that two hours I can only epitomize. At a picnic where . . . the girls as well as the boys swill beer I cannot talk at all. . . . If it comes to my ears that I am advertised to speak at picnics I will prefer charges against the offenders for holding the executive head of the Order up to ridicule."

A tireless worker and an able, efficient organizer, Powderly, in the 1870s, built the Knights of Labor into an effective labor union. Ironically, while he disdained upheaval and violence, the union he led so successfully was embroiled in a number of violent labor disorders. The fact remains that Powderly's Knights of Labor, which died before he did, heralded the successful industrial unionism epitomized by the Congress of Industrial Organizations in the twentieth century.

See also Knights of Labor.

Presser, Jackie (1927–1988)

From the Buckeye State of Ohio, Jackie Presser, son of Teamster official Bill Presser, in 1983 rose to the presidency of one of the nation's most powerful and most corrupt labor unions, the Teamsters. A huge man and a notorious womanizer, Presser was regarded as a clown by many Teamster stalwarts.

As a labor leader, Presser continued the Teamsters in the mold of corruption it had known under Jimmy Hoffa. Shortly before his death, he faced indictment on federal counts of racketeering and embezzlement. Following his death in 1988, the Teamsters, in a sudden switch, elected Ron Carey as president.

Presser, in stark contrast to his peers in the labor movement, supported Ronald Reagan for president and George Bush for vice-president, and he was seen in public with both.

Like some of his predecessors, Presser was closely linked to the mafia. Unlike those who came before him he was an informant for the Federal Bureau of Investigation. Fortunately for him neither learned about his relationship with the other. Because he was an informer, Presser was devoid of all personal propriety and honor. He intensely disliked the Hoffa system, yet as Teamster president, Presser did nothing to stem the tidal wave of chicanery that had engulfed his organization.

The producers of the HBO movie *Teamster Boss: The Jackie Presser Story* conclude that the larger-than-life Presser was by no means a hero. Abby Mann, who has *Judgment at Nuremburg* to his credit, and John Kemeny, who produced

The Josephine Baker Story, both conclude that Jackie Presser was a villain and a thug.

Primary Boycott

As early as the late eighteenth century, employees utilized primary boycotts against employers. When an employer refused to grant a wage increase, for example, his business was targeted by a boycott; that is, workers refused to work, set up a picket line, and discouraged other workers from applying for a job at the boycotted workplace.

See also Secondary Boycott.

Professional Air Traffic Controllers Organization (PATCO)

The Professional Air Traffic Controllers Organization (PATCO) was a union composed of federal workers who oversaw takeoffs and landings at airports from coast to coast. Under normal circumstances federal employees do not strike against the federal government. That pattern changed, however, in the summer of 1981 when air controllers, because the government was unresponsive to their demands, walked off the job, leaving the nation's airports in a state of anxious uncertainty.

President Ronald Reagan, the only president who has been a union member (he was one-time president of the Screen Actors Guild), displayed an anti-labor stance by taking steps to abort the strike. Chastening the strikers verbally, the administration branded the work stoppage illegal and fired the controllers. Several PATCO leaders were arrested and jailed. The president's strong action dealt PATCO a death blow and demonstrated the general anti-union persuasion of the Reagan administration.

While PATCO was a somewhat fragile organization and not a close ally to the armies of labor, its defeat characterized a diminishing solidarity in the American labor movement. Equally disturbing to labor activists was the enthusiastic support that the public and labor's rank and file gave President Reagan in the PATCO dispute.

The great irony of the conflict was that a former union official, the president, used his office to break a strike and destroy a union. The president's action in the PATCO controversy was in line with what appeared to be a strict anti-labor stance typified by his appointment of businessman Raymond Donovan as secretary of labor in his first presidential cabinet.

Pullman, George (1831–1897)

George Pullman was an American tycoon who, shortly after the Civil War, introduced the Pullman sleeping car on U.S. railroads. In 1867, at age 36, he established the famous Pullman Palace Car Company, which designed and built customized private railroad cars for the nation's business leaders.

Near Chicago, Pullman built a company town, named Pullman, for his employees. In comparison to some company towns, Pullman, Illinois, was an upscale community: employees lived in brick dwellings surrounded by flower beds and shaded green lawns, all depicting a park-like scenario. Bubbling water fountains and shops of all types graced the town.

Pullman workers paid Pullman for the right to live in one of his houses. They also paid exorbitant prices for water, gas, groceries purchased in the company store, and garbage pickup. Industrialist Mark Hanna, in commenting on Pullman's feudalistic town, exclaimed on one occasion: "Oh, Hell! Go and live in Pullman and find out how much Pullman gets selling city water and gas 10 percent higher to those poor fools!" Once an employee received a check for 2 cents, which he promptly framed.

Pullman ran his town like a feudal manor. The workers were serfs and he was lord, strictly controlling and supervising them. In 1894, with an economic panic taking hold of the land, Pullman drastically slashed wages while rents and prices remained constant. That action caused the Pullman Strike of 1894.

George Pullman believed he was doing what was best for his workers. He looked out for them, supplied all their needs, took care of them; his system was regarded as benevolent paternalism. He was an anti-union boss who resisted all attempts of intervention into his relationship with his employees. To some he was a captain of industry, an industrial statesman. To others, he was a robber baron because he exploited his employees and denied them human dignity and quality of life. Pullman's system, however, was in tune with that practiced by many other corporate executives in the late nineteenth and twentieth centuries—build a company town, control the workers, and keep out the union. No matter how fine a company town was, one important ingredient was missing in all of them, including Pullman: freedom.

See also Pullman Strike.

Pullman Strike (1894)

In 1894 George Pullman cut workers' wages 25 to 40 percent. At the same time he did not reduce rental rates or prices in the company store. Pullman employees quit in protest. The strike lasted for about a month—21 June to 20 July 1894. The American Railway Union (ARU), led by Eugene Victor Debs, supported the strike by boycotting Pullman cars. In a little over a week, rail traffic moving in and out of the railroad hub of Chicago ground to a halt. Special deputies were dispatched to get the trains moving again. Violence erupted, and railroad owners went over Governor John Peter Altgeld's head to ask President Grover Cleveland for U.S. Army troops. With troops on the scene to quell the violence and to see that the mail and commerce got through, and with the issuance of a federal injunction against the ARU and the Pullman workers, the strike was broken. ARU leader Debs was hustled off to jail in Woodstock, Illinois.

The injunction enforced by federal troops brought a resounding defeat to labor. American workers did not get relief from government by injunction until the 1930s.

See also Pullman, George.

Pure and Simple Unionism

Pure and simple unionism referred to the class-consciousness of labor postulated by American Federation of Labor chief Samuel Gompers. To Gompers it was pure, it was simple: the American worker must be above all absolutely loyal to organized labor, to a labor union. The union and the labor movement must be first so the good of the workers might be advanced. Union members had to put the union ahead of all else—including their families. They must swear complete and unreserved loyalty to the union, and they must answer the call and demands of the union unhesitantly and enthusiastically. It might be necessary for union members, for the good of the workers, to profess secrecy in carrying out union strategy.

In at least a few instances, workers allegedly bound themselves loyally together with a blood oath. In taking the oath, union brothers swore that they would not let home, families, God, or church come between them and the work of the union. It was pure and simple unionism—the solidarity of the union forever.

See also Gompers, Samuel.

Railroad Strike of 1877

July 1877 was a violent month for the American labor movement. During that month, many of the nation's railroad workers walked out to protest a wage cut. First to go out were employees of the Baltimore and Ohio, joined by Pennsylvania, New York Central, and Erie Railroad workers. In a matter of days all was quiet on the Eastern railroads. As the strike continued and grew, Western railroad employees on the Missouri Pacific and the St. Louis, Kansas, and Northern walked out. The nation's railroads were in the throes of paralysis.

The strike featured denominators common to other railroad strikes—rioting, the stoppage of trains, destruction of railroad property (including train depots), and looting. Railroad environs in Baltimore, Pittsburgh, Chicago, St. Louis, and San Francisco were ablaze as striking railroad workers set fires to cars, locomotives, and railroad property. In an attempt to quell rioters and end the violence, local militia, state troops, and the U.S. Army were called out. Angry, out-of-control strikers fought with the troops, resulting in widespread bloodshed—the death of more than 30 persons and the wounding of many more.

The press editorialized that the strike and its attending violence was communist-inspired. Strikers were called hoodlums, the rabble, bums, tramps, incendiaries, brigands, riffraff, idiots. In the midst of the tumult the grievances of the workers were largely disregarded. American clergymen criticized the strikers with these words: "God intended the great to be great and the little to be little . . . ."

The month of turmoil finally ended. Its impact: labor lost, the railroad barons triumphed, and the public and private sectors more than ever were of the persuasion that the labor movement must be stopped. As for labor, despite an ignominious defeat, it now realized its potential and significant power.

Railroad Trainmen, Brotherhood of

See Brotherhood of Railroad Trainmen.

Railway Conductors and Brakemen, Order of

See Order of Railway Conductors and Brakemen.

Railway Labor Act of 1926

During labor's lean years of the 1920s, trade unionism received little encouragement from the federal government and courts. In fact, most governmental activity was designed to curb organized labor. Congress, however, during a time when labor was declining, passed the Railway Labor Act of 1926. The law allowed the establishment of railroad unions apart from intervention or pressure by railroad owners. It also provided for the arbitration of grievances lodged by railway workers.

The Railway Labor Act was upheld by the Supreme Court. Thus railroad workers were accorded a choice that most other American workers did not gain until the New Deal in the 1930s.

Railway Labor Board

The Railway Labor Board was established to arbitrate the grievances of railroad employees after the national emergency of World War I had subsided. The board set aside all wartime standards, eliminated overtime, and ordered substantial wage reductions. While railroad brotherhoods were not included in the pay cuts, shop workers were angry over the board's catering to the whims of railroad ownership. Because of the board's action, railroad shop employees, numbering in excess of 400,000, went out on strike on 1 July 1922. The board considered the walkout illegal, and the government used troops, scabs, and an injunction in an attempt to break the strike.

Strong action by the federal government ended the walkout. Some stranded workers went into company unions, others accepted employment on company terms. Organized labor and especially railway workers suffered yet another devastating setback at the hands of government by injunction.

Randolph, Asa Philip (1889–1979)

Asa Philip Randolph was born in Crescent City, Florida, in 1889. After finishing high school in Jacksonville, he moved to New York City and worked as an elevator operator, a porter, and a railroad waiter while attending City College of New York. During World War I he founded *The Messenger*, a radical, socialist monthly. Continuing his socialist activities, Randolph ran unsuccessfully for New York secretary of state on the Socialist ticket in 1921.

Retiring from the political arena, Randolph established the Brotherhood of Sleeping Car Porters (BSCP) in 1925. As president of the BSCP, he successfully negotiated a contract with the Pullman Palace Car Company. One of the country's foremost African American labor leaders, Randolph helped establish the Negro American Labor Council, serving as its president from 1960 to 1966. A principal African American spokesman on the AFL-CIO Executive Council, he was an AFL-CIO vice-president who often clashed with George Meany, all the while remaining loyal to the union. Toward the end of his life he backed New York's Liberal Party.

A civil rights activist, Randolph organized a march on Washington in 1941 to protest discrimination in federal hiring and job-holding practices. President Roosevelt, to head off the demonstration in wartime, agreed to set up the Fair Employment Practices Commission (FEPC). Two decades later, Randolph was back in the nation's capitol as one of the leaders in the 1963 civil rights march on Washington.

Randolph, throughout an eventful life, encouraged African Americans to join labor organizations. He also worked to bring about unity between black and white workers, serving as president of the National Negro Congress and as the first African American vice-president of the AFL-CIO.

Randolph retired as AFL-CIO vice-president in 1974. For nearly half a century he worked tirelessly for the improvement of workers' standards through labor unions. He was a pacesetter for African Americans in the American labor movement.

Reece, Florence

Florence Reece was the daughter of a coal miner who loaded a ton and a half of coal for 30 cents. At age 14 she married Sam Reece, a coal miner who went into the mines at age 11 to earn 60 cents per day. She bore ten children, some of whom went into the mines as boys to help support the family.

Florence Reece lived in Harlan County, Kentucky, in the 1930s when the United Mine Workers of America attempted to unionize coal miners. She saw miners and their families hungry for food. She saw gun thugs prowling the county to keep coal miners from affiliating with the union. She saw her husband Sam come home wearing frozen clothes after lying in water all day to mine coal. Conditions became so bad in Harlan County that she moved with her family to Pineville, Kentucky, in neighboring Bell County. She recalled the Battle of Evarts in May 1931 and the killing of organizer Harry Simms on Brush Creek in Knox County.

Having witnessed all the horrors of the coalfield conflict, Florence Reece, at age 30, removed a calendar from the wall of her home and wrote one of history's most famous labor songs, "Which Side Are You On?"

Come all you poor workers,
Good news to you I'll tell,
How the good old union
Has come in here to dwell.
Which side are you on?
Which side are you on?
We're starting our good battle,
We know we're sure to win,
Because we've got the gun thugs
A lookin' very thin.
Which side are you on?
Which side are you on?
If you go to Harlan County,
There is no neutral there,
You'll either be a union man
Or a thug for [Sheriff] J. H. Blair.
Which side are you on?
Which side are you on?

Republic Steel Corporation

Republic Steel Corporation, one of the four enterprises comprising the Little Steel combine, was another example of a powerful corporation that was determined to keep its workers from joining the union during the New Deal years. It was guided in the 1930s by Tom Girdler, a bitter labor foe who vehemently opposed all efforts by the Steel Workers Organizing Committee (SWOC) to organize steelworkers in May 1937.

Like most U.S. corporations in the 1930s, Republic Steel used all the standard methods to resist the union. Workers on strike were harassed, strikers and union organizers were arrested; union halls were tear gassed; picketing workers were assaulted; policemen, deputy sheriffs, and troops were used to protect company property; and scabs were brought in to replace the striking workers.

The company did not capitulate to SWOC until the federal government intervened to allow Republic's steelworkers to decide the question of unionization.

Reuther, Walter P. (1907–1970)

Walter P. Reuther was born in Wheeling, West Virginia. He was employed by the Wheeling Steel Corporation as a tool and die maker. Following his discharge for dabbling in the union, Reuther relocated in Detroit, where he took a job with the Ford Motor Company and was again fired for union involvement. Since he could not get a job, he went to Europe for a few years. On his return to the United States, he volunteered as an organizer for the United Automobile, Aircraft and Agricultural Implement Workers of America (UAW). Following a brief sojourn in the Socialist Party, Reuther became a strong supporter of the Democratic Party in 1933.

In the mid-1930s, after organizing Detroit auto workers into UAW Local 174, Reuther became its president. A year later he was named to the executive board of the UAW. Reuther led several important UAW strikes in Detroit, including a sit-down strike at the Kelsey-Hayes Wheel Company. In 1942 he became first vice-president of the UAW, and during World War II he served on several key government boards.

With the end of the war, Reuther's star on the labor horizon brightened considerably. In 1946 he was elected UAW president and vice-president of the Congress of Industrial Organizations (CIO). He participated in several postwar strikes and was successful in negotiating a contract with General Motors Corporation that included an escalator clause tied to the cost-of-living index.

Partially disabled by an assassination attempt in 1948, Reuther, as president of the CIO, helped to bring about the AFL-CIO merger in 1955. In 1968 he took the UAW out of the AFL-CIO and with the Teamsters created the Alliance for Labor

Action. Tragically he died in 1970 in a Michigan plane crash.

Reuther led the United Auto Workers for 25 years and was CIO president for nearly two decades. He presided over the merger of the nation's two major unions into the AFL-CIO. Throughout his entire adult life, Walter Reuther was a stalwart leader in the American labor movement.

See also United Automobile Workers.

Right-To-Work Laws

The Taft-Hartley Act, passed by Congress over President Harry S Truman's veto in 1947, contained Section 14(b), which legislated what are known as right-to-work laws. Basically, Section 14(b) enabled states, especially in the Deep South, to circumvent federal laws recognizing a union shop by passing legislation to prohibit it.

Section 14(b) was welcomed by Southern states, which historically have been anti-union. Its application came with the passage of right-to-work laws by Southern state legislatures. Seventeen states, many in the South, enacted right-to-work laws to retard the growth of unions. Once a state had passed the law, workers had the option to either join or refuse to enlist in a labor union. Union membership was not a condition of employment.

With the passage of right-to-work laws, unionization of workers in right-to-work states became virtually impossible. The Wagner Act imposed the closed shop, where union affiliation was a prerequisite for employment. The Taft-Hartley Act, in effect, inaugurated an open shop system in which workers did not have to join a union as a condition of employment. Organized labor adamantly opposed Section 14(b) and right-to-work laws, while management regarded them approvingly.

Rockefeller, John D., Jr. (1874–1960)

John D. Rockefeller, Jr., was the son of John Davison Rockefeller, the founder of Standard Oil Company. Active in social and civic circles and a devout man, the junior Rockefeller, in keeping with the gospel of wealth axiom, plowed about $50 million of the vast fortune inherited from his father into the Rockefeller Brothers Fund or the Rockefeller Foundation. He counseled his children, including Nelson Rockefeller, who later was governor of New York and vice-president of the United States, to do the same.

At the turn of the century, Rockefeller represented big business in the National Civic Federation. That organization in 1898 cited anti-union business leaders with undermining the stability of the nation's economy. It also embraced the principle of unionization as a proper channel to foment good employer-employee relationships.

Within a decade, however, Rockefeller, in response to a congressional probe of the Ludlow Massacre at the Rockefeller-controlled Colorado Fuel and Iron Company, stated that he and his company would take necessary steps to maintain an open shop and to resist unionization of the mines. He said that he would never capitulate to the United Mine Workers of America.

John D. Rockefeller, Jr.

In a similar vein, as a member of a national industrial commission convened by President Woodrow Wilson following the end of World War I, Rockefeller joined Elbert H. Gary, chairman of the board of United States Steel Corporation, in rejecting collective bargaining and labor unionism for the American working class.

While Rockefeller seemingly accepted labor organizations as a member of the National Civic Federation, he later assumed an uncompromising posture toward organized labor. His anti-union position was comparable to that of most American business leaders during the first decades of the twentieth century.

Rogers, John S. (1930–)

For over two decades, John S. Rogers, an outspoken advocate of big unions, has been an official in the United Brotherhood of Carpenters and Joiners of America (UBC). College-educated and a student of the Harvard University Trade Union Program, Rogers was secretary-treasurer of the Suffolk County (N.Y.) District Council of Carpenters from 1957 to 1958. In 1958 he became an international representative of the UBC first district, comprising New York and New England. After holding that post for seven years, he was assistant to the general president from 1966 to 1974 and served on the first district executive board from 1974 to 1978. In 1978 Rogers was elected general secretary of the UBC, a post he held until 1984.

Rogers is thoroughly committed to labor unionism. He now believes that a union must have a large membership if it is to be successful in today's economy. He rejects the view that a small union meeting twice a month can succeed in helping workers. As Rogers puts it, a union must help the "little guy."

Rogers also believes that for a union to have political clout, it must grow and develop new strategies to meet changing economic conditions. He especially advises that the UBC must be cognizant with regard to how union welfare contributions are spent, feeling that unionists who contribute to the welfare fund have a right to keep an eye on how their money is disbursed. He is also deeply concerned about health and safety programs for UBC members. His union educates its members by a staff knowledgeable in areas of health and safety.

A man who derives a great deal of satisfaction from his work, UBC official John D. Rogers is always seeking ways to improve conditions of employment for the working class.

See also United Brotherhood of Carpenters and Joiners.

Rough Shadowing

Rough shadowing has been defined as following or shadowing a person in such a way that he is aware he is being followed. In many instances a union man was shadowed so closely that he became uneasy and felt harassed by a thug, guard, or lawman. United Mine Workers of America organizer James Westmoreland reported being rough shadowed in Harlan County, Kentucky, by an antagonist who stepped on his heels as he walked. Obviously, following a union man that closely had an intimidating effect.

On other occasions, union men reported being followed into the company bathhouse where they showered after work. The rough shadowing in those situations was often done by company guards who wanted to watch the union organizer or union man at all times. The idea was to prevent solicitations for the union everywhere, even in the bathhouse.

The worst part of rough shadowing, at least as far as organized labor was concerned, was that it deterred unionization of workers in many areas. It was not until the federal government intervened to enforce the Wagner Act in the late 1930s and 1940s that most rough shadowing ended, yet during labor disputes in some areas of the country today, the harrowing practice continues.

Scabs

The term *scabs* refers to strike-breakers imported by an employer during a strike to take the jobs of strikers. Scabs were used to break a strike. Once the strike ended, scabs sometimes remained on the job while others moved on to break another strike. Since scabs were brought in to take the jobs of striking workers, scabbing was a hazardous occupation. More often than not, an employer using scabs was forced to protect them by using guards, policemen, or deputy sheriffs. Where scabs were used, violence often erupted because strikers forcibly opposed them. The term *scab* is somewhat outmoded today. Now employees used during a strike are referred to as replacement workers.

Jack London, American socialist author in the late nineteenth century, defined a strikebreaker in the following manner:

After God had finished the rattlesnake, the toad and the vampire, he had some awful substance left with which he made a strikebreaker. A strikebreaker is a two-legged animal with a corkscrew soul, a water-logged brain, and a combination backbone made of jelly and glue. Where others have hearts, he carries a tumor of rotten principles.

When a strikebreaker comes down the street men turn their backs and angels weep in Heaven, and the devil shuts the gates of Hell to keep him out. No man has the right to be a strikebreaker, so long as there is a pool of water deep enough to drown his body in, or a rope long enough to hang his carcass with. Judas Iscariot was a gentleman ... compared with a strikebreaker. For betraying his master, he had the character to hang himself ... a strikebreaker hasn't.

Esau sold his birthright for a mess of pottage. Judas Iscariot sold his savior for thirty pieces of silver, Benedict Arnold sold his country for a promise of a commission in the British Army. The modern strikebreaker sells his birthright, his country, his wife, his children, and his fellow men for an unfilled promise from his employer, trust or corporation.

Esau was a traitor to himself; Judas Iscariot was a traitor to his God; Benedict Arnold was a traitor to his country. A strikebreaker is a traitor to himself, a traitor to his God, a traitor to his country, a traitor to his family and a traitor to his class.

There is nothing lower than a strikebreaker.

Schechter Poultry Corporation v. United States (U.S., 1935)

In the short space of 16 months, the U.S. Supreme Court, presided over by Chief Justice Charles Evans Hughes, invalidated eight New Deal measures. In one of the decisions, *Schechter Poultry Corporation v. United States*, a unanimous court declared the National Industrial Recovery Act unconstitutional.

At stake in what was known as the "sick chicken" case (because unfit birds were being sold by Schechter Poultry Corporation) was the constitutionality of the live poultry code negotiated in New York State in compliance with the National Industrial Recovery Act (NIRA). In its lengthy opinion, written by Chief Justice Hughes, the Court ruled that the live poultry code, along with other NIRA codes, was in effect a law arranged by an executive agency (the National Recovery Administration, or NRA) under presidential authority. Therefore the NRA had unconstitutionally exercised legislative power reserved to Congress by the Constitution. The court also decided that the live poultry code applied to a business that operated principally within the state of New York, while code-making authority under NIRA was intended for interstate corporations. The code then had no application to an intrastate business. Code authority "to fix the hours and wages of employes [sic] of defendants [Schechter Corp.] in their intrastate business was not a valid exercise of federal power."

The Court's decision in the *Schechter* case also took from the American workers the right of collective bargaining embodied in Section 7a of NIRA. However, 11 days before the NRA was struck down by the Court, Congress passed the National Labor Relations Act, which gave labor a new lease on life.

See also National Industrial Recovery Act.

Schneiderman, Rose (1884–1972)

Polish-born Rose Schneiderman came to the United States at the age of six. She attended New York public schools until she was 13, then went to work in a department store. At age 15 Schneiderman took a job as a lining mailer for a hat and cap operation.

Her work as a labor union activist began in 1899 when she helped organize Local 23 of the United Cloth Hat and Cap Mailers of North America (UCHCM). When she was 20, Schneiderman was the first woman chosen to the executive board of UCHCM. In 1905 she affiliated with the Women's Trade Union League (WTUL).

For the next four decades, Rose Schneiderman was closely associated with the WTUL. First she was vice-president and part-time organizer for New York's WTUL. In a very short time she became a full-time organizer and a member of the executive board. Following a brief sojourn with the International Ladies Garment Workers Union (ILGWU), Schneiderman returned to the WTUL. From the post–World War I period into the 1940s, she was an active official in the WTUL, serving as both vice-president and president. In 1933 she was the lone woman-appointee to the Labor Advisory Board of the National Industrial Recovery Act. Other posts held by Schneiderman included secretary of the New York State Department of Labor, a term on Brookwood Labor College's board of trustees, and vice-president of United Hatters, Cap, and Millinery Workers' International Union.

A political activist, Schneiderman chaired the industrial section of the Woman Suffrage Party of New York City. An unsuccessful candidate for a New York U.S. Senate seat on the Farmer-Labor Party ticket, Schneiderman presided over the Women's Division of the American Labor Party.

Almost from the time she was employed in the United States in 1891, Rose Schneiderman devoted her life to the women's trade union movement as a political and union activist.

Scrip

Scrip was company money issued by U.S. corporations redeemable only in company stores. Metallic scrip included the name of the company, the company logo (where applicable), and the value of the coin. The metal tokens carried values of one cent, five cents, ten cents, etc. The purpose behind the issuance of scrip was to bind workers to the company store. Since scrip was not usable at a business outside the company domain, it was another method of control over workers.

The scrip system disappeared with company stores. In the late 1930s the General Assembly of the Commonwealth of Kentucky enacted a statewide law abolishing the use of scrip. The state law was passed following the passage of

Rose Schneiderman

the Wagner Act by Congress in 1935. The end of the scrip system was yet another step toward the emancipation of the American working class during the New Deal era.

See also Company Stores.

Seattle General Strike

The Seattle, Washington, general strike was one in a wave of strikes that swept the United States in the aftermath of World War I. The strike was occasioned by a call for higher wages by Seattle shipyard employees. When the wage hike was rejected by shipyard owners, the workers quit in protest.

A central labor committee, whose leaders had a pro-Soviet affinity, used the walkout to invoke a general strike throughout the city. When 60,000 workers answered the strike call, the entire city was thrust into paralysis for five days.

The strike was strongly opposed by both local and national authorities. Finally Seattle labor unions abandoned the central labor committee, bringing the strike to an end. Seattle Mayor Ole Hanson became an overnight sensation during the controversy by referring to the strike as a Bolshevist ploy that he alone had crushed.

The Seattle, Washington, general strike was one of several labor disputes blamed on the Bolsheviks or communists

Scrip for the Pais Pocahontas Coal Company

during the national hysteria known as the Red Scare immediately following World War I.

Secondary Boycott

A secondary boycott is one in which a union attempts to influence its members to coerce a third party, who is not a part of a labor dispute, to stop doing business with an employer who refuses to recognize the union or rejects the demands of union members. In the Danbury Hatters case, for example, United Hatters called for a national boycott of hats manufactured by D. E. Loewe and Company of Danbury, Connecticut, in order to force the company to grant recognition to a local union. The company challenged the boycott because it restrained interstate trade in violation of the Sherman Anti-Trust Act of 1890. The court agreed with the company, which in effect invalidated secondary boycotts.

While the secondary boycott was an effective weapon of the union, its use in labor disputes was invalidated by the courts under a law passed by Congress to restrain big business. Since that view by the courts did not change until the 1930s, antitrust laws hampered labor unions instead of business combinations.

Seniority Rights

Seniority rights refers to a status gained by employees based on length of service to a company. Normally seniority rights carries a number of benefits, including eligibility for promotion. Also, if a company finds it necessary to restructure in the face of technological changes or economic decline, workers who have been in its employ the longest usually are given first priority before layoffs are invoked.

In some businesses, seniority rights are a primary basis for promotion, wage, and salary increments. In other businesses, including educational institutions, length of service is not a factor when promotion and tenure decisions are made. Unless college and university faculty have the benefit of union representation, seniority carries little weight in promotion decisions. In nonunion colleges and universities, promotion is based on subjective standards and political factors. In the realm of business, however, seniority is accorded greater recognition to employees. If restructuring is inevitable and it becomes necessary to terminate senior employees, many companies make the option of early retirement available.

Certainly in view of increasing technological changes, American workers are more than ever concerned about seniority rights, and those rights are a topic for bargaining and negotiation between employers and employees.

Senn v. Tile Layers Union (U.S., 1937)

The Supreme Court, in *Senn v. Tile Layers Union*, decided in a 1937 case that picketing was an expression of free speech that came under the protection of the First Amendment to the U.S. Constitution. In its decision the Court upheld peaceful picketing allowed by the Wisconsin statute. Speaking for the five justices in the majority, judicial activist Louis D. Brandeis stated: "Clearly the means which the state authorizes—picketing and publicity—are not prohibited by the Fourteenth Amendment. Members of a union might, without special statutory authorization by a state, make known the facts of a labor dispute, for freedom of speech is guaranteed by the Federal Constitution."

The Court's decision in the *Senn* case recognized that "peaceful picketing was a form of free speech with which a state could not legally interfere." It also was a reversal of the Court's earlier decisions with regard to picketing.

See also Truax v. Corrigan.

Shanker, Albert (1928–)

A leader in the union movement among the nation's educators, Albert Shanker has headed one of the country's mainstream teachers' organizations, the American Federation of Teachers, since 1974. A classroom teacher, Shanker got his start in the union by helping organize the United Federation of Teachers, a local in New York City. A holder of honorary degrees from several colleges and universities, Shanker has served as president of the International Federation of Free Teachers' Unions (IFFTU), made up of teachers' unions in many democratic nations.

Shanker advocates strikes by teachers and favors collective bargaining so teachers can have input into contracts. He also believes that teachers should be in the vanguard of critiquing and reforming the educational systems in which they work.

Shanker believes current laws should be changed to give unions opportunity to organize workers. As he sees it, under present statutes unions have little chance if the employer is anti-union. He also feels that today's workers are more educated, more knowledgeable, and possess better skills than those of decades past. Therefore, unions should implement changes to attract this new breed of American worker, including teachers.

Sherman Anti-Trust Act (1890)

The Sherman Anti-Trust Act was passed by Congress in 1890 with only one congressman opposing the law. The intent of the measure was to counteract the growth of trusts and monopolies. It termed unlawful "every contract, combination in the form of trust or otherwise, or conspiracy, in restraint of trade and commerce unlawful." The law included fines, prison terms, and the breaking-up of trusts for violators.

The original purpose of the act was aimed at big business and business tycoons. However, as construed by the Supreme Court, the Sherman Act was used against labor in the Pullman Strike and in the Danbury Hatters' case. A law designed to curb the excesses of corporations, trusts, and monopolies was directed to outlaw strikes, picketing, and secondary boycotts. Labor, not business, became a combination, or conspiracy, to restrain interstate trade and commerce. The Clayton Anti-Trust Act (1914) attempted to remove labor unions as conspiracies, limit the use of injunctions, and condone strikes and picketing. The courts, however, continued to take a negative position toward organized labor for another two decades.

It was not until the late 1930s and 1940s, when a change in membership led to a changing view by the Court toward the labor movement, that the stigma of unions as conspiracies to restrain commerce was removed.

Shotgun Houses

Many companies built company towns filled with shotgun houses. These dwellings were long and narrow, with one room lined up directly behind the other. Companies constructed houses in this style so as many people as possible could be jammed on available land. The houses were similar—two to three rooms, with stoops or porches. Sanitary facilities were furnished by the "little brown shack out back." The structures were wooden and often unpainted; in some towns the houses were swabbed with a dull gray or olive green color. Where running water was not available, a company well or spigot furnished water to all. With the coming of electricity, the houses were lighted by a dropcord dangling from the ceiling. The walls of the rooms, if papered, featured pages from newspapers and Sears, Roebuck catalogs. These unpretentious dwellings were rented to the company's workers, who were required to live there. If a worker joined the union, immediate eviction by a company thug took place.

In some company towns, shotgun houses were poorly maintained. Rows of these houses lined lanes or streets near the mill or mine. When a company town disbanded, the shotgun houses were sold to the workers. Once they passed into private ownership, they were repainted white, yellow, or other more pleasant hues.

Shotgun houses can still be found today in former mill towns and mining villages.

Simons, Algie Martin (1870–1950)

A socialist, Algie M. Simons was editor of the *International Socialist Review*. He was a founding delegate at the convention of the Industrial Workers of the World in 1905, and was also one of the founding fathers of the Socialist Party of America (SPA). Simons believed infiltration was the best strategy for the growth and development of the Socialist Party. Other SPA delegates favored an activist strategy.

A member of Phi Beta Kappa, Simons was the intellectual writer in the nation's socialist movement. While he was not as prominent or as dominating as Big Bill Haywood, Mary "Mother" Jones, or Eugene Victor Debs, Simons was one of the significant movers and shakers in the socialist movement in the United States during the first two or three decades of the twentieth century.

Sit-Down Strikes

The sit-down strike was part of a new strategy adopted by labor in the 1930s in an attempt to unionize U.S. industries. As the name implies, workers, adopting the passive resistance tactics of Indian Premier Mohandas K. Gandhi, simply sat down in the factory and refused to leave. When the strike succeeded, the sit-downers could only be removed from the plant's premises by force.

The sit-down strike was effectively used by American workers against General Motors Corporation (GMC) at Flint, Michigan, from 3 December 1936 to 11 February 1937. Before the Flint GMC workers employed the sit-down strike, rubber workers at the Akron, Ohio, Firestone plant successfully implemented the technique. In the wake of the Flint sit-down strike, the method was utilized by glass and textile workers, bakers, dressmakers, and electrical workers. Even waitresses refused to wait on customers at department store lunch counters.

The sit-down strike was serious business to American workers. Two employees spent their honeymoons as sit-downers, and six wives delivered babies while their husbands sat it out. This is the spirited song of the sit-downers:

When they tie the can to a union man,
Sit down! Sit down!

When they give him the sack,
  they'll take him back,
Sit down! Sit down!
When the speed-up comes,
  just twiddle your thumbs,
Sit down! Sit down!
When the boss won't talk,
  don't take a walk,
Sit down! Sit down!

Slichter, Sumner Huber (1892–1959)

In the post–World War II era, Harvard economist Sumner H. Slichter observed, in the face of the rising power of organized labor, that the nation was making the transition from a society dominated by big business to one controlled by big labor. Slichter was right to a degree. While big business was the dominant special interest during the Gilded Age, the Progressive Era, and the Roaring Twenties, laws passed by Congress during the New Deal years gave rise to big labor. Almost overnight organized labor became a powerful force with which the president, Congress, courts, industrial states, and businessmen had to reckon. Politicians seeking electoral offices courted labor and labor leaders. Contributions from labor unions became a hot commodity for those running for public office.

Within a decade, organized labor was so powerful that Congress, in 1947, passed the Taft-Hartley Act over President Harry S Truman's veto in an attempt to limit labor's strength.

Slichter's observation was right on target. In the postwar years, organized labor became another special interest group in the U.S. economy and society.

Slugger

A slugger was a person who habitually took jobs in plants or factories with the avowed intent of breaking a strike. Being a slugger was equal to being a fink or a scab. Employers used sluggers for a special kind of duty. It was a slugger's job to spy on and hunt union men, strikers, or organizers and give them a "chouncing"

United Mine Workers sit down during a strike of the company facility near Carbo, Virginia.

(beating). To prevent a plant, factory, or mine from being organized, sluggers were told to attack workers with sufficient fury to injure them.

Many U.S. employers used sluggers to prevent the unionization of their workers in both the late nineteenth and twentieth centuries. A slugger was an important weapon in the hands of the employer in the American labor struggle.

Smith-Connally Act (1943)

A wartime measure sponsored by Congressman Howard Smith of Virginia and Senator Tom Connally of Texas, the Smith-Connally Act passed Congress in 1943 over Franklin D. Roosevelt's presidential veto.

The Smith-Connally Bill authorized FDR to seize any industry in which curtailment of production, because of a strike, jeopardized the nation's war effort. While the law did not explicitly outlaw strikes, it called for a 30-day cooling-off period while the National Labor Relations Board permitted workers to vote on whether a strike should be called. The bill also prohibited political contributions and invoked federal conciliation in labor disputes.

While labor strongly opposed the Smith-Connally Act, the law probably lessened the number of strikes during World War II. It may be noted that the president did intervene in a railroad dispute beyond the scope of the Smith-Connally Act; when mediation attempts broke down, FDR seized the railroads to avert disaster to the nation's war effort.

While the Smith-Connally Act was principally a wartime law, it looked forward, especially with its cooling-off proviso, to the postwar Taft-Hartley Act (1947).

Social Security Act (1935)

The Social Security Act of 1935, passed by Congress as part of the second New Deal and upheld by the Supreme Court in *Steward Machine Company v. Davis* in 1937, was referred to by FDR as the most important piece of legislation of his first presidential term.

The law was established for several purposes: (1) to provide retirement income based on employer-employee contributions for workers; (2) to furnish unemployment compensation for workers laid off because of loss of job or disability; (3) to allocate federal funds to states for old-age pensions to the needy elderly; and (4) to set aside grants to the states for the blind, homeless, dependent children, and child care.

The Social Security Act applied to a minority of American workers in the 1930s. Since then it has been revised so that presently many workers, both of the blue- and white-collar class, come under Social Security entitlement. In the 1960s, as part of Lyndon Baines Johnson's Great Society program, Medicare was added as a benefit under the Social Security Act.

Socialist Labor Party (SLP)

The Socialist Labor Party (SLP) had its origin in the Workingmen's Party formed in 1876. The party grew out of organizations of Marxian socialists, anarcho-communists led by Mikhail Bakunin, and Lassallean socialists, who were guided by German socialist Ferdinand Lassalle. The Marxists separated from the anarcho-communists and established headquarters in New York City as the First International headed by Friedrich A. Sorge, a follower of Karl Marx.

The name of the Workingmen's Party was changed to Socialist Labor Party in 1877. It became involved in unions largely through the Cigar Makers of Adolph Strasser. In the presidential election of 1892 the SLP nominated candidates for president and vice-president, then continued to present a national ticket for most of the presidential elections until 1948. Although its candidates received a smattering of popular votes and no electoral votes in presidential elections, the SLP for over four decades was a vehicle through which some laborists transmitted their agenda to the electorate.

Solidarity Day

Solidarity Day is a time when organized labor, its leaders, and its members converge on the nation's capitol to march in support of an agenda for the toiling masses. The first Solidarity Day was celebrated on 19 September 1981, when about half a million workers assembled in Washington to demonstrate against the economic program of President Ronald Reagan. As the name implies, workers from afar gathered to exhibit the unity of labor. The young and old, whites and members of various ethnic groups, men and women, and workers from both the private and public sectors all came together in one gigantic protest movement. Even the most conservative workers, including carpenters and joiners, joined in the rally.

In the days of Samuel Gompers, such a show of strength by labor would have been incredible. More recently AFL-CIO chief George Meany took a strong stand against public outpourings of sentiment favorable to the labor movement. However, the present spokesman of the AFL-CIO, President Lane Kirkland, is a new breed of labor executive who emphatically endorses the rally.

For the last decade, organized labor has convened in Washington to celebrate Solidarity Day toward the end of summer.

Southern Tenant Farmer's Union (STFU)

The Southern Tenant Farmers' Union (STFU) began in Tyronza, Arkansas, when 18 sharecroppers, both black and white, convened under the capable leadership of H. L. "Mitch" Mitchell and Clay East. From its inception, the STFU was biracial.

In the infancy of the New Deal, the Agricultural Adjustment Act, which allo-

cated money to landlords but not tenants, made bad times worse for cotton farmers. STFU locals were established in eastern Arkansas during this time.

In 1935 the STFU gathered in its first convention. A constitution was adopted and a biracial slate of officers was chosen. Since cotton planters resented the STFU, its members were often targets of violence and beatings.

Under the guidance of Mitchell, the executive secretary of the STFU, passive resistance was encouraged. However, in 1935 in the cotton fields of eastern Arkansas a reign of terror against tenant farmers was imposed by local officials, planters, and landowners. Still the sharecroppers enlisted support from the Socialist Party, the National Association for the Advancement of Colored People (NAACP), the American Civil Liberties Union (ACLU), theologians, and Protestant denominations.

The STFU invaded eastern Oklahoma in August 1935 as 12,000 STFU members struck for a $1 per day pay rate for 100 pounds of cotton. While terrorism marked the strike, the STFU enjoyed a bit of success as the rate was increased to 75 cents. In late 1935, evicted sharecroppers were driven into tent colonies in eastern Arkansas. Tenant farmers were blacklisted and forced to leave, and terroristic acts were directed at STFU organizers and meetings. Gardner Jackson lobbied for relief for the evicted tenants, who received promise of Works Progress Administration (WPA) aid. Local WPA leaders did not see it through, however, and the La Follette Committee did not assist the tenants because Southern senators cut off aid.

In spring of 1936, during the weeding and chopping seasons, an STFU strike was called, resulting in additional violence and terrorism. While the STFU failed to assist tenants, the strike publicized conditions in the cotton fields. As a result, President Roosevelt charged the FBI to investigate conditions, and federal grand juries indicted lawless lawmen.

STFU activity resulted in the passage of two federal laws designed to benefit tenants—the Bankhead-Jones Tenant Act and the Farm Security Administration.

Meanwhile, the STFU sought affiliation with both the American Federation of Labor (AFL) and the Congress of Industrial Organizations (CIO). The AFL rebuffed the STFU in 1935, while the CIO was at best lukewarm toward the farmers' union.

In July 1935 the United Cannery Packing and Allied Workers of America (UCAPAWA) was established as a CIO international union with Donald Henderson as president. The STFU wanted to affiliate with the UCAPAWA, but a question of STFU autonomy and the ordering of 60 cents per month dues to UCAPAWA diminished those efforts.

Schisms developed within STFU leadership in 1938. The main issue was an alleged communist takeover, since Henderson was a communist. With the STFU wracked by dissension, UCAPAWA rejected autonomy for the tenant farmers organization. Still some STFU locals joined UCAPAWA. A year later the STFU parted company with UCAPAWA as Mitchell publicly blasted its leadership. Mitchell then tried to take the STFU into the International Ladies Garment Workers Union (ILGWU) and the National Farmers' Union. Those efforts failed, and by 1943 the STFU had faded as a farmers' union.

Despite its failure, the STFU publicized tenant farmers' problems for nearly a decade. The publicity impacted the origins of the La Follette Civil Liberties Committee, which probed outrages against American workers and farmers.

Steel Strike of 1919

The steel strike of 1919, one in a wave of strikes that swept over the United States immediately following World War I, was occasioned by a breakdown in talks between strike managers and steel company management led by Elbert H. Gary, chairman of the board of United States Steel.

With the support of the American Federation of Labor and William Z. Foster, a communist labor agitator, the steelworkers walked out on 22 September 1919. The strikers presented steel executives with five demands: (1) recognition of the union; (2) collective bargaining; (3) a wage hike; (4) an end to the 12-hour day; and (5) dismantling of company unions. Management refused to accede to the strikers' requests. Instead, the companies used scabs, spies, guards, and policemen to break the strike. The U.S. Army, under the command of Major General Leonard Wood of Spanish-American War fame, was used to enforce martial law and keep order. The strike was a bloody one, resulting in the deaths of 20 people, 18 of whom were workers.

Finally on 9 January 1920 the strike came to an end. It had lasted over three months. The workers achieved none of their demands; they were a beaten lot. Not until the 1930s did steelworkers experience the right to affiliate with a union without fear of employer/company recrimination.

Steel Workers' Organizing Committee (SWOC)

The Steel Workers' Organizing Committee (SWOC) was established in 1936 to spearhead an organizing campaign among the nation's steelworkers. Financially supported by the United Mine Workers of America (UMW) and led by Philip Murray, organizers streamed into the nation's steel towns. Steelworkers enthusiastically responded to the union banner, and by the end of the year, 100,000 workers in 100 locals were in the union fold.

A major victory for SWOC was securing collective bargaining rights for United States Steel's largest subsidiary, Carnegie-Illinois Steel.

During SWOC organizing drives, UMW President John L. Lewis and

United States Steel Board Chairman Myron Taylor often met secretly to forestall any major confrontations. As the union campaign progressed, important hours and wages were gained. Then additional United States Steel subsidiaries accepted the union.

As the SWOC strengthened, it gobbled up the Amalgamated Association of Iron, Steel and Tin Workers (AAIST). The AAIST relinquished its charter and was replaced by the United Steel Workers of America. In 1944 the SWOC absorbed the Aluminum Workers of America.

Following World War II, SWOC called a major strike, which ended in a substantial wage increase for the steelworkers. Later the union concentrated mostly on fringe benefits. By 1956 SWOC had amassed 1.2 million members, and by 1972 it was the second largest U.S. labor union with 1.4 million workers in over 5,000 locals. By that time SWOC had gained control of the International Union of Mine, Mill, and Smelter Workers (IUMMSW).

While only about one-half of the union members were steelworkers, the organization concentrated on pension plans, elimination of the Southern wage differential, and unemployment benefit plans.

In the beginning, the SWOC enjoyed its greatest success among the larger steel companies such as United States Steel. As time passed, however, it successfully organized Little Steel companies such as Republic Steel.

See also United Steel Workers of America

Steelman, John R.

John R. Steelman was an arbitrator with the U.S. Conciliation Service during the New Deal era. His principal role as an impartial observer and conciliator was to assist in the settlement of labor disputes. Steelman's strategy involved bringing representatives of management and labor together in an attempt to iron out differ-

ences so a strike could be settled and a contract signed. At times the discussions between labor and management aides went on nonstop around the clock.

Representing the U.S. Conciliation Service, an arm of the Department of Labor, it was not Steelman's role to take sides. Instead, he was to assist in an amicable settlement of conflict acceptable to both parties.

One of Steelman's shining moments as an arbitrator came in the summer of 1939 in Knoxville, Tennessee, where he met with representatives of the Harlan County Coal Operators Association (HCCOA) and the United Mine Workers of America (UMW). Following four days of mostly nonstop deliberations, a contract agreement that included operator acceptance of the UMW as exclusive bargaining agent was reached. The two-year contract, a Harlan County first, ended almost a decade of strife in the coalfields. Steelman referred to 3 March 1941, the day the pact was consummated, as a "red-letter day for the people of Harlan County."

Steelman's role as a federal conciliator was invaluable during the labor turbulence of the 1930s and 1940s.

Stephens, Uriah Smith (1821–1882)

Schoolteacher, tailor, ministerial student, reformer, and abolitionist, Uriah Stephens finally found his niche as a labor activist. Born in Cape May, New Jersey, Stephens had worn many hats before the Civil War. In 1862, after supporting Abraham Lincoln for president, Stephens was an organizer for the Garment Cutters' Association. When it collapsed, he became a cofounder of the Noble Order of the Knights of Labor. Having been associated with several secret orders that emphasized tradition, secrecy, and ritualism, Stephens made those traits part of the customs of the Knights of Labor.

Stephens opposed the wage system, favoring cooperation instead. His vision for the working class was one big union for all workers, irrespective of race, color, or sex. Twenty Knights of Labor assemblies chose Stephens as grand master workman of District Assembly I. Following an unsuccessful campaign for Congress on the Greenback-Labor ticket in 1878, Stephens was installed as national grand master workman. After holding office for a year, he resigned because of illness and because he emphasized secrecy.

Stephens' true worth to the American labor movement was as leader of perhaps the nation's first major union for all workers.

Stetler v. O'Hara (U.S., 1917)

The Supreme Court, in *Stetler v. O'Hara*, (1917), by a 5 to 4 vote approved an Oregon court decision that legalized a minimum wage law. The Oregon statute was similar to those passed in other states during the Progressive Era from 1900 to 1920. Its intent was to legislate minimum wages for women and children workers. In Oregon, Louis D. Brandeis defended the law. When he was named to the Supreme Court by President Woodrow Wilson, Brandeis refused to participate in the Court's deliberations in the case. Harvard law professor Felix Frankfurter, later appointed to the Supreme Court by President Franklin D. Roosevelt, presented arguments with Brandeis abstaining. The Court's vote split 4 to 4, and thus the judgment of the Oregon court was upheld.

Stetler v. O'Hara was a victory for progressives on the state level, yet it was not until the New Deal era that the hopes of support for a national minimum wage were realized.

Steward, Ira (1831–1883)

Ira Steward, a union stalwart in Boston, was a leading proponent of the eight-hour day for American workers in the United States (particularly Boston) in the mid-1860s. A machinist by trade, Steward spoke at both rallies of workers and to the Massachusetts Assembly on the merits of the eight-hour day. He also was the author of numerous articles and established the Grand Eight Hour League of Massachusetts.

It was Steward's idea that the workday could be shortened without a corresponding reduction of wages. Steward's wife was the apparent author of this ditty:

> *Whether you work by the piece or*
> *work by the day,*
> *Decreasing the hour increases*
> *the pay.*

Through Steward's efforts, the federal government instated an eight-hour day for its workers in 1868, and six states also enacted an eight-hour day law. Ironically the eight-hour laws for the states were never really implemented. For most workers across the nation, the eight-hour day did not become a reality until the New Deal of Franklin D. Roosevelt.

Steward Machine Company v. Davis; Helvering v. Davis (U.S., 1937)

In these companion cases, the U.S. Supreme Court, by a 5 to 4 vote in both instances, declared the Social Security Act of 1935 constitutional. The *Steward* decision validated the law with regard to a tax paid by employers for retirement benefits for workers. In *Helvering*, the Court ruled in favor of the law's provisions for old-age pensions and other benefits.

With these two Court decisions, President Franklin D. Roosevelt's New Deal scored a significant victory. Simply put, from 1937 workers covered by Social Security could look forward to a retirement pension as well as unemployment compensation. Dependents of workers under the law were entitled to receive survivors' benefits.

The twin decisions in the *Steward* and *Helvering* cases enforced the Social Security system from 1937 to the present.

Strasser, Adolph (187?–1939)

A native of Austria-Hungary, Adolph Strasser emigrated to the United States in the early 1870s. A leading organizer of the Social Democratic Party and the Socialist Labor Party, Strasser was an activist in eight-hour day strikes.

Strasser's main function in the American labor movement was twofold. First, he organized the Cigar Makers International Union (CMIU), which he served as president for a decade and a half. Second, as CMIU head he joined with Samuel Gompers to form the American Federation of Labor (AFL) in the mid-1880s. Beginning in 1895 Strasser was active in AFL circles as a member of the legislative committee, as an arbitrator of jurisdictional controversies, and as a lecturer. During that same period, he also was a lecturer, organizer, and troubleshooter for the CMIU in Pennsylvania. On one occasion he testified before the U.S. Senate Committee on Education and Labor in favor of the exclusion of Chinese labor on the West Coast.

At one point Strasser was identified with the anarcho-communists, who were followers of European socialist Mikhail Bakunin. When World War I began, Strasser resigned his union activities. For a time he was a realtor in Buffalo, New York, before moving to Lakeland, Florida, where he died in 1939.

Stretch-Out

The stretch-out was a method imposed on textile mill operatives by textile mill owners. Basically it involved using one woman textile worker to attend to several machines at the same time, without and compensatory increase in wages. It was a way of cutting costs, getting as much work as possible out of as few employees as possible.

The practice of the stretch-out continued until unionization of textile mills forced the owners to abandon it and technological innovations called for fewer workers to tend huge machines.

Strikebreakers

See Scabs.

Sweeney, John J. (1934–)

John J. Sweeney, born in New York City, is one of a new breed of American labor leaders. A 1955 graduate of Iona College, Sweeney began his career in the labor movement three years later in the research department of the International Ladies Garment Workers' Union. In 1961 he accepted a similar position with the Service Employees International Union (SEIU).

For the past two decades Sweeney has been an officer in the SEIU. At first he was an official in a local in New York. In 1972 he was named to the union's executive board; a year later he became international vice-president of SEIU. Sweeney also held various other positions in the SEIU in New York City.

From his role in the SEIU, Sweeney moved into important posts in the AFL-CIO. In 1975 he was elected a vice-president of the New York City AFL-CIO organization. He served on the AFL-CIO New York State Advisory Committee and on the Committee on Political Education. In addition to being a facilitator for mergers of locals, Sweeney in 1980 became international secretary-treasurer of SEIU and its president that same year.

Under such a dedicated, devout union man, Sweeney's SEIU today represents 850,000 workers in the health care, health insurance, custodial, building, and clerical services.

Sylvis, William H. (1828–1869)

Born into poverty, William H. Sylvis received no formal education. At age 18 he was apprenticed to a Pennsylvania foundry, where he became a journeyman iron molder. After several years as an itinerant molder he found a permanent job in Philadelphia. During an iron molder's strike, he joined the union and soon was elected its secretary. In 1859 he helped establish the Iron Molders International Union (IMIU).

The Civil War disrupted the IMIU, but after hostilities ceased, Sylvis helped revive the union. He was elected IMIU president in 1863. For the next three or four years, Sylvis toured the country organizing locals, issuing union cards, setting dues, and centralizing union authority. As a result the IMIU grew into a large and effective organization.

Following his success as IMIU leader, Sylvis, in 1866, was the cofounder of the National Labor Union. Again he traveled across the nation, wearing his broadcloth suit until it was threadbare, urging the eight-hour day and currency reform to liberate the working class from the "money-power." Sylvis also supported the formation of a workingmen's party.

Sylvis died suddenly in 1869, a year after being elected NLU president. He impacted the American labor movement in that he was perhaps the first national labor leader in the United States, building the first national labor union. He literally gave himself and his life to the American labor cause about which he felt so deeply. On one occasion he said: "I love this union cause. I hold it more dear than I do my family or my life. I am willing to devote to it all I am or have or hope for in this world." On the day he died, the shawl Sylvis wore "was filled with little holes burned there by the splashing of molten iron from the ladles of molders in strange cities, whom he was beseeching to organize."

See also Iron Molders' Union; National Labor Union.

Taft-Hartley Act (1947)

The Taft-Hartley Act, passed by Congress in 1947 over President Harry S Truman's veto, placed several significant restrictions upon organized labor: (1) it banned the closed shop, which did not allow for the hiring of nonunion workers; (2) it granted employers the option of suing unions for loss of property during strikes; (3) it initiated a 60-day cooling-off period before unions could call a strike; (4) it required unions to make their financial statements public; (5) it prohibited unions from making contributions to political campaigns; (6) it banned the check-off system, which permitted an employer to deduct union dues automatically; and (7) it required union leaders to pledge to an oath that they were not affiliated with the Communist Party.

The Taft-Hartley Act also included the famous Section 14b, which allowed states to enact right-to-work laws, which in effect did not make union membership a prerequisite for employment. In a right-to-work state, an employee either could or could not be a union member; workers had freedom of choice with regard to union membership.

The Taft-Hartley Act was passed in response to widespread anti-labor and anti-union sentiment following the close of World War II.

Teamsters, Chauffeurs, Warehousemen and Helpers of America, International Brotherhood of

See International Brotherhood of Teamsters, Chauffeurs, Warehousemen and Helpers of America.

Ten-Hour Day

The ten-hour day movement began in the building trades industry in the East where such cities as Boston and Philadelphia adopted a 6:00 A.M. to 6:00 P.M. workday with an hour off for dinner and an hour off for supper. During Andrew Jackson's administration, the secretary of the navy decreed a ten-hour day in the Philadelphia naval yards. President Martin van Buren, in 1840, ordered a ten-hour day for all workers laboring on government construction projects.

In 1844 a New England convention called for the ten-hour day throughout the Northeast and elsewhere. As a result, New Hampshire (1847), Maine (1848), Pennsylvania (1848), Ohio (1852), Rhode Island (1853), California (1853), Connecticut (1855), and other states enacted ten-hour laws. While the laws were often evaded, by the outbreak of the Civil War the ten-hour day was widespread for both skilled workers and common laborers. Notable exceptions to the ten-hour day could be found in the textile mills of Lowell and Salem in Massachusetts, where most of the workers were women.

The Supreme Court decisions in *Muller v. Oregon* and *Bunting v. Oregon* upheld the constitutionality of state statutes establishing the ten-hour working day.

See also Eight-Hour Day.

Textile Labor Relations Board

The year was 1934. Labor unrest was rampant throughout the country. Strikes abounded. Maritime workers on the West Coast and factory workers in Toledo, Ohio, walked out. In terms of sheer numbers, the textile strike, which involved workers from Maine to Alabama, was the country's major dispute. Between 400,000 and 500,000 men and women employees struck in support of a 30-hour week, the prevailing minimum wage of $13 per day, the end of the stretch-out, and acceptance of the United Textile Workers as chief bargaining agent.

Violence flared everywhere. In the Deep South, hordes of workers congregated in the mill villages to enforce the strike and establish picket lines, and battles raged between strikers and local police and deputy sheriffs. In Georgia, four-time Governor Eugene Talmadge dispatched the National Guard to quell disorder.

President Roosevelt, in an effort to stem the violence and end the strike, appointed a labor relations board for the textile industry. Union officials asked workers to return to their machines. As the strike ended, employers continued their policies of refusing to recognize the union and employing nonunion workers in jobs previously held by strikers. The textile strike of 1934 doomed the union and devastated textile mill employees.

Textile Workers' Organizing Committee (TWOC)

Textile workers' organizing reaches back to the year 1834, when 2,000 female employees walked out in Lowell, Massachusetts, to protest a wage cut.

The first national textile workers union was born in 1901. Known as the United Textile Workers of America (UTWA), it addressed the issue of job security. The UTWA struggled because mill owners stopped the spindles and looms rather than give in to the union. There were serious problems besetting the UTWA: rural millhands were suspicious of outside organizers; women and children were regarded as unorganizable; and immigrants in the Northeast were difficult to unionize, often being used as scabs. The mill town climate that featured company towns and paternalistic bosses was not conducive to union-organizing campaigns.

The UTWA, already beset with problems, was nearly dealt a knockout punch

by the national textile strike of 1934. The strike was a violent one, featuring concentration camps for arrested workers, lockouts, scabs, and the use of guards, including the National Guard. In the end the UTWA was forced to agree to a compromise that favored the powerful mill owners.

In 1937, the Textile Workers' Organizing Committee (TWOC), in conjunction with the UTWA and the Amalgamated Clothing Workers of America (ACWA), led by union stalwart Sidney Hillman, was formed in an effort to unionize the industry. The TWOC established the Textile Workers Union of America (TWUA), which enjoyed some initial success but was handicapped by internal instability and boom-bust economic cycles. Competition from other textile-producing nations and from the nylon and synthetic fiber industry also damaged the TWUA. With World War II, a wage freeze and no-strike pledges by workers further set back the union.

After the end of the war, automation and the use of synthetic fibers led to a decline in the TWUA membership. Despite tariffs designed to protect domestic textiles, the TWUA, gripped by internal fighting, lost its position as a leading textile union. The ACWA is perhaps the most viable union for textile employees today.

See also Amalgamated Clothing Workers of America; Hillman, Sidney; United Textile Workers of America.

Thirty-Hour Week

In an effort to stem the rising tide of unemployment during the depression year of 1933, Alabama Senator Hugo Black and Massachusetts Congressman William P. Connery cosponsored the Black-Connery Bill calling for a 30-hour work week. The concept behind the proposal was to limit the hours in a work week to provide jobs for more unemployed workers. Tied to the Black-Connery Bill was a stipulation that invoked a minimum wage law.

Neither Congress nor the public was eager to swallow a minimum wage law in 1933. At first President Roosevelt and Labor Secretary Frances Perkins threw their support behind the bill. As opposition mounted, they withdrew their assent. Ultimately the proposal succumbed in Congress. However, most of what the Black-Connery Bill proposed was incorporated into the National Industrial Recovery Act, which made it through Congress in June 1933.

Interestingly, Ira Steward in the 1860s urged a shortened workday and work week along with raising wages. The Black-Connery Bill was similar to the Steward notion, although in 1933 the intent was to put a floor under a diminishing wage scale.

Thomas v. Collins (U.S., 1945)

A Texas statute mandated state registration of union organizers who had to obtain a license in order to recruit union members.

In *Thomas v. Collins* the Supreme Court overturned the Texas law because it infringed on freedom of speech and assembly guaranteed by the First Amendment. In the majority opinion, the Court rendered a "preferred freedoms" status to the guarantees of the First Amendment. The freedoms of the First Amendment, the Court held, must not be restricted unless such speech and assembly constituted a clear and present danger to the republic.

Thornhill v. Alabama (U.S., 1940)

The Supreme Court decision in *Thornhill v. Alabama* struck down an Alabama law outlawing picketing. Justice Louis D. Brandeis had earlier hinted that picketing could be considered free speech protected by the First Amendment. Concurring with the Brandeis dictum, Justice Frank Murphy wrote in the majority opinion that peaceful picketing was a form of free communication guaranteed by the First Amendment. Thus a state could not outlaw picketing because labor used it as a vehicle to publicize its grievances in labor disputes.

See also Picketing.

Thugs

Thugs were hired by companies and charged with keeping unions out by terrorizing union organizers and members. Employers used company guards, company policemen, company security men, and deputy sheriffs in this capacity. The thugs harassed workers who attended union meetings, talked to organizers, or joined the union.

Thugs were often armed; some carried revolvers strapped around their waists. They had at their disposal all types of weaponry and ammunition to use against unionists. They typically received training relating to crowd and riot control. Thugs did not always have to use force; their mere presence had an intimidating effect on workers. At times thugs were imported by employers to dissuade employees from affiliating with a union. The Pinkerton and Baldwin-Felts companies were suppliers of thugs for use in labor disturbances.

Armed and cloaked with authority to suppress union men, thugs were arrogant in their work. During committee hearings in 1937, Senator Robert M. La Follette engaged in an interesting exchange with a thug. William C. Johnson, a former Baldwin-Felts guard who gave his nickname as "Thug," told La Follette that he was a thug and that his work involved "thugging." When La Follette asked what that meant, the mine guard replied that it meant "catchin' union organizers, takin' 'em for a ride, and bumpin' 'em off." Thuggery, as Johnson described it, was quite prevalent throughout the country.

Many thugs were ex-convicts who had spent time either in state or federal prisons for felonies, including even manslaughter and murder. As one coal corporation executive put it, "Of course, they are not Sunday School superintendents. That is not the type of man you want."

Titler, George Joy

Of Scot and German ancestry, George Joy Titler had a great-grandfather who fought at Valley Forge during the American Revolution and a grandfather who died in the Wilderness during the Civil War. Five feet nine inches tall and weighing about 250 pounds, Titler served in the U.S. Army during World War I. Prior to a two-year stint in the military, this son of a coal miner worked in the mines. Following his discharge, Titler resumed work as a coal miner in Iowa where he toiled for thirteen years. There he became involved with the United Mine Workers of America (UMW) as a board member of Subdistrict 13.

In the early 1930s Titler was an international organizer for the UMW. He moved to Tennessee where, under District 19 President William Turnblazer, he did organizing work in the Jellico-Chattanooga field. In 1937 he was tapped to head the organizational campaign in Harlan County, Kentucky, a post he held until 1941. It was under Titler's watch that Harlan's 12,000 coal miners joined the UMW as the county's coal operators signed a two-year standard contract with the union.

With Harlan County safely in the union fold, Titler, in 1941, relocated in Beckley, West Virginia, where he headed District 29. He remained District 29 president until UMW President Tony Boyle handpicked him to be international vice-president in 1964. In that position he was a Boyle loyalist who, from his Charleston, West Virginia, hospital bed, passionately criticized Jock Yablonski as a crook. After a federal judge in 1972 overturned the election of Boyle and Titler, the UMW vice-president declined to run for reelection. He had served the union faithfully for 59 years. He was a tired, physically ill old man. At age 77 George Joy Titler's career as a UMW official, a career which spanned four decades, came to an end.

See also Black Mountain.

Tobin, Daniel J. (1875–1955)

Irish-born Daniel J. Tobin came to the United States at the age of 15. He took a job in a Boston sheet metal factory while he attended night school in Cambridge, Massachusetts. From the factory, Tobin became a driver for the Boston Street Railway Company. While driving for a Beantown meatpacking firm, he got his first taste of unionism when he affiliated with the International Brotherhood of Teamsters (IBT). In 1904 Tobin was elected IBT business representative; three years later he was chosen IBT president, a position he held until 1952.

As IBT president, Tobin served as a labor consultant, both at home and abroad, to Presidents Woodrow Wilson and Franklin D. Roosevelt. Beginning in 1917, he was also an American Federation of Labor officer. A loyal supporter of Roosevelt, Tobin helped get out the labor vote in each of FDR's four presidential campaigns.

Tobin was an influential member of the so-called old guard of labor, refusing to yield to the mass-production unionism typified by the CIO of the 1930s.

Tompkins Square Riot (1874)

The Tompkins Square Riot occurred in New York City on 13 January 1874. An outgrowth of the depression of 1873, the disturbance was provoked by massive unemployment. A mass rally to protest the closing of workplaces was at first approved by city authorities and then canceled because representatives of the radical International Workingmen's Association were scheduled to speak. Meanwhile, workers, unaware of the postponement, filled Tompkins Square. Suddenly armed mounted policemen rode into the throng flailing away at women, children, and men. Many workers and onlookers were injured in the wild melee.

One interested observer at Tompkins Square that day was Samuel Gompers. Only a youngster, Gompers escaped uninjured by throwing himself into a nearby cellar. The events at Tompkins Square made a lasting impression on the future American Federation of Labor president. From that day forward, Gompers was convinced that the plight of the working class could be improved only by those thoroughly committed to the cause of the labor movement.

Trade Union Educational League (TUEL)

Organized in 1920 by communist leader William Z. Foster, the Trade Union Educational League (TUEL) was a Communist Party affiliate and the arm of the Red International of Labor Unions in the United States. It sought through its boring-from-within strategy to convert U.S. labor unions to the principles of Marxism. Targeted first by the TUEL were the needle trades industry and textile workers in the Northeast. While gaining headway in the New Bedford, Massachusetts, textile strike of 1928, the overall efforts of TUEL among American workers were short-lived. By the late 1920s the TUEL was dissolved, and the boring-from-within strategy was abandoned in the United States as textile unions were disrupted by internal conflicts.

See also Foster, William Z.; Trade Union Unity League.

Trade Union Unity League (TUUL)

The Trade Union Unity League (TUUL) was established in 1929 at Cleveland, Ohio. A loose federation affiliated with the Red International of Labor Unions, it was set up to rival the American Federation of Labor (AFL). The first convention of the TUUL was heavily attended by women, African Americans,

and young workers. Its agenda included low dues, transfers within unions, and officers' salaries that did not exceed the average industrial wage. William Z. Foster was the general secretary of TUUL. The union, completely class-conscious, favored a seven-hour day, equal treatment of African Americans, and defense of the Soviet Union.

At the time of the formation of TUUL, the National Miners Union (NMU), the Needle Trades Workers Industrial Union (NTWIU), and the National Textile Workers Union (NTWU) already existed. First to merge with the TUUL was the NTWU. Later auto workers, food and packing house employees, lumber workers, marine workers, metal workers, railway employees, and shoe and leather workers joined the ranks of TUUL. It was involved in textile strikes in Gastonia and Bessemer City, North Carolina; miners' strikes in Pennsylvania, West Virginia, and Ohio; and agricultural strikes in California.

By 1935 the TUUL had ceased to exist as a viable leftist labor organization. Some communists opposed dual unionism while others led workers to rejoin the AFL.

See also Foster, William Z.; Trade Union Educational League.

Triangle Shirtwaist Fire (1911)

The Triangle Shirtwaist factory fire occurred in New York City's garment workers' district on 25 March 1911. In the inferno 146 employees, mostly women, lost their lives. Charges were brought against the owners but resulted in acquittals. The New York State legislature responded to the disaster by passing a strict building code and by establishing the New York Factory Investigating Commission. Two notable commission members were Alfred E. Smith, Democratic presidential nominee in 1928, and Robert F. Wagner, sponsor of the National Labor Relations Act in 1935. The efforts of Smith and Wagner,

"This is one of a hundred murdered—is anyone to be punished for this?" *The New York Evening Journal* pleads for justice for the victims of the Triangle fire (1911). (FROM SWEATSHOP TO DEATH)

An editorial cartoon from the New York Evening Journal *decries the tragedy of the fire at the Triangle Shirtwaist Company in New York in 1911.*

with those of other commission members, resulted in numerous state reforms to improve health and safety standards in the workplace.

Investigations conducted following the disaster showed that there had been inadequate inspections of the building for some time before the incident. Exit doors had been secured to keep out union organizers and to contain the employees. The single fire escape ended in midair. Darkened stairs and hallways were dead-ends; fire drills were nonexistent. The three top floors of the factory were a death trap because the doors were kept locked. And the inquiries showed that these conditions were prevalent throughout the garment district.

The victims of the fire became martyrs in the cause of organized labor. Their deaths led to a series of much-needed labor reforms.

See also O'Reilly, Lenora.

Trumka, Richard (1949–)

A native of southwest Pennsylvania, Richard Lovis Trumka, like his father and grandfathers before him, was a coal miner. As a mine employee for over seven years,

Trumka did nearly every job the mine offered: shuttle car operator, roof bolter, motorman, trackman, loading machine operator, continuous miner operator, cutting machine operator, pipeman, and rock duster. From age 19 he was involved with his local union in Pennsylvania, and like John L. Lewis, he came out of the pits to become president of the United Mine Workers of America (UMW). He has held that positon since 1982. Trumka is married to the daughter of a coal miner, and the couple has one son.

Trumka, like several other modern labor leaders, is a well-educated man. He received a B.S. degree in accounting and economics from Penn State in 1971. While at Penn State he was tapped as a member of Phi Kappa Phi, a national academic honors society. Three years later he received his law degree from Villanova University Law School with an emphasis in labor law.

From 1974 to the present, Trumka has been deeply involved in the legal, health, safety, and collective bargaining issues of the UMW. In 1982 he was elected UMW president by a 2 to 1 majority over his opponent. At age 33, he was the youngest president of a major union in both the United States and Canada. In 1987 he was reelected by acclamation to head the UMW.

Under Trumka's leadership, the UMW has experienced stability and success in the negotiation of contracts with the nation's coal operators. Among the highlights of the Trumka regime are the 1984 national agreement with the Bituminous Coal Operators Association (BCOA) and the 1988 renewal of the national agreement, the agreements reached in both cases without a strike. The 1988 contract included a new UMW cash-deferred savings plan that permitted miners to set aside retirement funds. Also included was an education incentive program for unemployed UMW family members.

In 1989, when the UMW affiliated with the AFL-CIO, Trumka was elected to the latter organization's Executive Council. He stands today as a part of the new generation of young, educated labor leaders.

Turnblazer, William Jenkins, Jr. (1921–)

The son of a career UMW activist, William Jenkins Turnblazer, Jr., was the president of United Mine Workers of America (UMW) District 19 in 1969, when a group of UMW officials hatched a plot to murder Joseph "Jock" Yablonski after Yablonski opposed William A. "Tony" Boyle for the UMW presidency.

For four years following the murders of Yablonski, his wife Margaret, and their daughter Charlotte, Turnblazer kept quiet about the plot. But in August 1973, suffering emotionally from his guilt in the affair, Turnblazer revealed in a 36-page document that the order to kill Yablonski had come from UMW President Boyle. He told of meeting with Boyle and District 19 Secretary Albert Pass just outside International Executive Board Headquarters on the third floor of the UMW building in Washington three weeks after Yablonski's press conference announcing his candidacy. At that meeting, according

to Turnblazer, Boyle suggested that Yablonski would have "to be killed or done away with."

Turnblazer's statement led to the indictment of Boyle in connection with the Yablonski murders. In spring of 1974 Tony Boyle was tried in the town of Media, Pennsylvania, a suburb of Philadelphia. Testifying against the union chief was Turnblazer, who earlier claimed he knew nothing about a plan to get rid of Yablonski. This time he fingered Boyle as the man who gave the orders, carried out by the District 19 hierarchy, to murder Yablonski. With Turnblazer's incriminating testimony, Boyle was convicted.

Because he decided to come clean about the Yablonski killings, murder charges were dropped against Turnblazer at the request of special prosecutor Richard A. Sprague. Guilty of lesser charges, the former District 19 chief received a 5- to 15-year sentence in federal prison. He was incarcerated in a federal correctional institution in Maryland, where he joined several Watergate defendants as inmates.

See also Boyle, William Anthony; Pass, Albert Edward; United Mine Workers of America; Yablonski, Joseph.

Turnblazer, William Jenkins, Sr.

A veteran of the coal mines in western Pennsylvania, William Turnblazer, Sr., toward the end of World War I, became a union organizer in the southern Appalachian area. In 1917 he entered Harlan County, Kentucky, to organize that county's coal miners. A fiery, emotional type in the mold of the American Federation of Labor's Samuel Gompers, Turnblazer stirred miners to action with rousing speeches. After speaking to 2,500 miners at the Harlan, Kentucky, courthouse square in June 1917, three locals with a total membership of 1,500 were established in Kentucky's coal capitol.

Turnblazer later became president of District 19, United Mine Workers of America (UMW), with headquarters in Jellico, Tennessee. District 19 included coal counties in southeastern Kentucky and east Tennessee. It was during Turnblazer's tenure that the UMW poured money and organizers into Harlan County to unionize 12,000 miners. The struggle, which began in earnest in 1931, was finally completed in 1939 when the UMW secured its first standard two-year contract with the Harlan County Coal Operators Association (HCCOA).

It was through the tireless, energetic efforts of President William Turnblazer and a host of organizers that District 19 became union territory in the 1930s.

See also Black Mountain; United Mine Workers of America.

Union Organizers

A union organizer is a person sent into an area by union hierarchy to spread the gospel of unionism and to organize nonunion workers. In the past, when nonunion regions were often hostile to the union, organizers were usually veterans of union wars. In many instances organizers literally laid their lives on the line in anti-union territory. Organizers were shadowed, rough shadowed, shot at, ambushed, beaten, kidnapped, taken for a ride, whipped into unconsciousness, and dumped out and left for dead. They were often targets of terrorism by company policemen or guards, deputy sheriffs, Pinkerton detectives, and Baldwin-Felts detectives.

In the union wars of the 1920s and 1930s, organizers faced continual harassment as they went about the business of attempting to organize in nonunion strongholds. It can be said that in many areas it was open season on union organizers. To keep organizers from unionizing workers, employers often violated First Amendment freedoms—freedom of speech, press, and assembly. Organizers had few or no civil liberties. It was not until the federal government intervened to guarantee organizers the right to solicit union members, and workers the right to join a union, that the role of the union organizer changed.

Still, in staunch nonunion regions in the South today, union organizers face hostility, threats, and intimidation as they try to do their jobs. Despite recent changes in the labor laws, organizers sometimes face scenarios comparable to those encountered by most organizers during the 1920s and 1930s.

Union Shop

A union shop was an establishment in which an employer agreed to hire nonunionists as well as union members on the condition that nonunion workers in time would join the union.

The union shop became a controversial issue during World War II. Union leaders, notably John L. Lewis, insisted on the union shop, while employers such as Myron C. Taylor and Benjamin Fairless of United States Steel Corporation opposed it. Lewis attempted to get the federal government to impose the union shop, but President Franklin D. Roosevelt refused. As a stalemate developed between the union and steel executives, John R. Steelman, representing the U.S. Conciliation Service, intervened to produce a settlement that included a provision for the union shop.

While Lewis gained a temporary victory, anti-labor sentiment grew in the private sector and in Congress. There was considerable opinion that labor had grown so powerful that by threatening a work stoppage over an issue like the union shop, the nation's war effort would be seriously impaired. In the postwar era Congress went about the business of trying to curb powerful labor unions. Its efforts culminated in the passage of the Taft-Hartley Act in 1947.

United Association of Journeymen Plumbers and Steamfitters (UA)

Plumbers' unions developed in Philadelphia, Chicago, and New York before the Civil War. In Philadelphia, for example, plumbers participated in a strike with the building trades for a ten-hour day. These localized unions were of short duration since there was no national union.

With the end of the Civil War, unionism among plumbers resurfaced. The Knights of Labor organized plumbers, gas fitters, and steam fitters. In 1884 a national association of plumbers, steam fitters, and gas fitters appeared in New York. In one year 19 locals with 2,000 members were organized. When the Knights of Labor delayed action on a union charter, the International Association of Plumbers, Steam Fitters and Gas Fitters (IA) was formed. The IA experienced steady growth at first, but after New York and Brooklyn locals dropped out, it soon collapsed.

Five years later 40 delegates from 23 locals met in the nation's capital to establish the United Association of Journeymen Plumbers and Steamfitters (UA), which joined the American Federation of Labor (AFL) in 1897. In its infancy the UA consisted of a loose federation of autonomous locals. It grew rapidly until the depression of the 1890s caused its decline. Jurisdictional disputes and technological changes led to conflict between the UA and the International Association of Steam and Hot Water Fitters (IASHWF), which was organized in 1888 and chartered by the AFL in 1898.

Between the years 1898 and 1914 the UA was firmly established with employer recognition. Meanwhile, the controversy between IASHWF and the UA grew into bitterness. When the AFL ordered the two unions to merge, the IASHWF refused, whereupon the UA launched a campaign against IASHWF, leading to its demise. Meanwhile, the UA continued its growth into the World War I era, declined during the depression, and picked back up following the end of World War II.

In the postwar period, the UA profited from technological advances in the refrigeration, air-conditioning, and aerospace industries. It also organized the oil, chemical, and atomic energy fields. By the 1960s the UA had grown into one of the country's most powerful labor unions.

United Automobile Workers (UAW)

The United Automobile Workers (UAW) had its roots in the organization of the Carriage and Wagon Workers International Union (CWWIU), which, at the turn of the century, added the word *Automobile* to its title, making it the CWWAIU. Following jurisdictional disputes with other metal trades unions, the CWWAIU was suspended by the American Federation of Labor (AFL). It later adopted a new name: Automobile, Aircraft and Vehicle Workers of America (AAVWA). By 1920 the union had 40,000 members, but it collapsed during the Great Depression.

With the inception of the New Deal and the passage of the National Industrial Recovery Act (NIRA) in 1933, the United Automobile Workers (UAW) was established. In the beginning, the UAW was resisted by employers who formed company unions. When President Roosevelt refused to enforce NIRA, William Green, AFL president, chartered the UAW in 1935. A year later the UAW joined the Congress of Industrial Organizations (CIO). In 1937, as the UAW launched organizing drives at General Motors, Chrysler, and Ford, UAW President Homer Martin threw his support in with the Flint sit-downers.

The UAW suffered temporarily as factionalism appeared in the ranks of auto workers. One Martin-led faction rejoined the AFL, while a larger rival group stayed in the CIO. Under National Labor Relations Board auspices, auto workers won strikes and elections as UAW-CIO outdistanced UAW-AFL. When Henry Ford finally capitulated, most of the industry had been organized. By 1941 the UAW had enrolled 650,000 members.

In the mid-1940s, Walter Reuther assumed the UAW presidency after serious infighting with left-wingers. He led a successful strike against General Motors, which ended with a contract containing an escalator clause. Reuther also was instrumental in the AFL-CIO merger that took place in 1952. The UAW broke with the AFL-CIO in 1968 following a conflict between Reuther and George

Meany. It merged with the International Brotherhood of Teamsters in 1969 to form the Alliance for Labor Action.

Today the UAW remains one of the country's most powerful labor organizations. Recent figures reveal a union of 922,000 members in 1,231 locals.

See also Reuther, Walter P.

United Brewery Workers (UBW)

The first brewery workers union was established in 1879 in Cincinnati, Ohio. Two years later a similar union was formed in New York City. Both unions had a short existence. In 1886 a brewery workers national union, the United Brewery Workers (UBW), was organized at a Baltimore convention. Locals were founded at Newark, New York City, Philadelphia, Detroit, and Baltimore. The new union enlisted 40,000 members in four months and was chartered by the American Federation of Labor (AFL) in 1887.

The union, which was open to all brewery workers, was the first really independent union in the United States. Since little skill was required for most brewery jobs, it was rather easy to train workers to replace strikers. In the main, brewery employees were from German stock, with English and Irish workers the next most common groups.

Prohibition days set back the UBW, since many workers were idled. With the repeal of prohibition in 1933, the union made a substantial but not complete recovery.

In 1972 the UBW merged with the rival Teamsters, putting an end to the 75-year struggle between the two unions. Recent statistics show 47,304 unionized brewery workers in 211 locals.

United Brotherhood of Carpenters and Joiners of America (UBC)

The United Brotherhood of Carpenters and Joiners (UBC) followed the example of the International Cigar Makers' Union of America in the late nineteenth century. The latter organization, ably administered by three of the country's most militant labor organizers—Adolph Strasser, Samuel Gompers, and Ferdinand Laurrell—was a forerunner of the American Federation of Labor (AFL). Its goals were pure and simple (bread and butter) unionism—an emphasis on higher wages, shorter hours, and a shorter work week. The union also implemented union dues, union benefits, and the union label.

The Cigar Makers' Union pioneered these immediate goals of organized labor, the Carpenters and Joiners followed the same program. It may be said that both unions established the foundation for the new unionism that looked toward the rise of big labor in the twentieth century. The new unionism sought to organize skilled labor, the craftsmen, into associations focusing on hours and wages instead of land and currency reforms and cooperatives like the mass unions of the post–Civil War era.

Thirty-six delegates from 11 cities gathered in Chicago in August 1881 to establish the United Brotherhood of Carpenters and Joiners (UBC). From the outset the UBC was a permanent organization, drawing on an organizing tradition begun during the colonial period. UBC's founding father was Peter J. McGuire, under whose leadership membership increased from 2,000 in 1881 to 70,000 by 1900.

The UBC, campaigning for an eight-hour day, was rejected by the Knights of Labor, then chartered by the AFL in 1886. Two years later it was the number one union for carpenters and one of the AFL's most successful affiliates. Selected by the AFL to head the eight-hour movement, it led a successful strike for the eight-hour day in 1890.

Between 1890 and 1910, professional organizers transformed the UBC into a centralized federation. As union label contractors raided other unions, UBC membership increased to 350,000 by 1924.

In 1915 William Hutcheson assumed the UBC presidency. Under rigid leadership, in which authority was centralized and opposition crushed, Hutcheson gained firm control of the UBC by 1934. He opposed alignment with the Congress of Industrial Organizations (CIO) as well as the AFL-CIO merger in the mid-1950s. He was succeeded by his son, Maurice, and UBC membership climbed to 800,000 by 1972 before dipping to 700,000.

The UBC currently ranks as one of the nation's largest and most cohesive labor organizations.

See also Hutcheson, William L.; Rogers, John S.

United Brotherhood of Railway Employees (UBRE)

The United Brotherhood of Railway Employees (UBRE), an affiliate of the American Labor Union, was committed to direct political action in pursuit of its goals. Its philosophy was syndicalist, and it identified with the Socialist Party of America (SPA).

As an affiliate of the SPA, the UBRE was represented at the 1905 Chicago convention at which the Industrial Workers of the World (IWW) was organized. While the UBRE offered no charismatic personalities to rival Big Bill Haywood, Eugene V. Debs, Daniel De Leon, and Mother Jones, its approach to the American labor movement was similar to that of the Western Federation of Miners and the IWW.

United Farm Workers Union of America (UFW)

The roots of the United Farm Workers Union of America (UFW) are found in a grass roots organization of the 1960s called the National Farm Workers Association (FWA), led by Cesar Chavez. From its inception the FWA stressed total worker involvement. Monthly dues were assessed at $3.50. Emotional mass meetings and strikes were shunned as the union concentrated on home visits and the development of leadership. Mexican Americans made up most of the membership, which also included Filipinos, African Americans, and Anglos.

A self-supporting union, the FWA had 50 locals with 1,000 dues-paying members by 1964. Although a social organization in the beginning, two strikes led to higher wages and the rehiring of discharged workers.

In fall of 1965 California Public Law 78 was repealed, ending the bracero system. When it was continued under another name by the Labor Department, Filipino workers grew restless. The Agricultural Workers Organizing Committee (AWOC) of the AFL-CIO moved in to lead a Delano, California, grape workers strike. The FWA honored picket lines set up by AWOC, joined the strike, and called for a consumer boycott of California grapes. Cesar Chavez made a 230-mile trek to Sacramento to petition Governor Pat Brown to support collective bargaining rights for the farm workers. The strike-boycott was successful, as the FWA was recognized and signed contracts with Schenley Industries. The pact called for a wage hike from $1.20 to $1.75 per hour, a union hiring hall, and fringe benefits.

In August 1966 the FWA merged with the AWOC to form the modern UFW, and by 1967 the union represented the employees of major California wineries. The UFW recorded some remarkable gains in the late 1960s and early 1970s. First, in California the "Great Grape Boycott" against grape growers resulted in a three-year contract. The UFW then moved into the lettuce and strawberry fields and into Florida's citrus industry. In February 1972 Minute Maid agreed to a three-year contract covering 55,000 workers. The agreement called for higher wages, union hiring halls, the replacement of contract labor contractors, toilet facilities in the fields, rest periods, ice water, health benefits, and a pension fund. A five-man committee was appointed to supervise the implementation of the contract.

In the spring of 1973 trouble developed as the Teamsters entered the lettuce fields, despite a previous "no-raiding" agreement between the Teamsters and the UFW. While the UFW fought the Teamsters over the lettuce growers, the Teamsters managed to sign up the grape growers. UFW head Cesar Chavez called the grape growers pact a "sweetheart deal." George Meany termed it "disgraceful union busting."

The UFW received $1.6 million in strike funds from the AFL-CIO, as well as aid from the United Automobile Workers. Violence erupted as UFW pickets were brutalized. Two people were killed and 300 injured—60 by gunshot wounds, as Teamster "guards" hit UFW freight handlers. The UFW was forced to abandon picketing after some 3,000 were jailed. By the end of the year strike funds were exhausted and the UFW was left with only 12 contracts covering 5,000 workers. The Teamsters won, bringing back the labor contract system. Under Teamsters authority, neither membership meetings nor elections were held. David B. Castro became head of the Teamsters Farm Workers Union in 1973. The next year growers negotiated 350 contracts with the Teamsters that called for an hourly wage ten cents lower than the UFW scale. The agreements also included a medical plan and a pension plan.

Into the mid-1970s strikes continued in the California agricultural industry. Governor Jerry Brown called an emergency legislative session to deal with the conflict. As a result, a law was passed calling for elections seven days after workers petitioned for the union. The Agricultural Labor Relations Board was set up to supervise elections. The union could still invoke consumer boycotts, but secondary boycotts of distributors and retailers ceased.

See also Chavez, Cesar.

United Garment Workers of America (UGWA)

The United Garment Workers began in 1865 with locals of the short-lived Journeymen Tailors' National Trades Union. Ethnic diversity and changes in production methods led to the formation of the Journeymen Tailors' Union of America (JTUA) by 1883. The JTUA consisted principally of native workers. The less-skilled, eastern European Jews and more radical workers first affiliated with the Knights of Labor, then established the Tailors' National Progressive Union (TNPU).

In 1891, 47 delegates representing 18 locals gathered in New York City to organize the United Garment Workers of America (UGWA). Soon chartered by the American Federation of Labor (AFL), it included Americans as well as German, Irish, and Jewish immigrants. Attempts by employers to break the union failed, and in 1894 a strike of 16,000 cloak makers in New York City was highly successful. Strike losses in the mid-1890s caused UGWA leadership to become conservative as the union label was adopted.

In the early decades of the twentieth century, clashes between conservatives and radicals took place. The Hart, Schaffner, and Marx strike in 1910 led to a general strike. The insurgents broke with the UGWA, met in New York City, and organized the Amalgamated Clothing Workers of America (ACWA). It soon dominated the clothing industry as the UGWA declined. Today the ACWA remains a major labor union for employees in the clothing industry.

See also Amalgamated Clothing Workers of America (ACWA).

United Hatters of North America (UH)

Hatters' unions were active in the 1820s when New York hat makers attempted to establish closed shops. By 1833, New York City had three hatters unions with unions also in Philadelphia, Cincinnati, Baltimore, Newark, and Schenectady, New York. There was no national organization, but the locals cooperated.

The panic of 1837 destroyed most of the locals. There was a revival in the 1850s as the National Association of United States Hat Finishers Trade Organization was conceived by 27 delegates representing 12 unions. The new union grew rapidly to 2,100 members by 1868.

A battle over apprenticeship rules and an exclusionary craft policy divided the union and led to the creation of the National Hatmakers Association of the United States at Norwalk, Connecticut, in 1883. The hat finishers and hat makers both campaigned against contract convict labor and in favor of a union label. Both joined the American Federation of Labor (AFL) near the end of the century.

The panic of 1893 curbed the success of the hatters' unions. There were wage cuts, and employers adopted hostile anti-union stances. Despite the temporary setbacks, the 1896 United Hatters campaign was successful until the Danbury case temporarily bankrupted the union. By 1911 the UH had broadened its base to include trimmers, wool hatters, and millinery workers. Still, the union experienced decline through World War I and into the 1920s. The men's hat industry suffered the most because of technological changes and conflict with the United Cloth Hat, Cap, and Millinery Workers Union. UH attempted to organize the millinery workers and was endorsed by the AFL. Cap workers ignored the move, leading to a lengthy jurisdictional controversy.

Amicable relations between the two unions emerged in the 1920s and remained into the 1930s. The UH then claimed workers in the women's felt hat industry, which the cap workers had organized by default.

Finally, during the depression years of the 1930s, the presidents of UH and the cap workers agreed to merge their orga-

nizations, and the cap workers were subsumed within the UH in 1934.

See also Loewe v. Lawlor.

United Metal Workers (UMW)

The United Metal Workers (UMW) was an independent union represented at the 1905 Chicago convention where the Industrial Workers of the World was born. A radical organization, with socialist and syndicalist ties, the UMW was close to the Socialist Party of America. Charles O. Sherman (general secretary of the UMW), Big Bill Haywood, Algie Simons, and Mother Jones added color and excitement to the Chicago conclave.

While the United Metal Workers was one of the nation's smaller unions, it lent its approval to those leftist-oriented workers and unions at the turn of the century.

United Mine Workers Journal

The *United Mine Workers Journal* is the official publication of the United Mine Workers of America (UMW). The illustrated publication contains articles of interest to coal miners, including up-to-date information on black lung disease and other health and safety issues.

The *United Mine Workers Journal* has belonged to the membership most of the time. Union members are encouraged to write letters to the editor as well as to submit poems and articles for publication. For example, the November 1991 issue contained articles entitled "Does It Really Rain Acid?" by a Kentucky union miner; "Scott's Run: A 1930s West Virginia Coal Camp," by the wife of a West Virginia coal miner; and "If I Saw a Picket Line," by the 14-year-old daughter of a Pennsylvania union man.

During the Tony Boyle administration of the 1960s the *United Mine Workers Journal* was used as a mouthpiece for Boyle to enhance his regime and promote his reelection as UMW president in 1969. In the post-Boyle years, the

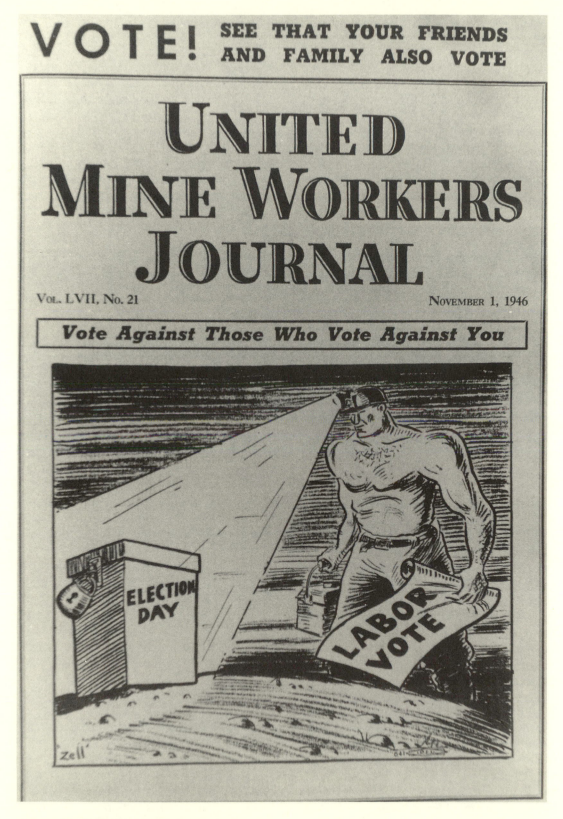

A cover of the United Mine Workers Journal

journal was returned to the rank-and-file coal miners. The November 1991 issue was one in which UMW members, their wives, and children could tell it to the world. Arnold Miller, who succeeded Boyle, and current president Richard Trumka have made the *United Mine Workers Journal* responsive to the needs of UMW coal miners, pensioners, and their families.

See also United Mine Workers of America.

United Mine Workers of America (UMW)

The United Mine Workers of America (UMW) was formed from the merger of two miners' unions at a convention in Columbus, Ohio, in 1890. It affiliated with the American Federation of Labor (AFL) and began organization efforts in the bituminous coalfields. After achieving some success in organizing miners in the upper Midwest, the union extended its efforts to the anthracite industry.

The influence of the UMW was undermined through the 1920s by competition from the nonunion Southern coalfields of Kentucky and West Virginia. Organizing efforts there during the early years of the New Deal were widely successful, despite the violence of Bloody Harlan.

In 1935, the UMW, under the leadership of John L. Lewis, who had become UMW president in 1920, helped form the Congress of Industrial Organizations (CIO). The UMW was formally expelled from the AFL in 1937. Lewis led the UMW out of the CIO in 1942, and except for a brief reaffiliation with the AFL between 1946 and 1947, the UMW remained independent until its affiliation with the AFL-CIO in 1989.

Lewis wielded enormous personal influence as president of the UMW until his retirement in 1960. When his successor, Thomas Kennedy, died in 1963, William A. "Tony" Boyle succeeded to the presidency. His regime, which was marked by charges of corruption and inattention to the needs of miners, collapsed after Boyle and other UMW officials were implicated in the 1969 murder of Joseph "Jock" Yablonski, Boyle's major rival for the UMW presidency.

The current leadership of the UMW, headed since 1982 by President Richard Trumka, has continued to rebuild the direction and solidarity that were so damaged during the divisive 1960s and early 1970s. Trumka led the move by the UMW into the AFL-CIO, and has worked out many mutually beneficial agreements with the Bituminous Coal Operators Association.

See also Black Mountain; Bloody Mingo; Bloody Williamson; Boyle, William Anthony; Duke Power Company; Lewis, John L.; Trumka, Richard; *United Mine Workers Journal*; Yablonski, Joseph.

United States v. Darby Lumber Company (U.S., 1941)

In 1941, Supreme Court Justice Harlan F. Stone, writing the majority opinion, upheld the Fair Labor Standards Act. Passed by Congress in 1938, the legislation enacted a national child labor law as well as a minimum wage and maximum hours law. In essence, the law suggested that a firm could not ship in interstate commerce products made by employees whose wages were below the minimum allowed by the law and whose hours were beyond the maximum allowed by the act.

In its decision the Court ruled that Congress, under the commerce clause of the Constitution, could regulate hours, wages, and child labor. The Court, known as the Roosevelt Court because of several new appointments by FDR, was comprised of Stanley A. Reed, Hugo Black, Felix Frankfurter, William O. Douglas, and Frank Murphy. This activist, liberal Court overturned the 1918 *Hammer v. Dagenhart* decision.

The *Darby Lumber Company* decision was a clear victory for the New Deal, following setbacks in *United States v. Butler* and *Schechter*. Because of the *Darby* decision, a national minimum wage law, child labor law, and maximum hours law continue today as part of the American labor scene.

United States v. Hutcheson (U.S., 1941)

In *United States v. Hutcheson*, the U.S. Supreme Court again ruled in favor of the 1932 Norris-LaGuardia Act. The 1890 Sherman Anti-Trust Act had been used by the Court to curb activities of labor unions that, according to Court interpretation, restrained interstate commerce. In *Hutcheson*, the Court held that the Norris-LaGuardia Act protected labor unions from criminal prosecutions, and it decided that a jurisdictional strike, picketing, and boycotting by a carpenter's union against a construction company was not illegal under the Sherman Act, since such activity did not interfere with interstate commerce.

The impact of the *Hutcheson* decision was to relieve labor unions from prosecution under the Sherman Act and to bring them under the Clayton Act by way of the Norris-LaGuardia statute. The bottom line in the *Hutcheson* case was that organized labor could engage in strikes, picketing, and boycotts without judicial interference arising from the Sherman Anti-Trust Act.

See also Clayton Anti-Trust Act; Norris-LaGuardia Act; Sherman Anti-Trust Act.

United Steel Workers of America (USWA)

The Steel Workers Organizing Committee (SWOC) was the base on which the United Steel Workers of America (USWA) was established. In 1936 Philip Murray, vice-president of the United Mine Workers of America (UMW), led an organizing campaign for the steelworkers. The next year United States Steel Corporation, also referred to as Big Steel, signed a union contract covering 200,000 workers. Independent producers (Little Steel) did not reach an agreement with the union at that time, leading to a strike in May 1937. The four Little Steel companies finally capitulated to unionization in 1938.

During World War II, the National Labor Relations Board (NLRB), in cooperation with the SWOC, were successful in getting Little Steel to bargain. Even before Pearl Harbor, the steel industry had agreed to a no-strike pledge. During the war, the National War Labor Board saw that the union received wage increases and job security. By the end of the war, the USWA had secured a strong foothold among steel and iron ore workers, except in the South.

Philip Murray was succeeded as USWA president by David McDonald in 1952. At first union membership jumped to 1.2 million. Chronic unemployment, however, caused a decline to 960,000 in the late 1950s. Under McDonald's leadership, contracts with only modest wage hikes were negotiated. As a result, steelworkers grew restless and membership continued to decline. In the 1965 election, David J. McDonald lost his bid to continue as union president to I. W. Abel.

Abel's presidency made major changes in union bargaining. Provisions were put in place for the rank and file to air grievances; racial job discrimination was terminated; and there were separate bargaining sessions on an industry-wide basis. In 1973 an experimental negotiating agreement provided for the arbitration of unresolved national contract issues. The USWA also absorbed the International Union of Mine, Mill, and Smelter Workers (IUMMS) and allied and technical workers. It also began organizing activities in the fabricating industry, which made USWA the country's second largest union.

See also Little Steel.

United Textile Workers of America (UTWA)

The United Textile Workers of America (UTWA) was established in Washington,

D.C., in 1901 by delegates of the International Union of Textile Workers (IUTW) and the American Federation of Textile Operatives (AFTO). In 1902 the UTWA enrolled over 10,000 workers in 185 locals. It drew most of its members from skilled workers and from unskilled employees in New England and the South. The UTWA experienced substantial growth during the New Deal years, with membership soaring to 350,000.

The Great Textile Strike of 1934 involved many employees who were members of the UTWA. The strike turned violent, and many workers were killed and wounded. In Georgia, Governor Eugene Talmadge incarcerated textile operatives in concentration camps. The month-long disturbance finally ended when the UTWA accepted a compromise, causing it to lose considerable prestige in the South.

The UTWA, in conjunction with the Textile Workers Organizing Committee, continued its extensive organizing campaign, which had only limited success in Southern mills until the Danville, Virginia mills were unionized in 1974. Meanwhile, the union received stiff competition from the rival Textile Workers Union of America (TWUA). That rivalry ended when George Baldanzi, a TWUA official, switched to UTWA, bringing with him 20,000 members. His move all but eliminated the TWUA in the South, and at the same time it strengthened UTWA, which continues as a viable organization today.

See also Textile Workers Organizing Committee.

United Transportation Union
See Brotherhood of Locomotive Firemen and Enginemen; Brotherhood of Railroad Trainmen.

Violence

The American labor movement has been characterized by violence, especially from the end of the Civil War to the 1930s. As American workers began to form national unions, employers counteracted the movement in several ways: (1) they brought in strikebreakers (scabs) when workers walked out on strike in support of the union; (2) they hired guards or thugs to protect the scabs who took the strikers' jobs, keep out union organizers, and keep workers under strict surveillance in an effort to keep out the union; and (3) they placed in the hands of thugs all types of material and weapons to use against strikers and union personnel. The workers, or strikers, fought back with weapons of their own in order to keep scabs from taking their jobs. They also bushwhacked bosses and thugs, especially in mountainous areas.

In the midst of such a scenario, the stage for violence was set. Key examples of labor-management violence in the late nineteenth century may be found in the Haymarket Riots (1886), the Homestead Lockout (1892), and the Pullman Strike (1894). In the twentieth century, violence erupted in the Flint Sit-down Strike (1936–1937), the Memorial Day Massacre (1937), and in the Harlan County, Kentucky, coalfield (1931–1939). Although workers opposed company methods to restrain unions, in most instances they could not match the resources and manpower hurled against them by management. Strikes led to violence, which in turn led to bloodshed.

One author has dismissed "feuding, pistol toting, racial composition, poverty, low-status occupations, and ruralness" as leading factors in the excessive violence found among coal miners in the southern Appalachians. The same author suggests that at least one study posits that where a "lower level of educational attainment" exists, there also exists greater violence. One other important factor that produced violence among workers, according to a recent study, was the sudden transition brought on by the twin forces of industrialization and urbanization, which overnight permanently altered the lives of isolated workers.

Whatever the reasons, the one constant is that the organization of the American working class was violent. The history of American labor is marked by the blood of many martyrs who gave their lives so American workers could achieve union recognition.

Voluntarism

Voluntarism, which developed during the Progressive Era, found expression in the leadership of Samuel Gompers and the American Federation of Labor. To Gompers, the progressive reforms that benefited labor were acceptable, yet he did not expect the government, through legislation, to give labor all it needed. Labor, he believed, could achieve its goals if allowed to pursue them without interference from management. Protect women and children workers, said Gompers, but let labor achieve other benefits in an unfettered fashion devoid of governmental involvement.

Voluntarism, Gompers challenged, would advance labor unionism in a number of ways: (1) it would bind workers to an entity that would take care of them in joblessness, sickness, retirement, and when they were injured; (2) it would prevent intervention of and regulation of labor by the government; (3) it would make workers immune from courts that assumed an anti-labor stance; and (4) it would emphasize the values of individual ingenuity and initiative.

The government, Gompers harped, need not be empowered to intervene directly in the affairs of the working class. Through free, voluntary associations, if labor was allowed such freedom, workers could bring enough pressure on bosses to force them to recognize the right of employees to self-organization.

Wabash Railroad Strike (1877)

A resounding victory for the Knights of Labor, the Wabash Railroad Strike occurred in April and May 1877 as Jay Gould's Wabash Railroad began to lay off workers in an apparent attempt to crush the union. The union responded by ordering a strike on the Wabash, and as additional workers were idled, the strike call included the Union Pacific and most Southwest railroads. In short, Jay Gould's entire railroad empire ground to a halt. The strike, accompanied by violence and destruction of company property, forced Gould to the negotiating table. Following conferences in New York City, Gould recognized the Knights of Labor and agreed it could represent his employees. Terence V. Powderly ordered the railroad employees back to work, and the Knights of Labor gained one of labor's few victories with management in the late nineteenth century.

The Wabash victory was a signal for workers in other industries to rally around the union banner. By 1886 the Knights of Labor had amassed over 700,000 members, up from 100,000.

Wagner, Robert Ferdinand (1877–1953)

German-born Robert F. Wagner migrated to the United States at the age of eight. In time he began the practice of law in New York State, where he also entered politics. At age 32 he was elected to the New York State Senate, where he became Democratic majority leader. In the New York Senate Wagner was a prolabor legislator. Cochairman of the Triangle Fire Commission, he sponsored legislation to enact factory safety laws along with other laws beneficial to labor. Truly he was a voice in the wilderness in behalf of organized labor. From the state senate, Wagner went to the New York State Supreme Court, where he handed down pro-labor decisions.

From 1926 to 1938, Wagner represented the state of New York in the U.S. Senate. As an esteemed member of the Senate, Wagner sponsored or cosponsored the National Industrial Recovery Act, the National Labor Relations Act (Wagner Act), and the Social Security Act. All three pieces of legislation contained provisions beneficial to workers and to organized labor. In fact the Wagner Act may be regarded as labor's Magna Carta, Declaration of Independence, and Emancipation Proclamation.

As a state senator, state supreme court judge, and U.S. senator, Wagner was truly a champion of organized labor. Upon his retirement from the U.S. Senate in 1949, Wagner was hailed as the "pilot of the New Deal."

See also National Industrial Recovery Act; National Labor Relations Act.

Wagner Act
See National Labor Relations Act.

Washington, D.C., Marches On

The first march on Washington, D.C., took place in spring of 1894. Discontent over the outcome of the Homestead Lockout and Pullman Strike led Jacob Coxey, an Ohio businessman, to organize a ragtag group of 5,400 unemployed workers to seek government relief. That year, as depression gripped the nation, unemployed workers wandered around the country in droves. To call attention to this serious problem and to request the federal government to fund a jobs program, Coxey marched with his group from Ohio. Other groups converged on the capitol from other parts of the nation. As the armies hit town, Coxey and several others were arrested for walking on the White House lawn. When policemen, armed with weapons, arrived on the scene, Coxey's army was driven from the premises, ending the first march on Washington.

During the 1930s, Asa Philip Randolph of the Brotherhood of Sleeping Car Porters threatened a civil rights march on Washington. Since it was wartime, President Roosevelt persuaded Randolph to call off the march. In return, he issued an executive order creating the Fair Employment Practices Commission to end discrimination in federal hiring practices.

Three decades later, Dr. Martin Luther King led a massive civil rights march on Washington. Although organized labor was supportive of social legislation, it turned thumbs-down on the August 1963 march. Finally, on 19 September 1981, the AFL-CIO, which had not supported previous demonstrations in the nation's capitol, changed courses, and a throng estimated at between 350,000 to 500,000 marched in Washington to protest Reaganomics. Thus was born labor's Solidarity Day, which is still celebrated with an annual mass march and demonstration in Washington.

Welfare Capitalism

Welfare capitalism was a creature of the Progressive Era. It was implemented by many executives in the form of company unions, which were to take the place of independent unions created by union organizers. The seminal idea behind welfare capitalism was an industrial democracy based on voluntary employer-employee cooperation. The plan, of course, called for an open shop. In return employees who joined the company unions were eligible to participate in profit-sharing, group insurance, and old-age pension plans. The concept also called for free

clinics for workers as well as employee cafeterias and lunch rooms.

A variety of recreational and social outings were also made available by the company. Employees could participate on company athletic teams, sing in choral groups, dance the night away, and indulge in a smorgasbord at company picnics. The image projected through welfare capitalism was that labor and management constituted one big happy family.

While welfare capitalism produced a number of benefits for the workers, and generally working conditions and wages improved, the entire system was corporate-controlled and managed. The main premise behind the plan was to keep workers from joining an independent union with which the company would be compelled to negotiate. In essence, the welfare capitalism of this century's first two or three decades caused a marked decline in union membership. Work stoppages were also less frequent. The bottom line, however, was that employees were entirely dependent on the good will of employers, and there was little job security inherent in the company union plan.

West Coast Hotel Company v. Parrish (U.S., 1937)

In a landmark case, the Supreme Court reversed an earlier decision invalidating a state minimum wage law. In *West Coast Hotel Company v. Parrish*, a Washington State law that provided a minimum wage for hotel maids was upheld. The year of the case, 1937, is significant in view of FDR's court-packing episode following his landslide victory over GOP candidate Alf Landon. The decision was made possible because two conservative justices, Chief Justice Charles Evans Hughes and Associate Justice Owen J. Roberts, changed their stances to vote with the Court's activists. Hughes wrote the majority opinion, while Associate Justice George Sutherland dissented. In its 5 to

4 decision, the court overturned *Adkins v. Children's Hospital* (1923), an earlier decision that had overruled a Washington, D.C., minimum wage law.

Western Federation of Miners (WFM)

In the aftermath of the Coeur d'Alene Mine War of 1892, Western miners from Rocky Mountain states and South Dakota convened in Butte, Montana, in 1893 to establish the Western Federation of Miners (WFM). The union of about 2,000 members opposed written contracts, preferring inclusive industrial unionism and solidarity. The WFM threw its support to the populists in the 1890s, and in 1896 affiliated with the American Federation of Labor (AFL). It later withdrew because of the AFL's conservatism.

The philosophy and agenda of the WFM may be summed up in one word—syndicalism. Most of the time it called strikes that involved violence—gun battles, bombings, and neo-vigilante activity. In short, it promoted radical unionism and class warfare. Most of the WFM strikes were called in attempts by the union to close a glaring gap in wages between skilled and unskilled workers. Almost overnight, Cripple Creek, Leadville, and Coeur d' Alene became household words as news of violent strikes in those locales were splashed on the front pages of the nation's newspapers. Management met the violent strikes with lockouts and mass deportation of strikers. Because of the violence associated with the WFM, mainstream labor organizations viewed it as a leftist union.

By 1905, with 30,000 members in the fold, the WFM in Chicago helped create the Industrial Workers of the World (IWW). Three years later the WFM withdrew from the IWW as President Charles Moyer renounced the union's revolutionary emphasis. In 1911 the WFM reaffiliated with the AFL, and in 1916 it changed its name to the International Union of Mine, Mill, and Smelter Workers (IUMMSW). Membership declined and the union almost collapsed as the IWW attracted workers in Arizona and Montana and the IUMMSW lost strikes in Michigan and Arizona.

The IUMMSW experienced a revival in the 1930s in the Mesabi iron ore area and in Alabama. It became a charter member of the Congress of Industrial Organizations (CIO), and as copper and Canadian nickel miners joined, membership jumped to an all-time high of 140,000 by 1948.

Trouble brewed within the ranks of the IUMMSW as communists infiltrated to divide the union into left- and right-wing factions. In 1950 the CIO expelled the union, and six years later 14 union officials were charged with false noncommunist affidavits in violation of the Taft-Hartley Act.

Both the United Automobile Workers (UAW) and the United Steel Workers of America (USWA) tried to raid the IUMMSW, but few workers were attracted to the mainstream organizations. In the 1960s, however, the USWA was successful in attracting Canadian workers, and IUMMSW membership plunged to 50,000. The IUMMSW then merged with the USWA.

Wildcat Strikes

A wildcat strike begins as a localized strike within one workplace in one plant, mill, or mine. Often the strike spreads to other locales as additional workers walk out to support those who initially went out. Since the wildcat strike occurs without the endorsement of the national union, it is an unauthorized work stoppage in violation of a national contract between the union and management.

A wildcat strike often results from a localized grievance between an employee or group of employees and an employer. It may be of short duration, with the cause of the controversy settled through local arbitration machinery. On rare occasions a wildcat strike may spread to become national in scope. In recent years, however, wildcat strikes have become more infrequent.

See also Strikes.

Williams, Lynn Russell (1924–)

A devout unionist, Lynn R. Williams in 1986 was tapped as the fifth president of the United Steel Workers of America (USWA), one of the nation's largest labor organizations. Actually Williams had been named to lead the USWA as acting president three years earlier upon the death of then-president Lloyd McBride.

Active in USWA affairs since the post–World War II period, Williams has served the union as an organizer, staff representative, district director, and international secretary. As district director he led the Toronto, Canada, district with a membership of 130,000. A native of the Canadian province of Ontario, Williams has been portrayed as a "toughminded but flexible negotiator and a shrewd strategist."

The USWA had its inception in the 1930s. Organized under the auspices of the Steel Workers Organizing Committee (SWOC), which was supported financially by the Congress of Industrial Organizations (CIO), the USWA by the end of the decade had over 300,000 members. From that impressive beginning, the USWA grew until it achieved a peak membership of 1.2 million members at the end of the 1970s. With the decline in the steel industry, as well as its affiliated industries, the USWA membership has decreased to its present enrollment of about 700,000.

Under the capable and astute leadership of Lynn Williams, in recent years the USWA has successfully organized workers in health care institutions, airport terminals, social work, and in the public sector. Today the USWA remains one of the nation's more viable unions.

Williams, Roy Lee (1915–)

Roy Lee Williams was born in Ottumwa, Iowa, in 1915. At age 20 he hired on as a truck driver in the Kansas City area. Almost at once he joined the local union of the International Brotherhood of Teamsters (IBT). From that humble start, his lifelong association with the IBT began. As the years passed Williams occupied the following Teamster positions: 1948–1954, business agent for several Midwestern locals; 1954, president of Local 41 in Kansas City; 1967, spokesperson for the negotiation committee; 1971, international president; 1971, director, central conference.

As in the case of several Teamster officials, Williams often ran afoul of the law. Three times he was indicted for the mismanagement and embezzlement of union funds in violation of the Landrum-Griffin Act (1957). While he was never convicted, he was discharged as trustee of the $3.3-billion Central States Pension Fund.

In the 1980s Williams was plagued by further criminal investigations. In 1981 a congressional committee probed his association with mafia chief Nick Civella. That same year he became acting president, then president of the IBT. The following year Williams was convicted of conspiracy in connection with attempts to bribe U.S. Senator Howard Cannon of Nevada with a Las Vegas land deal. In return Cannon was to assist in the deregulation of the nationwide trucking industry. Following his 1982 conviction, Williams was removed as IBT president. He was replaced by Jackie Presser.

See also International Brotherhood of Teamsters, Chauffeurs, Warehousemen and Helpers of America.

Wilson v. New (U.S., 1917)

The U.S. Supreme Court, in a 1917 Missouri case, upheld by a 5 to 4 vote the constitutionality of the Adamson Act, which established an eight-hour day for the nation's railroad workers. Although the law was passed during World War I,

Chief Justice Edward D. White, in the majority opinion, ruled that the "emergency character of the act did not make it less constitutional." His reasoning in upholding the law was that since railroads were in business to serve the public, Congress had the power to regulate them.

The *Wilson v. New* decision was a clear victory for eight-hour advocates. Further, it put into place one of the first nationwide eight-hour laws in the United States. The Supreme Court decision reversed the decision of the U.S. District Court for western Missouri.

See also Adamson Act; Eight-Hour Day.

Wilson, William B. (1862–1934)

A native of Scotland, William B. Wilson became the first U.S. secretary of labor,

appointed by President Woodrow Wilson in 1913. William Wilson's background for that important cabinet post was significant. After emigrating to the United States in 1870, he started working in Pennsylvania coal mines at age nine. In 1877, at age 15, he was chosen secretary of a local miner's union. The following year he joined the Knights of Labor, becoming district master workman from 1888 to 1894. Following an unsuccessful bid for a Pennsylvania legislative seat in 1888 on the Union Party ticket, Wilson joined the Populist crusade.

In the decade of the 1890s, Wilson was one of the charter members of the United Mine Workers of America (UMW). He was a member of the UMW's executive board from 1891 to 1894. He also served on a Pennsylvania

First Secretary of Labor William Wilson, right, shares the podium with President Woodrow Wilson, left, and American Federation of Labor President Samuel Gompers, middle.

board that revised state laws on coal mining. As a UMW official Wilson was involved in the coal strikes of 1899 and 1902. From 1900 to 1908 he was international secretary-treasurer of the UMW. Then President Wilson tapped him to head the Labor Department. He served in that capacity for both of President Wilson's terms in the Oval Office. As secretary of labor, Wilson's two principal achievements were reorganization of the Bureau of Immigration and Naturalization and organization of the U.S. Employment Service, which dealt with problems related to the wartime deployment and transfer of workers.

William Wilson's last bid for public office came in 1926, when he ran an unsuccessful campaign for the U.S. Senate. He died on a train near Savannah, Georgia, in 1934.

Winpisinger, William Wayne (1924–)

William Wayne Winpisinger was born in Cleveland, Ohio, in 1924. A high school dropout, he served as a diesel mechanic in the U.S. Navy during World War II. Following his discharge, he returned to Cleveland, where he became an automobile mechanic. Joining Lodge 1363 of the International Association of Machinists (IAM), Winpisinger immediately was an activist in union affairs. For the next three decades, from 1947 to 1977, he was an IAM official. Beginning as shop steward and recording secretary in his local, Winpisinger rose to lodge president and grand lodge representative in Cleveland. Following his transfer to IAM headquarters, he became an organizer of truck-automobile mechanics and a troubleshooter for IAM's air transport department. In 1965 he was named automotive coordinator for the International Association of Machinists and Aerospace Workers. The union then had 120,000 car and truck mechanics.

Winpisinger was chosen IAM vice-president in 1967. In that capacity railroad and airline mechanics were placed under his supervision. In 1977 he was elected IAM president at at time when the IAM was the AFL-CIO's third largest union. Winpisinger was named to the AFL-CIO's council as a vice-president in 1977. In that leadership role, he mounted a drive to increase IAM's declining membership. Immediately he locked horns with AFL-CIO President George Meany, whose reelection he opposed in 1980.

As founder of the Citizen-Labor Energy Coalition, Winpisinger in 1980 supported Ted Kennedy for the Democratic nomination for president. When the convention chose Jimmy Carter, he stalked out.

Presently the IAM represents 800,000 workers. Included are mechanics, machinists, and local, state, and federal employees. It has members in all 50 states and in Puerto Rico, Canada, and the District of Columbia. Aside from representing its members, the IAM, under Winpisinger's guidance, provides guide dogs for the blind and sponsors a disabled workers program. Its recent agenda included a Rebuilding America Act presented to Congress to remold the nation's infrastructure.

Winpisinger labels himself a "left-of-center progressive" who favors "western-European democratic Socialism" to remedy the ills of the American economic structure.

Wobblies

See Industrial Workers of the World.

Woll, Matthew (1880–1956)

Matthew Woll, president of the International Photo Engravers Union of North America (IPEU), was born in Luxembourg. He migrated to the United States in 1891, settled, and was educated in the public schools of Chicago. While apprenticed to a photoengraver, he studied law in night school. In 1904 he was admitted to the Illinois Bar Association.

As president of the IPEU, Woll was actively involved in the affairs of the American Federation of Labor (AFL). In 1915 and 1916 he was an AFL delegate to the British Trades Union Congress. Following World War I, during which he served on the War Labor Board, Woll was an AFL vice-president and executive board member. He also was president of the AFL's union label trades department and director of its legal bureau. Woll represented the AFL at overseas labor conclaves in Warsaw, Poland, and Oslo, Norway.

A conservative labor unionist who was strongly anticommunist, Woll was somewhat of a conciliator during the AFL-CIO organizing conflict of the 1930s. Usually, however, he favored the AFL agenda of craft unionism. With the AFL-CIO merger in 1955, Woll was both a vice-president and an executive council member. As in World War I, Matthew Woll served on the War Labor Board during World War II.

Women in the Labor Force

Women began to make their appearance in the American labor force in the 1820s. Female employees at a Pawtucket, Rhode Island, textile mill called what may have been the first strike by women workers in 1824. In the 1830s it was quite common to find women working as seamstresses, tailoresses, and shoe binders. Women also were employed as printers and cigar makers. Of course in those days women employees were paid less than their male counterparts.

During the early decades of the nineteenth century, women also established their own workers' associations. In Baltimore there was the United Seamstresses Society; New York had Ladies' Shoe Binders, Female Shoe Binders, and a Female Union Association; in Philadelphia there was a Female Improvement Society. Numerous female workers were employed in textile mills in the Northeast, where the Female Society of Lynn and Vicinity for the Protection and Promotion of Female Industry was formed at Lynn, Massachusetts. In the 1830s, as a decade earlier, women workers not only went on strike but on occasion made flaming speeches on the rights of women.

One of the most dramatic strikes of women textile operatives took place in Lowell, Massachusetts, in 1842. While working girls in that New England town had little to show for their efforts, the women's labor movement had begun in earnest.

With the establishment of national labor unions in the mid-nineteenth century, women workers joined both the National Labor Union and the Knights of Labor. Attending as delegates to the 1868 convention of the National Labor Union were Elizabeth Cady Stanton and Susan B. Anthony, who boldly supported women's suffrage. While their presence caused a stir in the convention, it did not impact the business at hand.

During both world wars, female workers were employed in large numbers in the nation's defense industries. Women also became important labor organizers and leaders, as epitomized by rebel girl Elizabeth Gurley Flynn and Mother Mary Jones.

In the New Deal years, the federal government threw its support behind organized labor, and major unions sprang up, notably the Congress of Industrial Organizations (CIO). Women workers affiliated with the CIO and its subsidiary unions, including the International Ladies Garment Workers Union (ILGWU). In fact 250,000 garment workers became CIO affiliates.

Another remarkable step in the advancement of women in the workplace and in the political realm came in 1933 when Franklin Delano Roosevelt named Frances Perkins Secretary of Labor.

In the 1960s women workers were about 34 percent of the total work force, up from 20 percent two decades earlier. Still, while more women entered the work force, on the whole they were not rewarded on the same pay scale as male workers were. In many cases they were treated as second-class citizens and targets of sexual harassment by superiors. On the other hand, labor recognized women workers as coequals, as exemplified by the appointment of ACTWU's Joyce Miller to the AFL-CIO executive council.

Women have made great strides in the realm of employment. Today they hold key positions in the American labor movement, in which they wield considerable influence. Still they are not always paid the same wage for doing the same job as male workers.

Women's Trade Union League (WTUL)

The Women's Trade Union League (WTUL) was organized in Boston in 1903 by William English Walling and Mary Kenny O'Sullivan. Its first president was Mary Morton Kehew, and serving on the WTUL executive board were settlement house workers Mary McDowell and Lillian Wald. The WTUL was the first national women's union to emphasize the organization of women employees. Its aim also was to develop educational and social activities as a means of improving women's environments.

From 1907 to 1922, the WTUL under the leadership of Margaret Dreier Robins was dominated by reformists instead of trade unionists. In the 1920s trade unionists took over, while the social settlement persuasion continued in cities such as New York and Chicago. Through weekly lectures, classes, and recreation, the WTUL attempted both to organize and to improve the quality of life for women workers. Various leagues, such as the Immigrant Protective League, were formed to protect immigrant women.

In the second and third decades of the twentieth century, the WTUL, still dominated by trade unionists, became politically active. It supported strikes by garment workers in New York and Chicago with pickets and relief. All the while the American Federation of Labor (AFL), led by Gompers, refused to support the strikes, rejected women delegates at AFL conventions, and refused to charter all-female locals. Finally after the Lawrence, Massachusetts, textile strike, the WTUL received minimal financial support from the AFL, the United Mine Workers of America, and the United Brotherhood of Carpenters and Joiners. Gompers provided aid because he feared the intrusion of the Industrial Workers of the World (IWW).

The WTUL joined the Women's Joint Congressional Committee in the 1920s to encourage the enactment of legislation for an eight-hour day, the elimination of night work for women, the abolition of child labor, factory inspection laws, and a minimum wage act.

During the 1920s and 1930s, the WTUL moved south in an effort to organize textile workers. Working with and through the YWCA and the League of Women Voters, the WTUL operated in the Carolinas, Virginia, and Tennessee. In the South the focus of the WTUL was on industrial unionism in the textile towns of Danville, Virginia, and Huntsville, Alabama.

The WTUL experienced financial difficulties from 1929 to 1935. As its financial woes became acute following World War II, and in the wake of new pro-labor legislation, the WTUL declined. President Rose Schneiderman resigned. The league died in 1947, although segments continued to operate until 1955 in New York City.

Work Hours

Concern over work hours dates back to the colonial period. In Massachusetts Bay Colony, for example, workers were expected to put in a complete day of work, probably from sunrise to sunset, with time off for sustenance and the necessary bodily functions. For about two centuries little attention was paid to limiting work hours.

Sparked by workers' demands, the ten-hour movement developed during the Jacksonian era. Employers protested and the press criticized, but the workers persisted. Finally in several communities the ten-hour day was adopted, and on the federal level President Martin Van Buren decreed a ten-hour day for workers engaged in government work.

The eight-hour movement sprang up in the post–Civil War period. Ira Steward of Boston, who was the high priest of the action, lectured and organized eight-hour leagues. The National Labor Union also placed the eight-hour day on its agenda, but the drive to limit the workday to eight hours was basically futile at that time. At the end of the century, however, the Populist Party adopted a platform that included the eight-hour day.

The progressives made maximum hours laws one of their objectives from 1900 to 1920. In more than 30 states laws were passed calling for the ten-hour day. Although employers challenged a ten-hour law for women laundry workers in Oregon, the U.S. Supreme Court upheld the law in the landmark *Muller v. Oregon* decision.

The New Deal years brought new emphasis for a national law incorporating an eight-hour day. Earlier the Adamson Act, which put into effect an eight-hour day for railroad workers, had become law under the Wilson administration. Roosevelt's National Industrial Recovery Act legislated an eight-hour law, but it was set aside by the Supreme Court in 1935. In 1938 Congress passed the Fair Labor Standards Act, which made the eight-hour workday mandatory nationwide in most instances. The Court upheld the law in *United States v. Darby Lumber* in 1941. From that point to the present most workers have enjoyed an eight-hour day and a 40-hour week.

See also Eight-Hour Day; Ten-Hour Day.

Worker's Compensation Laws

Worker's compensation laws date from the Progressive Era. By 1915 some 35 states had passed laws that basically made the employer responsible for injuries workers received while on the job. No longer was the motto Employees Beware valid in the workplace; with the passage of worker's compensation laws it became Employer Beware. For instance, when a worker suffered an injury on the job, he could file a claim charging the employer with negligence and with maintaining an unsafe workplace. A board of review heard the claim, listened to testimony from both sides, and took evidence from medical experts. If the board's decision favored the employee, the employer or his insurer was compelled to pay the employee for loss of time from work because of an injury as well as hospital and medical expenses. Worker's compensation laws called the employer into account, making him responsible for the health, welfare, and safety of his employees. Consequently employers began to provide safer workplaces along with all types of safety equipment for their workers, who were also drilled in proper safety techniques.

In recent times, coal miners in Appalachia claimed and were paid benefits under worker's compensation laws for pneumoconiosis, commonly known as black lung disease, which is contracted from working in poorly ventilated mines. As a result coal operators put in place high-tech ventilation systems that made the air in coal mines virtually free of coal dust. Coal miners were supplied masks to wear in areas where the continuous miner clawed coal from deep inside the mine. By the same token textile mill owners provided cleaner air in factories so workers would not be afflicted with brown lung disease from breathing lint as cotton was processed.

In short, worker's compensation laws forced mill and mine owners to provide a safer environment for their employees. Such laws were a major gain for workers in the twentieth century.

Workingmen's Parties

Workingmen's parties first appeared during the Jacksonian era in the Northeast in New York, Philadelphia, and several New England states. As time passed the parties encompassed a dozen or more states. They were established so the workers could have input into politics and government. A common thread that ran throughout all the parties was opposition to special interests, especially the Second Bank of the United States headquartered in Philadelphia. The parties came under strong criticism because of the involvement of radical reformers Robert Owen of New Harmony, Indiana, and Frances Wright of the Nashoba Colony in Tennesee, who saw in the workers' movement an opportunity to spread their communitarian doctrines. While the early workingmen's parties had vanished by the end of the Jacksonian era, the philosophy that capitalists should not take advantage of the workers survived.

In the postbellum period, another workingmen's party was organized, chiefly by those who favored socialism. Composed mainly of European immigrants, this party ultimately became the Socialist Labor Party (SLP). In the twentieth century workers in the Midwest organized the Farmer-Labor Party. The working classes also subscribed to the Greenback-Labor Party and the Populist Party in the late nineteenth century because their platforms represented many of the goals of the workers—abolition of the Pinkerton system, eight-hour day, and currency reform, to mention several.

While none of these parties survived, their agenda in the twentieth century was adopted by the Democratic and Republican parties. The Progressives from 1900 to 1920 and the New Dealers of the 1930s implemented many of the goals of the workingmen's parties. Perhaps historian Richard Hofstadter's evaluation of the Populist Party can be applied to all workers' political movements: "The true worth of the Populist Party was that it was the first political party to call attention to the fact that the federal government had a responsibility to promote the general welfare of all the people."

Workingmen's Party
See Socialist Labor Party.

Wright, Frances (1759–1852)

Scottish-born Frances Wright, a contemporary of Robert Owen, was a mid-nineteenth century feminist who advocated and supported women's rights, the abolition of slavery, and the workingmen's movement. In a time when few women dared speak publicly, Frances, or Fanny as she was affectionately known, mounted the platform to hold audiences—mostly male workers—spellbound.

A student of the famous English reformer Jeremy Bentham, Frances Wright became a militant American reformist. Famous for the Nashoba Colony in Tennessee, which she began as a pilot project to pave the way for the emancipation of slaves, Wright later joined Robert Owen's New Harmony colony. After Nashoba and New Harmony had failed to placate her fiery zealousness for reform, Fanny Wright became an ardent supporter of the workingmen's movement. An early champion of the "dump the bosses off your backs" theme, Wright may be compared to rebel girl Elizabeth Gurley Flynn of the Wobblies and Mary "Mother" Jones, a militant organizer of coal miners in the early years of the twentieth century. In fact, the media of her time branded Wright "the great red harlot of infidelity." Despite the abuse heaped upon her, Wright, like Flynn and Jones who followed in her footsteps, relentlessly pressed for reforms to benefit American workers during the Jacksonian era.

Wynn, William H. (1931–)

William H. Wynn was born in South Bend, Indiana, in 1931. Before he graduated from high school, at age 17 he joined South Bend Local 37 of the Retail Clerk's International Association (RCIA). After he finished high school in 1949, Wynn began a period of lengthy service with the RCIA. In 1954, Local 37 tapped him as its business agent. Five years later he became an organizer for District 12 council of RCIA. In the 1960s Wynn was director for RCIA's Northwest district, and as the 1960s ended, he was chosen assistant to RCIA's international president. In 1974 Wynn was elected international vice-president of RCIA, and three years later he was named president of his union. In 1979 Wynn headed the United Food and Commercial Workers (UFCW) following the merger of RCIA and the Amalgamated Meat Cutters and Butcher Workmen. In 1983 he was re-elected president of UFCW.

Wynn also has served as an AFL-CIO vice-president. Today his union, one of the largest AFL-CIO affiliates, represents supermarket employees, department store clerks, packinghouse workers, and manufacturing and processing plant employees, as well as those who work in health care facilities, nursing homes, banks, and insurance companies. The UFCW currently represents more than a million male and female employees throughout the United States and Canada.

Yablonski, Joseph (1910–1969)

Joseph "Jock" Yablonski, the son of a coal miner who was killed in a mining accident, was born in Pittsburgh, Pennsylvania, in 1919. At age 15 he went to work in the pits, where he joined the United Mine Workers of America (UMW). In 1934 Yablonski was elected president of his local union. From 1934 to 1942 he represented Pittsburgh on the UMW's District 5 executive board. In 1942 he was elected to the union's International Executive Board (IEB), serving until 1969. He was president of Pennsylvania' District 5 from 1958 to 1966, when UMW president W. A. "Tony" Boyle forced him to resign.

In the mid-1960s while Yablonski supported Boyle for the UMW presidency, he secretly supported insurgents for election to the UMW's executive board. In 1966 the UMW's IEB chose George Joy Titler over Yablonski for the UMW vice-presidency. Boyle then appointed Yablonski as director of labor's Non-Partisan League. In 1965, without union endorsement, Yablonski added pneumoconiosis (black lung disease) as a compensated illness in Pennsylvania.

From 1966 to his death in 1969, Yablonski became an antagonist and challenger to Tony Boyle's leadership of the UMW. He criticized Boyle for neglecting the health and safety of coal miners, for collusion with certain coal operators, and for running a dictatorial administration. He pledged to restore district autonomy, to end nepotism, and to launch an aggressive campaign to improve miners' health and safety.

In 1969, following the mine disaster at Consolidated Coal Company's No. 7 operation at Farmington, West Virginia, in which 78 miners were killed, Yablonski challenged Boyle for the UMW presidency. In a bitter campaign that ended in an election manipulated by Boyle and his lieutenants, the UMW president rolled over Yablonski by a margin of 81,056 to 45,872 votes. Yablonski immediately challenged the election because of reports that Boyle had rigged it.

Meanwhile, hired gunmen, who had stalked Yablonski in Washington, D.C., in his hometown of Clarksville, Pennsylvania, and in suburban Maryland before the election, slipped into his darkened Clarksville home on New Year's Eve in 1969 and shot and killed Jock Yablonski, his wife Margaret, and their daughter Charlotte as they slept.

Following the triple assassination, Pennsylvania authorities, with the assistance of the Federal Bureau of Investigation, trailed the killers to Cleveland, Ohio. Arrested in connection with the crime were Paul Gilly, Claude Vealey, and Aubran Martin. Subsequent investigations disclosed that the fund to pay the assassins was raised by District 19 of the UMW, which strongly opposed Yablonski's election. The master planner behind the murder plot, the evidence revealed, was UMW President Boyle. In trials that lasted into the mid-1970s, District 19 Field Representative William Prater, District 19 Secretary-Treasurer Albert Pass, District 19 President William Turnblazer, and President Tony Boyle were found guilty and sentenced to prison for conspiracy to murder the Yablonskis. Gilly, Vealey, and Martin were convicted as the assassins.

Ultimately Boyle's reelection was overturned by the federal government. In a new election, Arnold Miller, a West Virginia coal miner afflicted with black lung disease, was elected to lead the UMW. Miller's election was the culmination of a

Joseph Yablonski

movement by the Miners For Democracy (MFD) to restore the union to the rank-and-file membership.

Perhaps an accurate assessment of the Boyle-Yablonski imbroglio is that Jock Yablonski was a martyr to the miners, their health and safety, their retirement and welfare fund. The UMW today is perhaps a more democratic union because of Jock Yablonski's life and untimely death.

See also Boyle, William Anthony; Pass, Albert Edward; Turnblazer, William Jenkins, Jr.

Yellow-Dog Contracts

A yellow-dog contract was one that an employer forced an employee to sign as a condition of employment, in which the employee stated that he would not join a labor union. Such contracts were used by most American employers from around 1900 to the New Deal era.

In 1898 the Erdman Act, a federal law, prohibited discrimination by employers against employees because of union membership. In 1908 the U.S. Supreme Court invalidated that provision of the Erdman Act in *Adair v. United States*. In effect the Adair decision legalized yellow-dog contracts. In 1915 the Court in *Coppage v. Kansas* threw out a state statute similar to the Erdman Act. In *Hitchman Coal and Coke Company v. Mitchell* (1917), the Court upheld an injunction that prohibited unions from trying to organize workers who had signed yellow-dog contracts. In essence these three Court decisions effectively made yellow-dog contracts lawful throughout the land. From 1917 to 1932, yellow-dog contracts bound more than a million workers to their employers.

In 1932 Congress passed the Norris-LaGuardia Act, outlawing yellow-dog contracts. Employers still required employees to sign the agreements until the Roosevelt Court in *Lauf v. Shinner and Company* (1935) and *United States v. Hutcheson* (1941) upheld the Norris-LaGuardia Act. Despite the passage of the law and the twin court cases, some employers, such as the owl-faced Pearl Bassham—head of the powerful Harlan-Wallins Coal Corporation, employers of more than 1,000 miners in "Bloody" Harlan County, Kentucky—still used yellow-dog contracts throughout the 1930s. Bassham defiantly told the La Follette Civil Liberties Committee in 1937 that he had never heard of the Norris-LaGuardia Act.

With the New Deal of the 1930s, yellow-dog contracts diminished. With Congress and the White House solidly on the side of labor, employers could no longer require employees to sign the contracts. Employees were free to join unions without employer interference. Big labor had come to stay.

See also Adair v. United States; Hitchman Coal and Coke Company v. Mitchell.

Youngstown Sheet and Tube Company

One of the four Little Steel companies, Youngstown Sheet and Tube Company was staunchly anti-union in the first three decades of the twentieth century. To enforce its anti-union policy, Youngstown Sheet and Tube, according to evidence uncovered by the La Follette Civil Liberties Committee in 1937, maintained a sizable arsenal consisting of 8 machine guns, 369 rifles, 190 shotguns, 450 revolvers, 6,000 rounds of ball ammunition, 3,950 rounds of shot ammunition, 109 gas guns, and 3,000 rounds of gas ammunition. The other Little Steel combines kept comparable arsenals to combat unionism in the 1930s.

It was not until Congress had passed the National Labor Relations Act (Wagner Act) and the Supreme Court upheld it in *National Labor Relations Board v. Jones-Laughlin Steel Company* (1937) that intervention by the federal government compelled Youngstown Sheet and Tube to recognize the United Steel Workers of America and capitulate to unionism. The arsenal it had stocked to resist the Steel Workers Organizing Committee (SWOC) was no longer necessary. The union and big labor now gave company employees hope for improved working conditions, including higher wages and shorter hours.

Chronology

1828 The New York Workingmen's Party is formed. It supports the ten-hour day and calls for direct political action by workers, but internal dissent soon leads to the organization's dissolution.

1834 Women textile workers in Lowell, Massachusetts, stage a walkout to protest wage cuts.

1830s The National Trades' Union, established by workers in New York, Philadelphia, and Boston, focuses on such issues as the ten-hour day and improved working conditions.

1845 The Boston Mechanics' and Laborers' Association is formed. Its platform criticizes monopolies and "money-power," and calls for employee ownership of businesses.

1858 A meeting of machinists and blacksmiths in Philadelphia, Pennsylvania, leads to the formation a year later of the Machinists and Blacksmiths National Union.

1859 The Iron Molders' Union is established under the leadership of William H. Sylvis.

1863 The Brotherhood of the Footboard, forerunner of the Brotherhood of Locomotive Engineers, is formed in Michigan.

1866 The first truly national labor organization in the United States, the short-lived National Labor Union, is established by a meeting of labor representatives in Baltimore.

1868 The Order of Railway Conductors and Brakemen is organized from the merger of conductors' unions in Illinois.

1869 The Knights of Labor is established in Philadelphia.

1873 The Brotherhood of Locomotive Firemen, forerunner of the Brotherhood of Locomotive Firemen and Enginemen, is organized at Port Jervis, New York.

1875 The undercover investigations of James McParlan help to break the Molly McGuires, a radical labor group that had resorted to terrorism in the eastern Pennsylvania coalfields.

1877 Wage cuts lead to a national strike by rail workers, which paralyzes the railroads and is attended by widespread violence. The strike fails to achieve its aims, but serves notice of the potential power of organized labor.

1881 The United Brotherhood of Carpenters and Joiners is established in Chicago. The union is chartered by the American Federation of Labor in 1886.

1883   The National Brotherhood of Electrical Workers (later the International Brotherhood of Electrical Workers) is established.

The Brotherhood of Railroad Brakemen, forerunner of the Brotherhood of Railroad Trainmen, is organized in Albany, New York.

1886   Clashes between striking McCormick workers and police culminate in a melée in Chicago's Haymarket Square; eight police officers and eight workers are killed in several days of violence. Six anarchists associated with the Black International are later tried and executed in connection with the deaths of the police officers.

The American Federation of Labor is organized under the leadership of Samuel Gompers.

The United Brewery Workers is established. The union is chartered by the American Federation of Labor in the following year.

1890   The Sherman Anti-Trust Act is passed into law. Although originally aimed at corporate monopolies, the act also functions to prevent secondary boycotts by labor unions.

The United Mine Workers of America is organized.

1892   Striking workers at Carnegie Steel's Homestead plant in Pittsburgh, Pennsylvania, are locked out on orders from plant manager Henry Clay Frick. Workers respond by driving away the guards and Pinkerton agents hired by the company to protect the plant and newly hired scabs. Pennsylvania state troops are finally brought in to crush the strike, but Frick is attacked and wounded by anarchist Alexander Berkman.

The People's Party is founded in Omaha, Nebraska.

1893   The Western Federation of Miners, later the International Union of Mine, Mill, and Smelter Workers, is founded in Butte, Montana.

1894   Ohio businessman Jacob S. Coxey leads a march on Washington— "Coxey's Army"—in support of a federal jobs program.

The strike by Pullman rail workers protesting wage cuts is broken by federal troops and court injunction in a resounding defeat for organized labor.

1898   The Erdman Act prohibits discrimination against union workers on interstate railroads. This provision is later struck down by the Supreme Court in *Adair v. United States.*

1899   The Team Driver International, forerunner of the International Brotherhood of Teamsters, Chauffeurs, Warehousemen and Helpers of America, or Teamsters, is chartered by the American Federation of Labor.

1900   The International Ladies Garment Workers Union is organized.

1901   The United Textile Workers of America, the first national textile union, is organized.

1902   The regional strike by anthracite miners in eastern Pennsylvania ends after President Theodore Roosevelt, threatening federal intervention, forces mine operators to the bargaining table.

1903   The Women's Trade Union League is organized in Boston by William Walling and Mary Kenny O'Sullivan.

The U.S. Department of Commerce and Labor is established under President Theodore Roosevelt's administration; its two major functions are separated a decade later and the Department of Labor is formed.

1905 The radical Industrial Workers of the World is established at a labor convention in Chicago, Illinois.

1906 The American Federation of Labor submits a "Bill of Grievances" to President Roosevelt and the Congress, presaging the entry of organized labor into national politics.

The American Federation of Labor supports a strike by metal polishers against Buck's Stove and Range Company and is held to be in violation of the 1890 Sherman Anti-Trust Act. The injunction against the AFL is made on the grounds that the AFL's action constitutes a conspiracy to restrain interstate commerce.

1908 The Supreme Court upholds a 1903 Oregon statute establishing a ten-hour work day for women laundry workers in *Muller v. Oregon*. Attorney Louis Brandeis, who will himself join the Court as an associate justice in 1916, leads the defense of the Oregon law.

1911 The Triangle fire in New York City's garment district, which kills 146 workers, draws attention to the poor working conditions in the industry and leads to labor reforms in New York State.

1913 The tent colony occupied by striking coal miners and their families in Ludlow, Colorado, is attacked by Colorado state militia, in what will become known as the Ludlow Massacre.

The failed strike by silk workers in Paterson, New Jersey, damages the power of the Industrial Workers of the World.

1914 Congress passes the Clayton Anti-Trust Act, which attempts to exempt labor unions from the anti-trust provisions of the 1890 Sherman Anti-Trust Act and limits the use of injunctions against unions in labor disputes.

1915 The Amalgamated Clothing Workers of America is formed to protect the interests of immigrant workers in the men's garment industry.

The Supreme Court, in *Coppage v. Kansas*, strikes down a Kansas state law prohibiting yellow-dog contracts, by which employers required employees to agree not to affiliate with labor unions.

Industrial Workers of the World organizer Joe Hill, convicted of two murders committed during a grocery store robbery, is executed by firing squad in Salt Lake City, Utah.

1916 The Adamson Act establishes an eight-hour working day for railroad employees engaged in interstate commerce.

Congress passes the first federal child labor law. It will be struck down by the Supreme Court in 1918. A further federal attempt to control child labor will be declared unconstitutional by the Supreme Court in *Bailey v. Drexel Furniture Company*.

In *Loewe v. Lawlor*, the Supreme Court holds that the United Hatters Union had conspired to restrain interstate commerce in its call for a national boycott of the Danville, Connecticut, firm of D. E. Lawlor and Company, in violation of the 1890 Sherman Anti-Trust Act.

In *Hitchman Coal and Coke Company v. Mitchell*, the Supreme Court upholds yellow-dog contracts.

1917 The Supreme Court upholds the Adamson Act in *Wilson v. New*.

1918 The first National War Labor Board is established to minimize labor-management conflict for the duration of World War I.

The Supreme Court in *Hammer v. Dagenhart* strikes down the Keating-Owen Act, passed in 1916 to restrict child labor.

1919 The failure of the Boston police strike sets a national precedent against the right to strike by police and firefighters.

1920 The Trade Union Educational League, the American arm of the Red International of Labor Unions, is established to convert American labor unions to the principles of communism.

1921 The Supreme Court curtails the use of picketing by striking workers in *American Steel Foundries v. Tri-City Central Trades Council.*

The Supreme Court denies the right of labor unions to institute secondary boycotts in *Duplex Printing Press Company v. Deering,* severely weakening the pro-labor provisions of the Clayton Anti-Trust Act.

Efforts by the United Mine Workers of America to organize miners in the coalfields of southwestern West Virginia precipitate a series of bloody clashes that include the Matewan Massacre and the Battle of Blair Mountain. Federal troops restore order, but the coal mine war sets back the union's attempt to organize the West Virginia coal miners until the New Deal years.

1922 The United Mine Workers of America organizes coal miners in the Central Competitive Field of Illinois, Indiana, and Ohio. The strike leads to an attack by miners in Williamson County, Illinois, against Southern Illinois Company scabs. The Herrin Massacre leaves 19 dead, most of them strikebreakers.

The nationwide strike by railroad shop workers is broken by the federal government.

1925 The Brotherhood of Sleeping Car Porters is established under the leadership of Asa Philip Randolph.

1928 The National Miners Union, a Communist Party affiliate, is established in Pittsburgh,

Pennsylvania. The organization collapses in 1932 after its failed attempt to organize miners in Harlan County, Kentucky.

1929 National Textile Workers Union organizer Fred Beal leads a strike by workers at the Manville-Jenckes textile mill in Gastonia, North Carolina. The strike collapses and Beal is arrested and convicted of conspiracy in the death of the local police chief. He is eventually pardoned in 1942.

The short-lived Trade Union Unity League, an affiliate of the Red International of Labor Unions, is established as a rival to the American Federation of Labor.

1931 The United Mine Workers of America attempts to organize coal miners at the Black Mountain mine in Harlan County, Kentucky, initiating years of labor strife in Bloody Harlan.

1932 Congress passes the Norris-LaGuardia Act, which limits the use of injunctions against workers in labor disputes and prohibits yellow-dog contracts.

1933 The National Industrial Recovery Act is signed into law, establishing minimum wages and maximum work hours, and guaranteeing the right of collective bargaining. The act also creates the National Recovery Administration.

Frances Perkins becomes the first woman to serve in the cabinet when named secretary of labor by President Roosevelt. In her 12-year tenure Perkins will spearhead the labor reforms of the New Deal.

1934 Workers organized by the United Textile Workers of America stage a nationwide strike, but the labor action breaks down amid violence and strikebreaking tactics by mill owners.

1935 The Supreme Court's decision in *Schechter Poultry Corporation v. United States* strikes down much of the National Industrial Recovery Act of 1933.

The National Labor Relations Act, or Wagner Act, establishes the right of collective bargaining, prohibits interference with employees' unions, and creates the National Labor Relations Board. The law finally and fundamentally changes the nature of labor relations in the United States.

The United Automobile Workers is chartered by the American Federation of Labor.

The Committee on Industrial Organization, forerunner of the Congress of Industrial Organizations, is formed under the leadership of John L. Lewis, Sidney Hillman, and other union activists.

1936 The first sit-down strike is carried out successfully by workers at the Firestone plant in Akron, Ohio.

A successful sit-down strike at General Motors' Chevrolet I plant in Flint, Michigan, establishes the primacy of the United Automobile Workers as the union representing the interests of General Motors workers.

The La Follette Civil Liberties Committee is formed as a Senate subcommittee to investigate the opposition of American business to organized labor. The subcommittee's work continues until 1940 and uncovers widespread abuses by corporations.

1937 The Supreme Court upholds the National Labor Relations Act in *National Labor Relations Board v. Jones-Laughlin Steel Company*.

United States Steel Corporation signs a union contract after successful organizing efforts by the Steel Workers Organizing Committee.

Efforts by the Steel Workers Organizing Committee to organize the workers of the Little Steel companies culminates in the Memorial Day Massacre, in which Chicago police fire into a crowd of workers on holiday, killing ten and wounding more than a hundred others. An investigation by the La Follette Committee eventually pressures the Little Steel firms into accepting unionization.

The Textile Workers Organizing Committee is formed with the cooperation of the Amalgamated Clothing Workers of America to organize workers in the textile industry.

1938 The National Federation of Telephone Workers is founded and organized. It will grow to become the Communications Workers of America, the largest communications union in the world.

The federal Fair Labor Standards Act becomes law. The act, a key piece of President Franklin Roosevelt's New Deal program, restricts child labor and establishes a minimum wage and a 44-hour work week.

1941 The second National War Labor Board is created by President Roosevelt to prevent labor-management disputes that might disrupt the war effort. Despite strikes in the coal and railway industries, the board is largely successful in forging a labor-management partnership for the duration of World War II.

1945 The Supreme Court overturns a Texas statute that requires the licensing and registration of union organizers in *Thomas v. Collins*.

1946 The coal strike of 1946 ends after the Supreme Court supports an anti-labor injunction on the grounds that the government can impose injunctions when strikes affect the national security.

1947 The Federal Mediation and Conciliation Service is established as part of the Taft-Hartley Act.

1949 The Congress of Industrial Organizations expels the International Longshoremen and Warehousemen's Union for its "communist" leanings.

The Supreme Court upholds a Missouri statute against picketing in *Giboney v. Empire Storage and Ice Company*.

1956 The National Football League Players Association is founded.

1957 The Senate's McClellan Committee begins investigations of wrongdoing by American labor unions. The hearings continue through 1959 and reveal widespread corruption among the Teamsters and several other labor organizations.

The Supreme Court restricts picketing in its decision in *International Brotherhood of Teamsters Local 695 v. Vogt*.

1963 William Anthony "Tony" Boyle succeeds Thomas Kennedy as president of the United Mine Workers of America.

1965 The Medicare program is implemented, providing a system of health insurance to retired workers.

1967 The National Hockey League Players Association is established.

1969 United Mine Workers of America dissident Joseph "Jock" Yablonski, his wife, and daughter are murdered in their Clarksville, Pennsylvania, home by killers employed by UMW President Tony Boyle and UMW District 19 official Albert Pass.

1973 A coal miner's strike against Eastover Mining Company in Harlan County, Kentucky, over the issue of United Mine Workers of America representation, leads to the second Bloody Harlan.

United Mine Workers official Albert Pass is convicted in the murders of Joseph "Jock" Yablonski and Yablonski's wife and daughter. William Anthony "Tony" Boyle is convicted the following year.

1981 The Reagan administration's action against a walkout by the Professional Air Traffic Controllers Association results in the firing of striking workers and the collapse of the union. The government's sharp response to the strike garners widespread public support.

Bibliography

Auerbach, Jerold S., ed. *American Labor: The Twentieth Century.* American Heritage Series 78. Indianapolis: Bobbs-Merrill, 1969.

Avrich, Paul. *The Haymarket Tragedy.* Princeton, NJ: Princeton University Press, 1984.

Barnard, John. *Walter Reuther and the Rise of the Auto Workers.* Boston: Little, Brown, 1983.

Bernstein, Irving. *The Lean Years: A History of the American Worker, 1920–1933.* Boston: Houghton Mifflin, 1960.

———. *The Turbulent Years: A History of the American Worker, 1933–1941.* Boston: Houghton Mifflin, 1969.

Brill, Steven. *The Teamsters.* New York: Simon and Schuster, 1978.

Brody, David. *Labor in Crisis: The Steel Strike of 1919.* Critical Periods of History series. Urbana, IL: University of Illinois Press, 1967.

Brody, David. *Steelworkers in America: The Nonunion Era.* Cambridge, MA: Harvard University Press, 1960.

———. *Workers in Industrial America: Essays on the Twentieth Century Struggle.* 2d ed. New York: Oxford University Press, 1993.

Broehl, Wayne G., Jr. *The Molly Maguires.* Cambridge, MA: Harvard University Press, 1965.

Brooks, Thomas R. *Communications Workers of America: The Story of a Union.* New York: Mason/Charter, 1977.

Brown, Stuart. *A Man Named Tony: The True Story of the Yablonski Murders.* New York: Norton, 1976.

Bruce, Robert V. *1877: Year of Violence.* Indianapolis: Bobbs-Merrill, 1959.

Carlson, Peter. *Roughneck: The Life and Times of Big Bill Haywood.* New York: Norton, 1983.

Caudill, Harry M. *Theirs Be the Power: The Moguls of Eastern Kentucky.* Urbana, IL: University of Illinois Press, 1983.

Chalberg, John C. *Emma Goldman: American Individualist.* Library of American Biography series. New York: HarperCollins, 1991.

Corbin, David A. *Life, Work, and Rebellion in the Coal Fields: The Southern West Virginia Miners, 1880–1922.* Urbana, IL: University of Illinois Press, 1981.

———, ed. *The West Virginia Mine Wars: An Anthology.* Charleston: Appalachian Editions, 1990.

Daniel, Cletus. *Bitter Harvest: A History of California Farmworkers, 1870–1941.* Ithaca, NY: Cornell University Press, 1981.

Dubinsky, David and A. H. Raskin. *David Dubinsky: A Life with Labor.* New York: Simon and Schuster, 1977.

Dubofsky, Melvyn. *Industrialism and the American Worker, 1865–1920.* 2d ed. Arlington Heights, IL: Davidson, 1985.

———. *We Shall Be All: A History of the Industrial Workers of the World.* Chicago: Quadrangle, 1969.

Dubofsky, Melvyn, and Warren Van Tine. *John L. Lewis: A Biography.* New York: Quadrangle/New York Times Book Company, 1977.

———, ed. *Labor Leaders in America.* Urbana, IL: University of Illinois Press, 1987.

Dulles, Foster Rhea and Melvyn Dubofsky. *Labor in America.* 5th ed. Arlington Heights, IL: Harlan Davidson, 1993.

Eller, Ronald D. *Miners, Millhands, and Mountaineers: Industrialization of the Appalachian South, 1880–1930.* Knoxville, TN: University of Tennessee Press, 1982.

Fine, Sidney. *Sit-Down: The General Motors Strike of 1936–1937.* Ann Arbor, MI: University of Michigan Press, 1969.

Fink, Gary M., ed. *Biographical Dictionary of American Labor.* Westport, CT: Greenwood, 1984.

———, ed. *Labor Unions.* Greenwood Encyclopedia of American Institutions. Westport, CT: Greenwood, 1977.

Fink, Leon. *Workingmen's Democracy: The Knights of Labor and American Politics.* Urbana, IL: University of Illinois Press, 1983.

Fox, Maier B. *United We Stand: The United Mine Workers of America, 1890–1990.* Washington, DC, United Mine Workers of America, 1990.

Franco, Joseph with Richard Hammer. *Hoffa's Man: The Rise and Fall of Jimmy Hoffa as Witnessed by His Strongest Arm.* New York: Prentice Hall, 1987.

Fraser, Steven. *Labor Will Rule: Sidney Hillman and the Rise of American Labor.* New York: Free Press, 1991.

Fried, Albert, ed. *Except to Walk Free: Documents and Notes in the History of American Labor.* Garden City, NY: Anchor, 1974.

Garland, Jim. *Welcome the Traveler Home! Jim Garland's Story of the Kentucky Mountains.* Julia S. Ardery, ed. Lexington, KY: University of Kentucky Press, 1983.

Gifford, Courtney D. *Directory of United States Labor Organizations.* Washington, DC, n.d.

Golin, Steve. *The Fragile Bridge: Paterson Silk Strike, 1913.* Philadelphia: Temple University Press, 1988.

Green, James R. *The World of the Worker: Labor in Twentieth-Century America.* New York: Hill and Wang, 1980.

Grossman, Jonathan. *William Sylvis, Pioneer of American Labor: A Study of the Labor Movement during the Era of the Civil War.* New York: Columbia University Press, 1945.

Harris, William H. *The Harder We Run: Black Workers since the Civil War.* New York: Oxford University Press, 1982.

———. *Keeping the Faith: A. Philip Randolph, Milton P. Webster, and the Brotherhood of Sleeping Car Porters, 1925–37.* Urbana, IL: University of Illinois Press, 1977.

Heckscher, Charles C. *The New Unionism: Employee Involvement in the Changing Corporation.* New York: Basic Books, 1988.

Hevener, John W. *Which Side Are You On? The Harlan County Coal Miners, 1931–39.* Urbana, IL: University of Illinois Press, 1978.

Hill, Jacquelyn D. et al. *Like a Family: The Making of a Southern Cotton Mill World.* Fred W. Morrison Series in Southern Studies. Chapel Hill, NC: University of North Carolina Press, 1987.

Huberman, Leo. *The Labor Spy Racket.* New York: Modern Age Books, 1937.

Hume, Brit. *Death and the Mines: Rebellion and Murder in the United Mine Workers.* New York: Grossman, 1971.

Hutchinson, John. *The Imperfect Union: A History of Corruption in American Trade Unions.* New York: Dutton, 1970.

Jaynes, Gerald David. *Branches without Roots: Genesis of the Black Working Class in the American South, 1862–1882.* New York: Oxford University Press, 1986.

Jones, Jacqueline. *Labor of Love, Labor of Sorrow: Black Women, Work, and the Family from Slavery to the Present.* New York: Basic Books, 1985.

Kelly, Alfred H. and Winfred A. Harbison. *The American Constitution: Its Origins and Development.* New York: Norton, 1963.

Kennedy, Robert F. *The Enemy Within.* New York: Harper, 1960.

Larrowe, Charles P. *Harry Bridges: The Rise and Fall of Radical Labor in the United States.* New York: Hill, 1972.

Lindsey, Almont. *The Pullman Strike: The Story of a Unique Experiment and of a Great Labor Upheaval.* Chicago: University of Chicago Press, 1942.

Litwack, Leon. *The American Labor Movement.* Englewood Cliffs, NJ: Prentice Hall, 1962.

Livesay, Harold C. *Samuel Gompers and Organized Labor in America.* Boston: Little, Brown, 1978.

McGovern George S. and Leonard F. Guttridge. *The Great Coalfield War.* Boston: Houghton Mifflin, 1972.

Marshall, F. Ray. *Labor in the South.* Cambridge, MA: Harvard University Press, 1967.

Meier, August and Elliott Rudwick. *Black Detroit and the Rise of the UAW.* New York: Oxford University Press, 1979.

Montgomery, David. *The Fall of the House of Labor: the Workplace, the State, and American Labor Activism, 1865–1925.* New York: Cambridge University Press, 1987.

Moody, Kim. *An Injury to All: The Decline of American Unionism.* Haymarket Series. New York: Verso, 1988.

Nelson, Bruce. *Workers on the Waterfront: Seamen, Longshoremen, and Unionism in the 1930s.* Urbana, IL: University of Illinois Press, 1988.

Nelson, Daniel. *American Rubber Workers and Organized Labor, 1900–1941.* Princeton, NJ: Princeton University Press, 1988.

Pelling, Henry. *American Labor.* Chicago: University of Chicago Press, 1960.

Pessen, Edward. *Most Uncommon Jacksonians: The Radical Leaders of the Early Labor Movement.* Albany, NY: State University of New York Press, 1967.

Pfeffer, Paula F. *A. Philip Randolph, Pioneer of the Civil Rights Movement.* Baton Rouge, LA: Louisiana State University Press, 1990.

Quaglieri, Philip L., ed. *America's Labor Leaders.* Lexington, MA: Lexington Books, 1989.

Renshaw, Patrick. *The Wobblies: The Story of Syndicalism in the United States.* Garden City, NY: Doubleday, 1967.

Salvatore, Nick. *Eugene V. Debs: Citizen and Socialist.* Urbana, IL: University of Illinois Press, 1982.

Schatz, Ronald W. *The Electrical Workers: A History of Labor at General Electric and Westinghouse, 1923–1960.* Urbana, IL: University of Illinois Press, 1983.

Schmidhauser, John R. *Constitutional Law in American Politics.* Monterey, CA: Brooks/Cole, 1984.

Smith, Robert Wayne. *The Coeur d'Alene Mining War of 1892: A Case Study of an Industrial Dispute.* Corvallis, OR: Oregon State University Press, 1961.

Stein, Leon. *The Triangle Fire.* Philadelphia: Lippincott, 1962.

Taylor, Paul F. *Bloody Harlan: The United Mine Workers of America in Harlan County, Kentucky, 1931–1941.* Lanham, MD: University Presses of America, 1990.

Titler, George J. *Hell in Harlan.* Beckley, WV: n.d.

Trotter, Joe William, Jr. *Coal, Class, and Color: Blacks in Southern West Virginia, 1915–32.* Urbana, IL: University of Illinois Press, 1990.

Weiler, Paul C. *Governing the Workplace: The Future of Labor and Employment Law.* Cambridge, MA: Harvard University Press, 1990.

Weiner, Lynn Y. *From Working Girl to Working Mother: The Female Labor Force in the United States, 1820–1980.* Chapel Hill, NC: University of North Carolina Press, 1985.

Bibliography

Wolff, Leon. *Lockout: The Story of the Homestead Strike of 1892: A Study of Violence, Unionism, and the Carnegie Steel Empire.* New York: Harper & Row, 1965.

Woolley, Bryan and Ford Reid, photog. *We Be Here When the Morning Comes.* Lexington, KY: University Press of Kentucky, 1975.

Zieger, Robert H. *American Workers, American Unions.* Baltimore: Johns Hopkins University Press, 1986.

———. *John L. Lewis, Labor Leader.* Twayne's Twentieth-Century American Biography Series 8. Boston: Twayne, 1988.

———. *Rebuilding the Pulp and Paper Workers' Union, 1933–1941.* Twentieth Century America series. Knoxville, TN: University of Tennessee Press, 1984.

Illustration Credits

Index